Completely
Mixed
Up

Mixed Heritage Asian North American Writing and Art

Rabbit Fool Press
Vancouver

Cover artwork by Michael Tora Speier, from *Nectarine River: The Tale of a Mixed Race Surfer*
Rabbit Fool Press
www.rabbitfoolpress.com
ISBN 978-0-9783607-9-5

Contents of Ingredients

Preface

Brandy Liên Worrall-Soriano

It's funny how things happen. In 1999 I began the Master's program in Asian American Studies at UCLA. That's when I met Irene Suico Soriano, who asked me and fellow graduate student James Lawrence Ardeña, or Jamie as I know him, to put together a hapa reading in Los Angeles at the Japanese American Cultural and Community Center in Little Tokyo. Neither Jamie nor I even knew what "hapa" meant when she asked us to do this reading. We quickly learned that it meant people like us~halfers~and that's why she asked us to do it. Because Jamie and I both liked having products to show off, rather than just doing something as fleeting as a reading, we decided to do a chapbook. And then we decided to do another. And another. Except that the last one~that took a while because after graduate school, we were faced with the realities of jobs and children. So something that we used to be able to previously knock out in a month now took six years.

In 2006 when we released the final chapbook, people asked what was going to happen when all these handmade beauties were sold out. What was going to happen to the works within those pages? Again, because we strove for posterity, we proclaimed that we would compile all three handmade chapbooks into one print anthology. Others rejoiced with us at this idea. We were pumped! Viva Hapa Nation!

Then I got diagnosed with cancer in 2007. This wasn't something that was in anyone's plans. And that changed everything. I learned that being multiracial could have its disadvantages when facing a life threatening illness (like Jeff Chiba Stearns writes about in his essay). For one, oftentimes the Asian part of you has an undocumented, unknown medical history, which proves tricky when determining things like your medical family tree for genetic testing. Another issue is that you are hard pressed to find a match if, for example, you need a bone marrow donor if you're diagnosed with leukaemia. These were the new real-life lessons I was learning about what it meant to be a hapa.

The good news is, I got to live. However, to this day I'm still dealing with long-terms side effects from chemotherapy, radiation, and never-ending surgeries. That's one reason why it's taken us so long to put out this anthology. The other is that since 2007, I got divorced and fell in love with my hapa Romeo, and despite the great chance that the chemo would destroy my reproductive abilities, we had a miracle hapa baby. All that set the publication schedule back a few years. And this is why it's funny how things happen: my hapa Romeo is the brother of Irene Suico Soriano, the originator of this project almost 16 years ago~and he is the one who has helped me tremendously in creating this book!

Of course I must acknowledge Jamie. Without him, this book would not exist. We've made a great team for the last decade and a half, and I can only hope that I make him proud.

This is how this book works: each section is a reproduction of each chapbook, as closely as possible (I even included the original editors' notes that appeared in each chapbook). Some contributors decided that they didn't want to take part in this anthology because the works they created were of a particular time and therefore would remain as such and not be carried forward to the present day. But most recognized that even if they've changed in the last 15 years~and who hasn't?~their works either historically represent the politics of that era or would resonate with new readers who are at a particular point of identity discovery.

One hundred years ago, Edith and Winnifred Eaton~under the pen names of Sui Sin Far and Onoto Watanna, respectively~were two sisters out of fourteen children in a Chinese and British family who immigrated to Canada~and who would later be considered the first Asian North American writers. They were acutely aware of the racial struggles of the time. Edith, adopting a Chinese-sounding pen name~was a journalist who often reported on the trials of being in-between and of disenfranchised Chinese immigrants. Winnifred assumed a pseudo-Japanese pen name because, as many people surmise, Japanese immigrants were not as vilified during those years. She wrote a hearty number of romance novels and short stories. These sisters were the godmothers of mixed race and Asian American/Canadian writing.

Here we are in 2015, when the echoes of the Civil Rights movement 50 years ago are becoming louder because of how, it seems to me anyway, racial relations, understanding, compassion, and inclusion are taking a few big steps backward with violence against black and brown bodies on the rise, with legislation piling up against non-Whites, with people being killed because of who they are. What has become of us, of our society?

Just a few days ago, as I was working on this book, my next-door neighbour, a Vietnamese Canadian, warned me about doing this kind of work. I laughed at his notion that the Vietnamese communists would actually be interested in my work enough to come kill me–hey, I live in Canada–things like that don't happen here. But you know, it occurred to me to check my privilege. Even if I am safe here, or perceive myself as such, as a cultural worker, I would not be in other parts of the world, like Vietnam, where my mom comes from. That's why it is even more important to do this work, to take the risk–because we can and we should. Yes, race does exist. Yes, racism is something that is alive and well today, in all parts of the world. If I were a *con lai* (or half breed) in Vietnam, I don't think I'd be so brave and brazen to do this kind of work because of how stigmatized my body would be there. Here in North America, I have that privilege to do this work. And use it I shall.

I dedicate this book to my parents, who were love revolutionaries during a war with a legacy that is still being felt. I dedicate this book to my comrades, who are impassioned enough to share their stories, even and especially under this darkened cloud of racial strife. Finally, I dedicate this book to my children and their generation, as they learn yet in other ways what it means to be multiracial in this new technological era in which the world is made both smaller and more divided.

I sum up the book's contents with this: it's funny how some things change, and it's funny how some things stay the same.

April 2015

Foreword

James Lawrence Ardeña

Resiliency, Persistence, Completion.

Those are the buzz words on the tip of my tongue, having worked in higher education since the beginning of the Mixed Up Trilogy. Working in a college setting has been the one sort of constant over many years of my life. A lifetime for some, like my differently mixed nephews just learning to drive, or the blink of an eye in my memory.

That is why I am awed that the time has come, after so many years of this and that. My interests have shifted and changed during these fifteen years. Ask me about gardening, fungi, or backpacking, and you'll have to interrupt me in order to get away from the profusion/excitement of my verbal babble. These are stalwarts for my own spirit and resiliency allowing me to persist. I wish I had known them sooner, as I never finished the degree I started—which is why I am so grateful and in admiration of Brandy's embodiment of those three words above.

I anticipate the reverie on revisiting writings from the turn of the century, witness to the evolutions of voice and thought. Others have moved into other genres of self-expression, still craft with words, or never wrote again. I am particularly excited to hear new voices in the section of more recent works, mindfully chewing on the issues and concepts explored by authors centering Asian mixed race heritage. Have things changed while I've been away? Are they the same? How will these expressions of life fall on new ears old and young? Is it still back and white? Are mixed heritage folks still fetishized? Is the term "hapa" still in? What's a hapa'ning now anyways?

For me this all started when I left home to attend a graduate program in Los Angeles. When I first arrived there, I was fresh and new, all of 25, and I met an Asian American Studies alum who was also from Seattle. She was returning to "finally complete" her degree just under the wire of ten years after having left after coursework. In naiveté I ask why she hadn't completed earlier, and in her wise years she simply replied, "Life." That's where Brandy and I met all those years ago and how this project got started.

Although the credentials don't follow my name, I still carry the punk-rock attitude we embodied those years ago. Some may call it Do-It-Yourself, or DIY, which is exactly what we did when searching for something that spoke to our experiences. I am forever grateful for the friendship, partnership, and life lessons with my co-editor/conspirator of the trilogy and am honored that our evolving vision of a "side project" reaches a milestone in her publication of *Completely Mixed Up*, demonstrating that poetry is not a luxury—it is a vital necessity. Resiliency + Persistence = *Completely Mixed Up*. Cheers, B ! Thank you for this completion.

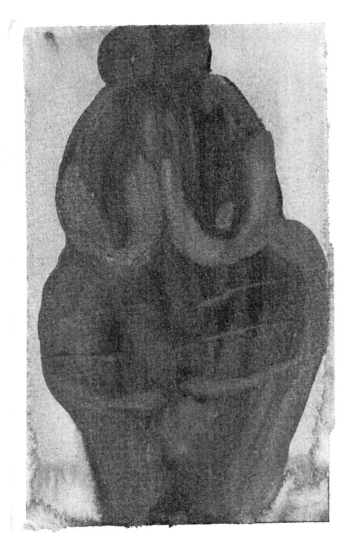

mixed up

✗ 2000 ✗

Co-editor's Note (2000)

James Lawrence Ardeña

> "...to be seen and not known is the ultimate abandonment"
> ~ bell hooks

I come to los angeles from Seattle, the green wooded west. I have been priveldged to work alongside many great artists through isangmahal arts kollective. It is within this tradition of collective action that my work continues. In the act of creation, there is subversion. Quite often the signifier that precipitates the common question that we are asked is how we are "seen" visually. Although the question is an attempt, it is merely undertaken by checking a box in which the questioner has a pretext in which to inscribe us, without truly knowing.

The work that I have done and will do is not a solitary one. There have been many individuals who have influenced, supported, hindered, and challenged me all along. I would not have it any other way. I have been blessed with the opportunity to more fully know them, and they me. It has always been those individuals whose spoken words and vivid images I have appreciated the most in my growth. I hope that this claim of space begins that path with those whose works are shared and those who will read their words. We must claim authority of our own voice, regardless of others' notions and values that are anointed. They seek to silence, and our silences will not save us.

Initially, I told myself and many friends back home that I would not write creatively or organize events while attending UCLA. Fortunately, the opportunity arose, and with that I remembered.

> "...Poetry is not a luxury. It is a vital necessity of our existence. It forms the quality of light within which we predicate our hopes and dreams toward survival and change..."
> ~audre lorde

Co-editor's Note (2000)

Brandy Worrall

"She's the Mixed One." Those were the last words I heard before I left the Vietnamese Students Association of Regis College—never to return.

"Hey, why don't you go back to the country you came from?" Those were the last words I heard before I decided that the kids in my hometown were not only racist but also very stupid. I was born in the same town in which they were born.

Maybe
I am a cultural let down
A biological put down
I have fucked up
hang ups
but god bless this country~
we are MADE IN THE USA!

Yet we're also made in Saigon, Manila, Tokyo~don't you know~ what we are?

****

This chapbook, *Mixed Up*, reads like the title. Childhood dreams turn to defiance of expectations~but the road is not easy, not linear. We are a jumbled Amerasian map~East Coast, West Coast, Midwest, Far East, Down South, Across the Border and Back Again~We were born from afar and have travelled quite wide. The languages each of us speaks~within ourselves and outside of ourselves~are foreign to each other, but somehow, they understand just perfectly what's being said to and within one another. Yet this chapbook is not a dictionary, but rather a photo album, because pictures are worth a gajillion words~and that's how many words it takes just to show you how Mixed Up we really are.

Peace and Pancakes

ka

James Lawrence Ardeña

ka said wise words to me
this day, my daily bread
speaking in revelations
I hear in a child's breath
crushed under the weight of doubt
in an unorganized time
fettered away in traffic lights
of
red light–green light
in the Sinden's hopscotch driveway
throwing stones
and, catching them in chipped teeth.
me not atomo me superman

"do you have a problem?"
"you need to keep moving?"

cabin fever
love
warmth
in this day not torment lines my tongue
recognitions of rapture
definitions are broadened
to areas that remain untouched
via connotations of evil
reading lies, as interest moves
and wise words are whispered once again by ka
as institutions kill ka
and the path
with neutral tones of emancipation
community beckons to be realized
birthed through direct experience
insight begets a base a faith
yet I still want to cry

singing
"goodnight sweetheart it's time to go"
"goodnight sweet heart it's time to go"

her head is nestled in my palm
as I caress graying blond hairs
of the one whose hands were the softest
this child will ever touch
tears rip across consciousness
and love, lands loudly in facial gestures
I am the child she is and becomes
coldness enters the body, permeates emotions
and I escape to warmth
to vaccinations of cabin fever
longing to stay/depart/stay
and home is here
as god is love
as buddah is love
as ka is love
and she will live on in people she will never know of
but they know of her as the light
which took care of me
excavated daily to dwell decidedly
to love
to choose to love

"what did you do yesterday?"

bells ring quietly against ribbed walls of flesh
and I want to know its melody
as palm trees know the sun
as I crave—I begin to know
as I walk —I understand
time takes slow turns

"visit me in kalifornia" she says
"yes nay, I shall."

and I will roll lumpia until 3 am responding
"yes nay, I shall."
"yes nay, I shall."
"yes nay,
          I shall."

Gifts come

Leilani Chan

Gifts come in tattered packages
past down from generation
                    to generation
sometimes never opened
only wrapped again and again
in tattered wrappings

made of newspaper headlines
which stole our souls
made mothers weep
and fathers angry

paper bags,
soaked with meat scraps
                chitlins, chicharones, and spam
tied with blood soaked wires and rope
that now
in this generation
our soft hands
that hold no scars
dig deep
and try to reach the gold within
cutting our hands
re-opening wounds
and shedding tears
our fathers never could

and if we can
and if we do
and if we are able
to get to the gift inside
our eyes
dulled by wrappings
would be so blinded

from the shine
that the joy of the gift
would first come
only, by way of pain.

Eulogy to My Multi-Racial Multi-Cultural Ancestors

also known as the ANTI-Eulogy to My Multi-Racial Multi-Cultural Ancestors

Leilani Chan

PROLOGUE

People always ask me
to break it down for them
what races?
which parent was what?
I indulge them often
just to appease their curiosity
but if I break it down for you
you still won't understand
     5 races by blood
     3 more by culture
     8 altogether
     and growing still
     as life winds around me

You see, it is not the races of my ancestors
who have made me who I am
but their personalities
Which are made up
of the races and the places that they come from

So I invite you
to join me
in the journey
of my multiplistic mind

For some,
this might be confusing
But for me
it is just natural
the way it has always been

Anything else
is too simplistic for me to comprehend
So often, I feel stupid

I have never been comfortable with categories
None TRULY fit
there is no one exactly of my race
exactly of my heritage
on the planet earth but me
The only category that might fit
is the category of people
who also have no category

So,
I welcome the many doors
which open up to claim me.
And, I return their love times two
if and when I can

But I know my home is not in the room,
but on the window sill
in the doorway
a kaleidoscope of visions

Here, is where I set up shop
plant a plant
hang a painting
store a postcard from a friend
plug in my computer
to the
world
wide
web...

THE POEM

I exist on currents
of the wind
of the sea

I am the descendent
of survivors
of voyagers
of travelers

my restlessness
has been inherited
Why stay too long?
Why wait until someone runs us out of town?
What is life by a voyage anyway?

ROOTS?
      Roads
      Boats
      and Aeroplanes
the faces of my ancestors fill each and every seat

OCEANS are the borders
that wrap around my homelands
and the rivers that divide them
are like the vessels that are my veins
In me, they unify

I live on currents and tides

I carry rains
left over from typhoons and hurricanes
in the bow of my ship

I scoop what's left over
from wars that were not mine

and dump them back
into the rivers from which they came

I am used
       to the bob and sway of the ocean
       the head wind
       the tail wind
       the turbulence
           is home to me

as calm and comforting
       as the winds
       through the leaves
       of rain forest trees

as white blue moonlight
       through a wide open window
       on a humid island night

the buzz of a mosquito
the crack of a gecko
or the sound of a passing siren
is always there
to disturb by serenity

Nothing stands still
though sometimes I long for it to do so
If it did
       I'd rip it down
           like a paper cage
                that could never keep me in

The world
is ALREADY littered
with my paper carcasses

cocoons and incubators

HOW MANY TIMES MUST A PHOENIX RISE?

I am learning to understand the smell of ashes

welcome it like the smell of fresh baked bread

burnt civilizations
hallowed ghettos
bullet trailed foot paths

gun smoke, gas chambers
poisonous gases
all have built my lungs

ashes
laced around the trunks of trees
that uproot easily
and travel well

an unusual thick of forest vines
grows comfortably
around the ruins of war
as if the leaking diesel fuel
were water from the heavens

I cry
I gasp
I melt
and rise for more.

The glimmer of beauty
amidst the fall of rain
and the crack of thunder
is what I live for
is what I long for

rains from the heavens
could be bullets you know?

EPILOGUE

You see me standing here before you
and you think it's only me

I am a moment in time
my body a mere marker
of what has come before
and what is yet to come

Before I was born
My death was wished
      one hundred times
and in my life
      one hundred times more
and with each wish
      I grow
      one hundred times stronger
and I will live
      one hundred days longer

~ PAU ~

Pickle

an excerpt from the solo show "Sungka"

Alison M. De La Cruz

LIGHTS UP ON ANNALYN (Multiracial Pinay (Filipina American) 20s), ON 1st BASE. SQUATTING, MOVING BACK AND FORTH.

ANNALYN

You've always gotta keep your eye on the ball, and your mind in the game. When you are out here on base - you never know when it's your opportunity to steal 2nd...and that's how I met Georgia. Okay, I know lesbians and softball. It's really stereotypical. But I sweartagawd ~ I didn't know that I was a lesbian when I started playing softball. I just looked up one day and realized that there were all of these FINE! Women! (BEAT) Then CRACK! My teammate, she hits one straight down center field, so I take off running.

SHE TAKES OFF RUNNING

And I pass second and Georgia, she's shortstop, and I keep running to 3rd, but then I STOP! Cuz the 3rd basewoman, she's got the ball, so I turn around and run back to 2nd. But I have to STOP! because now Georgia, she's got the ball, and it's like ~ I'm in this pickle. So I turn around and run back to 3rd and then I stop! The 3rd basewoman, she's dropped the ball. So I can run forward to 3rd or back to Georgia. (PAUSE) I run back!

ANNALYN LANDS ON 2nd BASE

Georgia leans over in between pitches, "Your coach looks pissed."

I know, I know.

Georgia asks, "Was it worth it?"

(Beat) I don't know, I'll tell you during dessert? (TO AUDIENCE) It was cheesy, but it worked!!!

So a couple of days later, we went to dinner. We're talkin' about being women, about being queer, about playing softball and the whole time I'm just lookin' at her.

Wow, she's so FOINE and we're here together. (Beat). Then I realize that we aren't saying anything. So I panic, and I look at her, I say,

You look exotic, are you *Hapa?*

And she's like, "What's hapa?"

You know, when you're part Asian Pacific Islander and part something else.

She says, "I don't know about the *exotic* part, but my dad is Filipino and my mom is White."

Wow, me too. (TO AUDIENCE.) It was soo cool, cuz I'd never met anyone whose mom was White and dad was Filipino. And then we started to bond about how when we were growing up, people always tried to tell us who to be, and how to be... gotta try to

SHE RUNS BACK AND FORTH BETWEEN BASES

to be more white... or to be more Asian.... to be more straight or to be more gay... to be who our friends thought we should be ... or what our family thought we should be...

STOPS IN BETWEEN

and never just being ourselves. And I thought wow, finally someone understands. After that - conversation just seemed to flow between us.

ANNALYN LEAVES THE BASES

We hung out. Got to know each other. You know, she's a *Performance Poet!* (PAUSE) I didn't know what that was either. She reads poetry in a theater, with lights and shit. But she warned me I'd never come see her read because people she knows make her nervous. She set a boundary. I respected that. And... we've been going out for a couple of weeks now. Things are ok.

But last night at dinner she asks me if I want to come with her to the theater. Since it's *her* solo project she needs *me* to fill in while *she* looks at the lights. (MINI-BEAT) Bring me?!, Someone she knows to the theater?! So I say *yeah*, and she takes me downtown.

ANNALYN MOVES. LIGHTS CHANGE.

She has me stand on stage and they test all the lights: the blue, the green, and the red, orange, amber, yellow and purple lights. And I stand there. And stand there. And then I realize: I ain't never *been* on a stage before. (LOOKING AROUND) and I look GOOD! And then I start to think about how I can't see her, but all she is doing is looking at me. No one has ever looked at me for this long.

So I start to think to myself. She sees me. She really knows me, understands me. I think that I'll tell her right now: that it's just you. Just me. And we're good together. And then as if she senses what I'm going to say she says, "The red light, the red light is best."

Oh, I said, Is it the color of desire? And ecstasy...

"No." she says, "It's the color that looks best on brown skin tones."

Oh. I said. (Shit!)

But then she says, "But it looks really good on *you*."

Oh?!! I say. But then I start to think about how she does that all the time, pulls me out and flirts with me, and then pushes me back in. It's like we're in a pickle, running back and forth between friends and *more-than-friends*. You know, like *friends with energy*!

And I realize that I can't do it anymore. I get it. I see you. I know that we could be good together. And so I yell into the darkness: I don't wanna play anymore. Please be my girl or dump me.

Then-CRACK! My teammate hits another, so I take off running and leave Georgia, just like I did last night.

RUNS TO 3RD

Last night she dumped me. And tonight ~ we're in this game and she's in her usual position right there, but I can't look at her. I need to win, I need to get home so I start praying for the... CRACK!

My teammate hits a base hit. Finally I run towards home and then STOP ~ the Catcher, she's got the ball. So I turn around to run back to 3rd. Georgia's on 3rd. She doesn't have the ball, but she has this funny look on her face. So I keep running. Once I touch my foot to the base, I stand and take my position.

She isn't going away. Everything is her and me in this moment, the times in-between pitches.

RED LIGHTS UP AS GEORGIA STEPS TO ANNALYN

"The red light," she says, "The red light is best."

Oh?! I say. Should I repeat last night's lines about the color of ecstasy?

"No." she says, "It's the color that looks best on brown skin tones ~ flushes out the shadows and warms the bones."

Oh, I say. Then it's probably best to hide the pain in my chest. But it can't hide the cracks in my shells, or the knicks and knacks gathered by my living.

"No it can't," she says (BEAT) but "It's the color of FIRE, DESIRE and Ecstasy and my love for you!"

Oh! I say. Me Too!

"I know," she says, "I know, I just wanna walk you home."

FADE TO BLACK. END OF EXCERPT

Suppose Revolution

Cheryl Deptowicz-Diaz

We weren't supposed to...grow up complete
in ourselves
in our dreams
in our trusts.

We weren't supposed to...want
change
time for leisure
a better life.

We weren't supposed to...
know words like justice or call each other comrades.
We weren't supposed to...feel when we saw
a homeless man on the streets
a hungry child too weak to cry
a wife recently beaten
a co-worker fired.

We're supposed to...
say it's okay
turn our backs
roll up our car windows
look the other way
celebrate our nonchalance.

He's only a lazy bum.
It's only a dirty child.
She's only a weak woman who probably asked for it.
He's only a slacker.

We weren't supposed to...grow up red.
Red like the silk robes of imprisoned prostitutes in Bangkok.
Like the eyes of a fiery bull or the flag of his Spanish matador.
Red like a dew-dropped Hawaiian hibiscus flower.

Like the flushed cheeks of a newly-sexed teenager.
Red like the swollen bulging tear ducts of an abandoned child.
Like the blood dripping from the bruised lip of my hip hop lover pulled
over by cops.
Red like the fire of a ghetto rebellion.
Like the rage of a million workers laid-off.
Red like the molten lava beneath our feet ready to erupt.

We weren't supposed to...know you.
Yet for millions, billions, trillions everywhere,
You are the ardor of desire
The fire in excitement
The infatuation of craving
The affection of fancy
The love in warmth
The emotion in tenderness
The intensity of anger
The passion in souls...

Revolution, worldwide.

Daughters

Cheryl Deptowicz-Diaz

I am the daughter of imperialism and revolution
In these veins, fight the two, searching for solution.
I brought clothes to a naked village
I was the land that was pillaged.
I am the gun of that trigger.
I am the blood of their fallen nigger.

I am the daughter of imperialism and revolution.
In my blood flows the mortal combination.
My skin is of the coconut brown.
My eyes are of color amber you want to drown.
I am the multiracial, multiethnic.
I'm the amerasian putting you in panic.

I come from a land of history untold.
I come from a land where slavery was bold.
I am whom you hate. I am whom you reject.
In the fight for freedom, I'm the unspoken project.

I am told I'm not brown enough.
I act too strong, too tough.
Told this.
Told that.
Might I change my last name? Get a tan?
Possibly my white comrades I can abandon?
Might I never speak of my gay and lesbian friends?
Forget too the feminist ones.
Shunned by each community,
I search...search...I search for immunity.

I begin to question, is it really my skin or is it my...
Not small enough waist
Not big enough smile
Not parted enough legs

Not big enough boobs
Not short enough skirt
Not red enough lips
Not nip enough eyes?

Today I help raise other daughters to be
Womanly women in this man's world,
Never compromising, never apologizing.
Not for breast that bounce with every confident stride.
Not for tongues that speak boldly.

Daughters becoming women.
Linguists who give us the language to name our oppression.
Rollercoaster rides that teach us to scream.
Mothers who tell us to love deeply.
Mapmakers who erase all borders, connecting our lives.
Comics who make us laugh, at life's drama.
Architects who build windows in a world full of walls.

Child Transplanted

Cheryl Deptowicz-Diaz

Over two decades ago, April 9, 1982, I was 8½ years of experience
I stepped off a plane to a land called America
Little did I know back then the significance of that step
From one plane to a big unknown land,
The significance of that trip
The consequence of cooperating with my mother
Her requests to make the travel easier

Carry the duffel bags
Watch my brother
Don't cry
Obey her and my two older sisters
Help *ate* (older sister) change my baby sister's dirty diaper
Don't cry
Stand guard of our big boxes with our last name and a foreign address
written on them
Eat the weird tasting vegetables served in the plane
Don't ask for *toyo, suka, at patis* (soy sauce, vinegar, or fish sauce)

Pretend you don't feel the tension in the air
Pretend you don't notice mama having a hard time speaking a language
not our own
Pretend you don't see the tears from her eye
Just crack a joke
Just don't cry

Neither did I understand what all the commotion was the night before
At the *despedida* (going away) party
People were crying
Everyone making us promise to always remember them

Tita Mila, the so-called, "less refined" of all my aunts, knelt down to her knees
Looked me at eye level
Peered through her glasses

Turned serious and
Made me promise never to forget our language, *Tagalog*

She knew about the English tutoring classes we've been taking
She's heard us practice, as Mama demanded, the tongue twisters

"Peter Piper the pepper picket picked a pack of pickled pepper."
"She sells seashells by the seashore"
"Full of fun, full of flight, forty-five fun fat flies."
"Full of fun, full of flight, forty-five fun fat flies."
"Full of fun, full of flight, forty-five fun fat flies."

I looked at Tita Mila's sad face, confused in her emotion
I nodded my head, yes
Intent on keeping my promise

I didn't realize then the goodbyes I said to all
My aunts, uncles, cousins, neighbors, teachers, friends, crushes
Were such permanent ones

I didn't think then, that day, at the Philippine Airport
Was the last day I'd touch my grandmother's hand
Last time she'd sneak me candy from our *sari-sari* (variety) store
Last time I'd taste her cooking,
Yummy *paksiw* (fish dish) over white rice, best eaten with bare hands
The week before, the last time I'd handwash my school uniforms with her
Soak them in a big *palangana* (tub) filled with water and suds
The sound of wet sounds crunching between my fingers,
Sweet to my ear along with praises from *Lola* (grandmother), telling me I
was her favorite

I can go on forever because I remember so much
I remember just about everything
The home we left
The keepsakes we couldn't bring
The alley in which we played
The meals we sold from our store to the university students across the way

The floor Papa always wanted washed.
The wooden stairs I'd shine with a *bunot* (coconut shell)
The baker we bought *pandisal* (bread roll) from everyday for breakfast and
merienda (afternoon snack)
The traffic
The stuffy churches and the long sermons
The food
The *palengke* (open air market)
The trips to Pampanga where my childhood lives
The classes in Tagalog, English, and Chinese
The jeepney rides
Beng-Beng the loyal dog we left behind
And on and on...and on

Years later...
What am I supposed to do with these memories?
How do they fit in my "American" life?
How will they help release my falsely-imprisoned mother
Who now knows prison lingo, like "lights out" and "lock down?"
How do they help find a job for my father where he's not insulted
everyday?
How do they feed my family too proud to apply for welfare?
How do they free
the people I promised never to forget?
the land I left behind?

Spoken from the Neck

Lance Dougherty

i live in a place
where right and wrong mean the same as
do what it takes to survive, and the concept of tolerance
is only recognized by people who make museums
i'm from a place where prejudice is something people do for fun
and peace is a prize only given to those of a nobel stature
that confused place is called earth

we are in a crazy place
to those in positions to make important judgments i am strength
little to their knowledge i'm nothing more than a fabled character
waving his pen in the air and proclaiming that
it is mightier than your knife, your sword, and your gun
i do all for the sake of the lost cause, but words become misconstrued
and actions become friends to contradiction
do you understand that we live in a problematic society made even
more complex
by our own personal inquisitions of self worth

i continuously wonder about this place
i have answerless questions, and then have people of
immeasurable brainpower
answering these questions with greatest of ease
i perpetuate the solutions only to find the same people
telling me, there are none. can things be put into proper perspective
changed to never happen, a new beginning sprung from birth

I think it's time that I stop listening to people that
speak from the neck, speak from the neck,
aybe I should stop speaking from the neck

The Wish

Hazel H. Hill

Today I wish I can stop being a woman
Not to be a man, but to be sexless.
Today I wish I could stop being Black and Filipina
Not to be white, but to be a generic being
Today I wish I could stop being heterosexual,
Not to be homosexual, but to have no sexuality
That defines me.
Today I wish I could stop being poor, not to be rich but
To have a chance, a fair shake.
Today I am removing all the categories that
Define
Mold
Shape
Constrict
Me.
Today I erase these notion of my being
No more class
No more race
No more sexuality
No more gender
No more categories that
Determine my opportunities
Today I am creating a free and boundless me!
But doesn't this sound like the. . .
The American Dream
That regardless of my background
As long as I work hard
I shall succeed
        SUCCEED.
Then I wake up and see
That my life has already been carved out for me.
I am socialized to be
A brown skin, feminized, heterosexual, Black and Filipina,
working class, woman.
That have meanings that can destroy me
But what about the American dream,

I've been lied to . . .
So what about my wish?
I want not to obliterate the categories,
But the meanings and consequences behind them.
My daily revolution, or I should say
Evolution is to make the limits that
Confine me, Boundless.

I am proud to be
A women
Black and Filipina
Working class
Heterosexual
To be me and to celebrate me
On my terms

This women, feminized not by any social standard,
But of my choosing,
So if I decide to wear my sweats,
Don't give me shit and tell me that I'm not the proper lady.
To be Black and Filipina, oh yes both, not by
What everyone else says, but what
I say is my Blackness and My Filipinaness
So don't tell me to choose one.
To be working class and to not let this determine my fate.

To celebrate all types of love and respect
The love we share with each other
As my sister Mary J. says
Cause everybody needs love

Can you love me?
Today I want you to
See me
To hear me
To feel me
Can you feel me?

We need to understand that these
Social categories bind and constrict

Our minds . . .Bodies and souls.
Can't we see how these notions control our lives.
These consequences invisible to our colonized minds.
I'm not say to give up our history
Or deny my ancestry.
Because my ancestors still live through me

But, But, But
Are we afraid to not have these. . . categories
That continue such pain and privilege.
Have we been so trained that this is the only way
We see to live.
To have hierarchies that make life unfair
To organize our lives in such harmful care
Are we afraid to think different
To think out of the box.

What happened to the child
That was born full of dreams?
Does becoming an "adult" mean
Dying and sacrificing yourself?
Does it mean being afraid to live as you truly feel?
Is it that scary not knowing
What to expect when you meet somebody?
To be open and not judge.

I say change that fear into excitement
For our lives are always uncertain.
Embrace the unknown for our future lies in it.
We can no longer fear difference and change.

And I say to you this
can you imagine my wish?

Storytelling

Dorian Sanae Merina

I had to walk three blocks
to the bus stop
juice from cooked squash
dampened the canvas bag,
clouds wouldn't stop moving~
is why I am here
with no oranges from the garden.

Remember the 215 route?
Well, it changed
goes down Catalina now.

"Uncle Talino?" the letters from overseas
question respectfully.
They hear the news
"cousin Ramon told me"
"we just found out"
"I remember he loved the mambo"

> *Oras para umuwi*
>> *Oras para umuwi*

"How do I say, *I am sorry?*
Is it difficult?"
We sit around a table
plates of chow mein, empanadas
plastic forks.
I ask the questions for the second time
but before I can translate

she says, "Yes, yes, it is difficult.
It is hard."

The soap operas distracted me.
That poor child doesn't know
who his father is
the lawyer with the green eyes
or the tall man with the mustache.
The woman with a pink dress
enters holding a coin in her palm,
"Where do you think
I found *this*?" she asks, thrusting
it in front of the green-eye man.

> *Oras para umuwi*
> > *Oras para umuwi*

"You better catch
that bus," says Grandma.
"And don't let that squash spill."

*oras para umuwi - It is time to go home

For My Cousins Who Will Choose Who They Are

Dorian Sanae Merina

running home this evening
I look for the san gabriels
to find only
a faint line above the haze
a razor-black definition
of home running

and, before I can help it, my mind
rushes in
fills the rest with detail and reference
so that I see
as if in mid-earthquake
a perfect memory of a mountain.

I tell you this, cousins, because you too
will find your landmarks
this way,
you too will find yourself
listening to others
on the bus in school on t.v.
who will tell you, "You can choose
who you will be
you have the responsibility
to see it this way."

***

what chose who blood
passages over the dark-rain ocean crossing
the border-blister heat

                to arrive

find that address in the suitcase
stolen

***

there is in you
       hot blood
       cool blood
       island blood
       lovers blood
       tribal blood
       white blood
       hungry blood
       city blood
american blood American blood AMERICAN blood

***

it is twenty-eight day since Grandpa die
we used to eat chilled plums from buckets
drink coke and play ping-pong
in the backyard

one of his countrymen once said,
America
is in the Heart
this after years and years away
from the mountain on the Island

***

we will be mis   taken
for everything
we will learn to trade the landmarks
for pictures of ourselves
we will be tempted by the temporary ease
of forgetfulness

but, my cousins, after years of pretending
to choose
we will learn: we only know how
to discriminate

you will find yourself
suddenly alone with no easy choices
nothing gets better
once it is gone
or taken
or given
you cannot get it back in one piece
not in one lifetime

so I give you no caution
just a cool eye in the hurricane
just a hot eye in the field
there is something
no one has told you
go to it

Drawing Dinosaurs

Victoria Namkung

Hapas
Hybrids
Haoles
Hesitation

He says we're different because I don't have an immigrant parent
I say I do
I have two

He says, no because my mom doesn't have an accent
And she doesn't ask for doggie bags at nice restaurants
And she doesn't keep the black and white photo that comes when you buy
a frame

He says it's on the mantle

I laugh
No I guess I don't have that.
And he says, your dad doesn't even speak Korean
And I say, neither does yours

We walk around the streets near Pike Place Market
It's getting cold.
We look inside furniture shop windows
at moss green chaise lounges

I tell him that I'd like to have one of those

We keep walking and he says there's a little mixed kid
And I say don't think about it so much
And he says aren't you scared of having a white baby?
I say no

He looks disappointed.
He has no idea that I plan on having his.

On Not Moving

Victoria Namkung

It ended at 1:24pm. It was at least 80 degrees outside. August.

Now it is through, he puts on a pair of Gap khakis and walks out of my bedroom. I hear the front door slam shut and then the screen door closes slowly after. My cordless phone rings in the living room and the black pug next door is barking. I stay on my full-size white bed lying on my side. From my bedroom window, I can see the black birds sitting high on the wooden telephone poles and I hear the kids from the nearby high school walking through the alley going to McDonald's. The vertical cream-colored blinds in my room are half-open, but the windows are closed. I look out for a minute and then realize that I am expected back at work. I go straight to the only bathroom in my one bedroom apartment. The sun is coming in strong through the tiny shower window, but I flip the light switch on anyway. I need as much light as possible. Leaning on the countertop, I look hard at my face first. My eyeliner is now under my swollen eyes, my bottom lip is bleeding slowly, and I realize I can hardly feel the linoleum under my feet. I wash my hands first. My neck is stinging badly, so I am careful when I lift my gray and white lace camisole off. I don't know what I am expecting to find. Lifting my messy nest of dark hair I look hard at my back. I count seventeen bluish-purple bruises that have already formed in clusters. Some are just the size of pennies. Others are not. There are four more on my freckled shoulders. The skin is broken in two places. And I continue to stare into that medicine cabinet mirror with the Broadway light bulbs above and realize that this is the first time I am seeing myself cry. And I never want to forget that image. So I keep staring into that mirror. Not hysterically, but tears drop in a steady stream and fall onto my naked chest. And I can't stop looking. Not just out of horror or disgust or fear, but because I know that if I look for a few seconds more, I will know that this is as bad as it is ever going to get.

Sometimes I feel...

Co-written and Directed by Felicia Perez

Erin O'Brien

Announcer (offstage with mike):
>   Hello and welcome all you fine brothers and sistas. I want to welcome you to our second annual "Tell It To Me Sista" Poetry Slam. Y'all looking mighty *revolutionary* tonight. I want you all to give it up for our first volunteer, a sweet little sistah by the name Errinn OhhBhryann! Teach sista teach.

Audience applause

Erin walks to center stage with a black shirt which has a huge fist of power on the front

Hi, my name is Erin. Sometimes I think of myself as a poet and so I'm gonna read you a little poem I wrote, it's called "Sometimes I Feel."

Erin breaths deeply and gets into spoken word mode

sometimes I feel
sometimes I feel
sometimes I feel
I feel you watching me
you watching
you watch, you watch, you watch
watch me, look mommy
watch me, look watch me
watch out
watch out for me
out for me, out for me
THEY are all out for me
I am out for me, for me
I am out

I am out
out out out
I am I am I am
I am not this or that
I am both/and
I am some of this
and I am some of that
and I am real cute
hapas are the cutest
you have an interesting look
well, that's because
I am interesting
inter esting
inter inside
enter my inside
my inside
in my side
on my side, my side
are you on my side?
are ya with me?
because if you're not with me
then you're against me
are ya with me?
do you want to BE with me?
you want to be with me?
you want to be with me!
be with me
be me
be like me
like me
please like me
please me
please lick me
me me me
love me please love me
why don't you love me?
you don't love me!

don't leave me
don't leave
don't don't
don't touch me
please don't touch me like that
don't! it hurts!
don't! please stop
don't don't
oh don't stop baby
oh don't stop
stop stop
stop! you're under arrest
under arrest
under all the rest
all the rest think i'm an angel
underneath the angel is a bad girl
a very bad girl
BAD girl BAD girl
i'm just a girl
a girl a girl
I like a girl
a girl? a girl!
I fucked a girl
I fuck girls
I look girly
like a girl
too much like a girl
you don't act too much like a girl
girls don't spit
girls don't talk back
girls don't wear boots
girls don't have attitudes
and girls certainly do not challenge authority
and girls don't fuck girls
don't fuck girls
don't fuck don't fuck
don't fuck me over

don't fuck me up
don't fuck around on me
don't fuck around
she fucks around around
a fucking round of drinks
I'll have another fucking
round of drinks
drinks, drink up, drink this

sometimes I feel
sometimes I feel

like a target   Light cue: bright red special over head
no not the store
like a target, the object of someone's hate, someone's anger,
someone's fear, pain, passion, destruction. Like I'm under
attack for who I am. My identity under attack. Words,
fists, bullets hitting me on all sides. And sometimes I feel
like I'm just going to crack.

sometimes I feel
sometimes I feel   Light cue: spotlight
Like a communist.   *eggs are thrown*
Hey, I have the right to free speech, what do you think this
closet commie. What? who me dad no way I'm a registered
democrat, all power to the people.

Oh yeah where are you from?   (take off shirt) *eggs thrown*
sometimes I feel like an immigrant. Where is nowhere in
particular any way. Well you see i was born in Virginia and
then I moved to the Philippines and then back to Virginia and
then to Cameroon and Syria and back to Virginia and then to
London then Napa then Italy and back to Napa then to Santa
Barbara and then LA. Power to Los Angeles

Oh yeah what are you anyway?   (take off shirt)   *eggs thrown*
Actually, I'm bi-racial. You see this side of me is
Vietnamese and this side of me is Irish-American and that
make me bi-racial. O'Brien eh, you even Asian?
And sometimes they say O'Brien eh   (take off shirt)   *eggs thrown*
funny you don't look like an O'Brien
O'Brien O'Brien, I heard she's a lesbian
A what? A lesbian!

Actually, I'm Bi-sexual   (take off shirt)   *eggs thrown*
You see this side of me is a lesbian and this side of me is
straight and together that makes me bi-sexual

I had no idea Erin was straight, she's dating a boy. what's
happened? she's all in to that queer power queer power
or is girrrl power!   (take off shirt)   *eggs thrown*
you see because I'm a spice girls fan   (take off shirt)   *eggs thrown*
tell me what you want what you really really want I'll tell
you what I want what I really want I wanna I wanna I
wanna kill you and slit my throat. but no I wouldn't do that
to you no because you're my sista yeah that's right

Because I'm a feminist   (take off shirt)
Women have the right to walk alone at night   *eggs thrown*
hey, that's just cause you know you can't get a girl wet any
other way. but that was just when I was in school...

when I was a student   (take off shirt)   *eggs thrown*
but then again I feel like I will always be a student like I
am constantly learning even though I think I know everything
I learned that sometimes I feel
Sometimes I feel like I'm walking on eggshells like I'm
walking on eggshells and I feel like I'm just going to crack.
like a target   Light cue: bright red special overhead
no not the store
like a target, the object of someone's hate, someone's anger,
someone's fear, pain, passion, destruction. Like I'm under

54

fists, bullets hitting me on all sides. And sometimes I feel
like I'm just going to crack.
Sometimes I feel like I'm walking on eggshells like I'm
walking on eggshells and I feel like I'm just going to crack.

Who's responsible for this, I ask you who is responsible for
this? this mess who? I'll tell you who's responsible no
wait, I'll show who is responsible you wait just wait right
there and I'll show you   (get mirror)
I'll show you who's responsible

(mirror facing audience)
sometime I feel
like a target   Light cue: bright red special over head
no not the store
like a target, the object of someone's hate, someone's anger,
someone's fear, pain, passion. destruction. Like I'm under
attack for who I am. My identity under attack. Words,
fist, bullets hitting me on all sides. And sometimes I feel
like I'm just going to crack.
Sometimes I feel like I'm walking on eggshells.
And sometimes I feel like the egg , hard on the outside soft on
the inside, white on the outside yellow on the inside and
sometimes I feel like I'm just gonna crack.

But I don't mind being an egg even a bad egg or a rotten egg
because at least, at least I'm not a chicken (drop mirror)

Light cue: lights out
music cue: Fight the power track 10

The One The One

Tony Osumi

Check it out, check it out
man loves a woman...
let's get it on...
brothers and sisters
ain't no woman...
like the one
the one—I got

I believe I believe
I've been touched
caressed
beyond words
my silent tongue
massaged
without a beat
to a higher desire—*fire fire*
thank you
the one the one

can it be can it be
for real—the real deal
straight and clean
scene to scene
always and forever...
time to hold tight
hold close
your time/our time
seize the time...
with her
the one the one
I got I got
your back
front/top and bottom
never ever

will you be cold/hungry
without laughter
livin' ever after
the one the one

which way, this way
foward/always forward
keep on pushin...
too much, so much
to be done
I
you
We
Us~must
it can be done
love and trust
you
the one the one

Sardines and Crackers

Tony Osumi

Alone with sardines and crackers
no one to cook for

My anger has chased you out
and you have not come back
Eating from another's pot?

Crackers dry
caught between my mouth
oil burns my throat

Liberation
will not take place
with anger like mine
against women like you
rhetoric and practice
have become contradictions

no one to talk to
no one to cook for
I have become a contradiction
alone with sardines and crackers

Los Angeles Nikkei

Tony Osumi

Westside Sansei
saying good riddance to scotch-tape and black mascara
as you board the Asian American Movement
gate number 1968
Next Stop...
S. F. State, Manzanar, Agbayani Village, Wounded Knee, I-Hotel...
armed with Issei comrades
Malcolm's ghost
and the Red Book
you hunt America's three-headed beast
race/sex/class
making Third World-class time
with a strong *East Wind* at your back
the People at your side

Sawtelle Sansei
pumping gas and checking oil
to pay the note on a new
maroon '65 Mustang
built by union hands
like those in Pico Rivera
before Ford dropped a bomb
3000 workers wide
front-line casualties
unfriendly fire
blue collar hollers
finding chorus at
Goodyear, Kaiser Steel, Firestone, GM-Southgate...

J-Town Nisei
losing a husband
in the 442nd
sent you paycheck to paycheck

earning 60 cents to a man's dollar
an Oriental dollar, a Third World dollar
Yes, you'll be a renter all your life
holed-up for fear and warmth
behind deadbolts and iron bars
over a noisy 4th Street storefront
your back curving
after years of holding up
half the sky

3 Poems for Kindergartners

Tony Osumi

Kids of the World

Birds of the world
do you have enough to eat?

And fish of the world
is your water sweet?

Trees of the world
do you ever cry?

Rivers of the world
are you free to run by

Kids of the world
do you dream?
People of the world
do you dream?

Little Seed

Little seed, little seed.
What do you need?
Water please, water please.

Little Plant, little plant.
What do you need?
Sunshine please, sunshine please.
Little girl, little boy.
What do you need?
*Water, sunshine and love please
and love please.*

I am the People

I am the People
and the People are me
I am the People
and the People are me
I won't be free
until the People are free
So let's work together
in harmony

too Mixed up

2000

Editors' Note (2000)

James Lawrence Ardeña and Brandy Liên Worrall

Too mixed up is the second installment of three chapbooks devoted to the multiracial Asian American (hapa) experience. The first chapbook, *mixed up,* was put together for a reading in Los Angeles; therefore, the majority of materials are by authors from the local area. This chapbook departs from the first in that respect; contributors' locales include San Diego, San Francisco, Seattle, the East coast, Canada, and Japan, among others. The collective experience of Asian American multiracial people cannot be essentialized into a singular notion of identity. With this in mind, we sought authors who are able to chime in with creative works and essays that integrate their various experiences of being multiracial with issues of body image/ size, sex, political ideology, activism, sexuality, and geographical space.

In conjunction with Asian American Studies ideology, we seek to create a dialogue that not only dismisses traditional stereotypes of hapas, but also asserts the decentralization of the hapa experience away from the California experience and ideology as the mainstream model. By invoking such wide and varied subject matter, we hope to elucidate further what does connect and bind us. The increased visibility of multiracials is often dramatically associated with a rise in population. However, our numbers have always existed. Scrutiny by the media and academia harkens back to the same notions of half-breed as freak or exotic object put under a social microscope for dissection and ill-formed classification. In order to debunk this construct, it is essential that we present ourselves in the most comprehensive manner as possible. It is our hope that this trilogy destroys the veil of exploitation and stereotypes, provides a lens through which to view the ever-evolving history of multiracial Asian American fluidity, and inspires others to continue "weaving the tapestry" that resists being tied up and boxed in.

Untitled

Ethelyn Abellanosa

You're too fat to be filipina
You're too white to be filipina
You're too tall to be filipina

I can't fit into your ideals
> *Hold my breath to hide my size*
Nothing good can come from selling myself (*short*) as
> *mestiza, exotic, erotic, filipina, hapa*
Since I will still be fat at the end of the day.

Your labels, so strong and persistant have made themselves my labels.
You expect Filipinas to be
> *petite. exotic. submissive. sexual.*
Yet I cannot balance
> *the other side of me, the other half of me, the other whole of me,*
my Irish/German ancestry. I come from large women. These are the genes
in my system.
> *I can no longer suck in my stomach to fit in an appropriate filipina size*
dress.
I can no longer pimp myself exotic to find love. Raking scissors over my
arms won't make me thin.
> *This is who I am.*

I can starve, I can exercise, I can beat my insides
until I am a shell. But I am so tired.
Tired of your exoticisms, of *your* labels, of *my* labels
> *covering me, suffocating me, engulfing me, drowning me, strangling me,*
killing me.

From my American homeland, I am expected to be thin smart thin funny
thin bright thin caring thin pretty thin outgoing thin serious thin patient
thin considerate thin strong thin devoted thin dedicated thin proud thin
witty thin perfect thin.

But the truth is, I am fat smart fat funny fat bright fat caring fat pretty fat outgoing fat smart fat serious fat patient fat angry fat considerate fat shamed fat perfectionist fat strong fat silly fat devoted fat bitter fat dedicated fat proud fat witty fat radical fat enraged fat resigned fat emotional fat conflicted fat.

Eating Dirt

Wei Ming Dariotis

Why does the vampyre eat dirt? She eats the dirt to become the land to
take it into her the earth becomes her body she eats the earth consumes it
becomes
consumed by it.

The vampire, traditionally, carries on its travels its native soil sleeps in it
a little piece of home
is only safe when embedded in it.

Final resting place. Native land
birth dirt
grave soil. From dust to dust.

This dirt-dust breathed into me
made of me. I eat the sand-dune dirt of San Francisco and taste the foot-
prints of Yerba Buena taste metallic aftertaste gold-dust dreams of '49ers
and sojourners taste the barefoot dreams of the ghosts of natives of this
place this spit of land-dirt surrounded three sides
by water.

Vampyres, traditionally, fear to travel over water. Ocean water
holy water
birth water.

Vampyres must be grounded. We need to be implanted in the soil of the
place we are located. We emerge from the ground we speak from the earth
we dracula-dragon-wyrm-serpent emissaries of the Earth our Mother she
speaks through us, but only if we remember to eat her.

Eat her flesh
into our flesh, which is borne of her.

I, having become a vampyre, ceased to menstruate ceased to give blood
(began only to take it). And then my female organs atrophied

that which made me a woman -gyne-hyster-omega-the center-first shrank
and then transformed
reformed merged with
into an ancient organ, the use of which had gone forgotten (had only been
guessed at).

But we remember. It was meant to help us digest our death
to digest our earth. We eat the earth we live at and it protects us. Pregnant
women crave clay and eat dirt like children. The instinct remains.

My organ digests the dirt the dirt becomes my body filters the blood I
drink in
the blood becomes my body
I become the earth the dirt the soil the sand-dune smudge of all the places
I have lived
I become the blood the body the cell-soul of all the people whose blood I
have sucked into me.

To be a vampyre is to be that which collects the genetic code of humanity
that which connects all things through the blood we share. To be a vampyre is to be the agent of the earth-mother. I am her child; I whisper her
secrets into the dreams of those from whom I consume and am consumed
by (they eat me alive). They bury me alive. I was alive in the bosom of my
mother earth
in the womb of my mother-I was buried in her flesh and now I eat it
                    placenta soup   placenta tare-tare
I have no placenta no ovaries no fallopian tubes
I have no woman-center. But, becoming a vampyre did I cease to be a
woman? I know I am a woman. I know Woman as I know Man because I
have eaten of them, drank of them, and dreamed of their dreams.

I have stalked them through nights threaded with wisps of cool fog and
nights throbbing with heat that turns the moon yellow and swollen.

It is different to hunt a man, the hunter. A woman is used to being
stalked—she knows she's prey. Am I a woman, being a huntress? Diana, the
hunter, she was a woman. A lesbian is a huntress woman-a woman-loving

woman. A Huntress by definition is not prey. Without these organs inside my body that define "womanhood"-these organs that define "woman" as "child-bearer," "life-giver"~I, life-taker, huntress, murderer-even without these organs I remain a woman.

I re/member my woman-ness: it is re/created in me re/born in me. What is the essence of Womyn? To create-destroy
to tend the soil in which things grow. I tend the soil, I attend the earth
am the Earth's attendant and hand-maid
her mistresss and lover
I lie in the Earth and caress her
my body naked into hers-my grave my lovers' bed. I slip into the moist dark caves of her.

In each place I search she tastes different. In each place I taste her I know her in her differences. I take into me her varied flavors: the special scent of loam, the grit of desert sand baked hard~but my favorite is always that earth licked by the sea touched by the thousand shores that sea has gently caressed; the earth made salty by the sea.

This Box's for You

Cheryl Deptowicz-Diaz

Ignorance indeed is indescribably insane.
I've bumped into him many times
at the doctor's office, the grocery line, the produce section
at the gym, in mass demonstrations, at the dinner table.
Even exchanged a few words, here and there.
But, it's not really what he says, but mostly the way he looks at me.

This look of difficulty, wanting to decipher, decode, what I am.
This look of upset because I don't fit his multitude of boxes
Neither do I fit his ready-made templates,
Pre-printed forms,
Small jars used to separate like spices.
Different looks for different gooks, not fitting the bill.

His confused look was evident in the numerous glances he's stolen my way
His own discomfort have, at times, made me shift in my seat, switch my stance,
my palms sweat, my stomach churn, fear for my life.
Is this how far we've not come?

Decipher, decode.
Finally, the brave, necessary, inevitable question, "what are you?"
Decipher, decode.
Need to put her in her place, her box
Miscellaneous contagious why isn't she obvious
Decipher, decode.
Need to remold, pigeon holed,
Congregate, separate, need to meditate
Meticulously put in your place
Different looks for different gooks, not fitting the bill

Without my cooperation,
I become his Italian bellalinda in Italian restaurants,
the one that's supposed to ask for extra virgin olive oil, expertly eating long

70

spaghettini in marinara sauce without one slurp falling on white shirts.
I become his Hawai'ian exotic dancer, at luaus, a pink hibiscus flower in
my ear, festive lei around my neck, grass skirt gyrating to the beat of his
Pacific Oceans.
I become his American Indian, at Annual Pow Wows, up Cachuma Lake,
near the res, selling my baskets, beaded necklaces, and turquoise rings.
I become his Mexican woman with tight braids down her back, selling
tamales down the street corners.
Ohh, and how exciting, might I also have, by happy chance,
a bit of African blood too.

All too well, I know this process of sifting the brown rice from the white
rice
One jar for brown sugar, one for white.
One box for straight, one for queer
One for female, one for male
One for love, one for hate
One for you, one for me
One for us, one for them
One for far, one for near

All or nothing
With me or against me
Day or night
Love me or hate me
Black or white,
Nothing in between
This tug-o-war,
this either/or
Good or bad
Happy or sad
Crying or laughing
Exclusive or inclusive
Temporary or permanent
My lover or my friend
Now or never

This dichotomy
Nothing in between
No gray areas
No *tal vez* (maybe), *baka* (maybe), perhaps

So...I respond to his "what are you?"
I am mid-day twilight
a bag of trail mix,
a bowl of fruit salad
I am the shaded gray
A bouquet of many flowers
A rainbow of colors
A cello the size of a viola that sounds like a saxophone.
I am the lead singer of a samba, kulintang, taiko dancing gospel troupe,
doing back up.
A red mountain bike slowly speeding on the fast lane
I am Chinese longbeans at a Jewish festival.
I am chicken and eggplant adobo served with falafels in the Greek Isles.
I am the four-inch high-heeled stiletto designed perfectly
for the 100-meter dash.
I am your stereotyped melting-pot, now grown up
Demanding you to do the same.

Decipher decode
Need to put her in her place, her box
Miscellaneous contagious why isn't she obvious
Decipher decode, need to remold, pigeon holed,
congregate, separate, need to meditate
Meticulously put in your place
Different looks for different gooks, not fitting the bill.

Let's Play Guess My Mix

Jason Kanjiro Howard

Hey let's play a game. I have been playing it ever since I can remember. It's fun. It's called "Guess what I am." Come on, guess. Don't be shy. Okay, I see you want a challenge. I'll give you five guesses and still bet you won't be able to guess.

I'll even give you a hint. I'll tell you my name ... Jason Kevin Howard. Does that help you out? Come on, that doesn't tell you anything?

Hell, let's go crazy, I'll even give you ten guesses? Do you feel comfortable now?

Let's begin.

"This is easy. Of course you're Hawaiian."
Hawaiian is always the #1 choice. It's not a bad guess. I don't mind it, but no, I'm not.

"Well then you're Filipino."
NO, but another good guess. You are in the ballpark. Come on you can do it.

"You gotta be Mexican or Latin or something?"
You're getting colder. Try something else.

"Samoan?"
Have you ever seen a Samoan this small? Try Again.

"Sicilian?"
NO, but I love pasta.
"Chinese?"
NO.

"Korean?"
NO, but my roommate is.

"Thai? No I mean Taiwanese?"
NO, and NO.

"Vietnamese War Baby ?"
Come on now. Be serious.

"Black, I mean Mulatto..."

You might laugh, but I've gotten all of them before.
So finally I give in and tell them what I am and watch them brainfart.
Their reaction is usually funny.

Just imagine two stoners passing a joint between each other.

He takes a hit. SNORT, SNORT~(hold my hit)

(Trying to hold it) That's really good shit. (Blows it out) What kind of bud is it?—Pass it.
"Japanese and Irish, man?"
No way, man (puff)~that's so cool man. (PAUSE-puff) That's so trippy. I can't handle it man. (MY BRAIN CAN'T CONTAIN THE INFO) You're bullshitting me, right? Wow! Japanese and Irish.
So where did you get it, man? It's so exotic. *But I dig the relationship though.* Two island countries. Sushi and Potatoes. Sake and Whiskey. Ha, Ha, Ha—just kidding man.
Hey man, I thought you could handle your high. Gimmie back that j...

As long as I can remember I knew I was different. I wasn't the same as everyone else. I wasn't one thing. I was two. But I didn't have to decide one or the other. I would be both. But I knew somehow that I was never going to be fully accepted into one or the other. I would always be on the outside looking in.
And because I wasn't like anyone else ... well, except for my sister. I went out of my way to be different, or do things that broke the stereotype or broke down any negative stereotypes which kept people off balance, This was fine with me I used this to my advantage. They didn't know what to make of me. So I didn't talk about my bi-racialness until they asked me.
And when it came up, I made a game out of it. This was my way of dealing with it, letting someone ask questions so they don't feel like an idiot.

This way I can control it. If they guess wrong it won't hurt me. I can show them that I can look like a million different people. I wouldn't let their confusion hurt me inside. This was reaffirming to me. I could be safe that it wasn't going to be blurted out in some weird way. Or that someone might make a racial comment in front of me, and make an ass out of themselves.

Instead of waiting for people to be shocked by my mix. . . I would shock them first and take great pleasure in watching their head spin.

After the cat is out of the bag. And they know what I am.

They try to put me together like I'm some Mr. Potatohead. They study my face, my nose, my lips, my tan, my hair, my eyes, my legs, and that they are empowered they feel like they can ask me a bunch of questions.

That is so weird. What is your Dad?
He's Irish?
Is your dad like in the military?
Is your mom like a geisha?
Does she speak English?
Does she talk with an accent?
Was she born here?
She was interned?
Wow.
So is she glad she got the money?
What did she spend it on?
Does she take a lot of pictures?
You know I've heard some weird stuff about Japanese moms.
Do you have a small penis?
Are you Catholic or Buddhist?
Have you been to Ireland?
You have cousins named Fergel and Finbar?
Have you been to Japan?
What kind of women do you date?
You don't like blondes?
You date Asian women?
Do you have a fetish?
Do you drink?
When you do, do you get red in the face and in the ears?
Is your dad an alcoholic?

The funny thing is that two generations of my family conspired to not illicit such reactions.

I was born as Jason Kevin Howard, but I always had problems with it. I didn't feel like it fit me. Do I look like a Jason Kevin Howard? Close your eyes and try to picture a Jason Kevin Howard. It's so boring and bland.

Jason is greek, Howard is English, and Kevin well Kevin is Irish but nobody these days knows that is Kevin is Irish.

My name could have easily been Kanjiro O'Hannrahain.

Now let's play the game again, except now I'll tell you my name first. Except now it's no fun. There's no mystery. Everything is right out in the open. But that's too easy in this country; sometimes you need a buffer or else you get labeled.

This buffer started with my grandfather. When my grandfather came over from Ireland to the US. and there was so much bigotry against the Irish that the only way he thought he would have a fighting chance was if he changed his name from O'Hannrahain to a more ethnically ambiguous last name like Howard.

My mother wanted to name me Kanjiro after my great grandfather, but there was already a division in our family from Father's mother.

When my father was dating my mother, my dad's mother, my grand-mother, was curious about the relationship.
So is she nice?
um hum
Does she cook?
yes?
What's her last name?
Hattori?
Hattori could almost be Italian.

During their relationship, my mother had never met my grand-mother until the day they decided to get married.

They arrived at the door holding hands.

My grandmother opened the door and screamed while slamming the door in my parents' face. She didn't talk to my parents for almost six years.

I didn't know this growing up--in fact, until she passed away. They didn't tell me.

Growing up I was always jealous that I didn't get a Japanese name or even a Japanese middle name like my sister. Her middle name is Natsuno, which means "summer child" in Japanese.

But she was born two years after me.

When I was christened my grandmother finally accepted my parents' marriage. So I don't think that giving me a Japanese name would have eased the tensions.

Names can make a difference.

I've thought about changing it back to O'Hannrahain and taking my great-grandfather's name. Jason Kanjiro O'Hannrahain. It's always bothered me that my grandfather had to change his name.

But I feel like I would get shit from people. Like I was trying to be trendy, or politically correct, or trying to get an inside track on a job, or be something that I wasn't.

It wasn't until this year that I became comfortable with my bi-racialness being out in the open. Like it proceeded me when I walked into the room. As if I was announcing it to the world by being involved in a group that is racially mixed.

Now I have to stop playing the game and step into the light.

One of the first things I did with the group was a Hapa and Parenting workshop at a large Japanese conference this year. There were a bunch of different Japanese hapas there, and they all offered their own experience to help out the Japanese parents whose children were marrying out.

So I'm feeling good. I'm in my element. Being mixed is something that I know about, and I can help them answer these embarrassing questions about identity, fitting in, and still maintaining a Japanese identity.

When the workshop ends, there are still a bunch of people still milling about asking questions, and looking at pamphlets.

I try to reach out to one of the people that attended the conference. He was a longtime teacher and a coach at a high school.

I thanked him for coming to the conference, and I asked him if he learned anything new.

And he looked at me funny. Like he was trying to break me down in his mind.

"I listened to what you said about your family and your experience. This is all new to me, but when you started talking, I looked over, and you mentioned you were Japanese. I was puzzled. Because you don't look Japanese at all."

And he shuffled out of the room and left me hanging there.

I was so stunned, I didn't know what to say. I am usually prepared for this. What is he trying to say...

And then I remember why I invented the game.

You Woke Me This Morning

(for Akili Tyson)

   Peter Kiang

You woke me this morning.
I reached out startled, maybe still dreaming,
thinking we could actually touch.

We met a year before Reagan.
In big, bold letters, your favorite t-shirt announced:
"Young, Gifted, and Black".
We who were older joked with you, saying
"well, maybe young and Black."

But our movement shook the campus that year
as we rallied for ethnic studies,
demanded a Third World Center,
boycotted the Crimson,
picketed the Hasty Pudding,
and sat in at Eliot House.
Proud of our unity,
in love with our colors.

Most of us were graduating
but you were a freshman.
What made you so active, I wondered.
One night you told me about your father,
a revolutionary, dedicated to Black liberation.
Your Swahili name, a reflection of his vision.
He trained you as a child how to drop to the floor on cue,
in case the Klan or the police were coming.

And I wondered why Black-Asian unity was so natural for you.
You told me about your Japanese grandmother,
living in Los Angeles.
A simple woman, a camp survivor.
She taught you about *gaman*[1] and tradition and honor.
You were her favorite.

Others from those days have preceded you.
Leroy, Keith, Marlon.
Young, gifted, and Black.
The conspiracy of *la sida*[2]
is deeper and more deadly than Cointelpro[3].

In D.C., we climbed your T Street stairs
just before the new year.
Your slow ascent
showing the effects of drugs and disease.

But inside your home
you served tea and fresh fruit.
Your almond eyes shining like always
with the brilliant beauty of African Kings and Queens.

Recalling old times,
Imagining new plans,
We laughed as Jazz's[4] eyes
sparkled back to you,
sharing the promise of
a new cycle of life.

Work was so hectic today,
I forgot about this morning
until the drive home
when those familiar voices on NPR[5]
shared the news.

Then I knew.
You woke me this morning
to say goodbye.

(Boston—1996 May 9)

1. *Gaman* in Japanese means "to endure."

2. *La sida* is the term for AIDS in Spanish.

3. Cointelpro stands for Counter Intelligence Program–the U.S. government's covert operation which infiltrated and destabilized Black Liberation Movement groups such as the Black Panther Party in the late 1960s.

4. My son, born in 1994, is named Jazz.

5. NPR stands for National Public Radio where Akili Tyson had worked as a sound engineer.

Letter To Gloria

Peter Kiang

[For Gloria Anzaldúa after re-reading *Borderlands/La Frontera: The New Mestiza* at a July 2000 institute sponsored by the Association of American Colleges & Universities on diversity and democracy in the curriculum.]

Estimada Gloria:

Your words have moved me for more than 20 years. Mestizo identity *y el movimiento sin fronteras*. The movement without borders. Two realities and two commitments in my own life.

Querida Gloria, how does it feel for you, for your revolutionary words and images to be canonized? Was it ever your intention to shape academic discourse and the realm of high theory? Forgive me for not being in touch with your most recent art or commentary. But I can't imagine that you are satisfied with any of this.

Yesterday, José, a master teacher/organizer, shared how he still uses *This Bridge Called My Back*, even now. That book meant so much to me so long ago. Do you remember those days? I was reading you and Fanon, side by side, and here you are together again. Yes, Fanon is here, too, invoked by Stuart Hall to describe how diasporic identities resist colonization–concepts at the center of much that I do now. Fanon was so clear in exposing how colonialism's distorted discourse is constructed and then imposed until the colonized call it their own.

But here, *la frontera* intersects with diaspora–making faces of resistance, making souls of *Regéneracion*. Yes, *el movimiento* must be for the land. And yes, *el movimiento* must be for the mind.

Ay, Gloria, you and your words, and those of Fanon, meet here again in my life, after so many years, helping me recall and reconnect with something important in my own learning. I have never really shared your work with my own students, but I am wondering now if perhaps it is time.

Estimada Gloria, I've missed you.

Cariñosamente,

pk

Untitled

Daniel Takeshi Krause

There were those who would say they loved me.
Some would say they could see the heart of me,
Not only vaguely almond eyes and tinged skin,
But no amount of Coca-Cola could turn my hair fair
Or my almonds blue
So I put down my Big Mac
And took my huddled mass to my new island home
Where hair runs black.

And there are those who would say they love me.
Some would say I'm a Japanese soul,
Not only a high nose and vaguely oval eyes.
Still others look up from their french fries
And I see how they bleach their hair
And burn their skin;
How they hate themselves from within.
But I won't judge because I've been there.
I've tasted that sin.
I know what it hurts like.

There are those who would say they love me,
But I've heard that before,
And I'm not looking for love anymore.
I only want someone to look like.

She Is

Noemi LaMotte-Serrano

she is
disheveled hair and smeared red lipstick
yesterday's fashions splattered with drippings of last week's adobo
eyes glazed over with memories her tired thoughts can no longer grasp
 she is
standing in the middle of the intersection of fifth and market
 waving her arms frantically at the angry san franciscan commuters
who are anxious to return to the safety and simplicity of iron-gated apartments
 a blond in a mercedes slams her finely manicured fingers against the
horn,
sneers to the man in the passenger seat, "Look at that crazy bitch, she
thinks she's directing traffic!"
she is not directing traffic
 she is dancing to an ancient rhythm of a jungle beat
on an island that is home
 on an island that is lost
 a home that is lost
 a people that is lost
she is lost in the longing to return
she is
 lost
in a dark bedroom
shades drawn so tight that even her six year old son cannot reach her
with his cries of "Mama if you love me you will open the door."
she is lost in a country of locked doors.
she is lost to a granddaughter who always let herself pass for mexican
her history is lost on the painted lips that speak more spanish than tagalog
she is a crumpled photograph in the back of a crowded drawer
she is a culture left to dissolve in a country that once was hope but never
home
she is what i was always afraid to become
she is beautiful in black in white
she is the words i can never find

to describe a lola that is only mine
in death
she is dancing to an ancient drum beat
 on an island that is home
she is waiting to teach me the steps
she is
home.

Scissors

Claire Light

Nothing can stain linoleum like photographic chemicals. Disgusting. You walk around the rest of the house in your socks, confident that they won't come up black. But on the linoleum of the back pantry she's taken over, with its sticky chemical patches, you tiptoe around, worrying that some sort of ethylphenolpolymuck will eat through the fibers and into your feet. That linoleum will come out of the deposit.

Her scissors are obviously going to be stored in a drawer. She puts things in drawers and takes them out of drawers to use and returns them to the drawers when she's done. She tends to take over unwanted furniture and ruin it. She cannibalizes the stuff to hold her chemical trays and the photo stains cover the blond surfaces (horizontal and vertical) of a small number of cheap Scandinavian modules. Few drawers in evidence. The scissors are in the first one you draw.

All you wanted was to cut the legs off yet another pair of jeans grown suddenly too short. She has several such pairs herself. It's summer. You two were talking friendly about the fashion viability of cut-offs and you asked for her scissors and her volatile mood broke down, the way it always does, before you get a chance to leave the room happy. On a dime she turned nasty and said no, they're my scissors. Ask Mom for hers. You say what you both already know: Mom can never find hers. Well, she says, you can't use mine, you'll lose them.

So you say that you'll use hers with or without her permission and she says, you'll have to find them first. I'll find them, you say.

She dignities out of the house to take a walk. You head straight for the pantry.

Five minutes later the legs are off the jeans, but you're still smoking. You've determined already to "lose" them deliberately, put them down on one of the clean, uncluttered surfaces in the kitchen or hallway that hide the stacks of junk drawers filled with things you can't either use or just get rid of. You know your mother will happen by and sweep them into a drawer and they will be lost forever. She'll forget the next minute that she ever saw the scissors and they'll just be gone. You'll ask her, Mom, did you see the scissors? and she'll say, I think there's one in the second drawer of the table in the family room. but of course there isn't.

Where should you put them? You could leave them in your room, too, to be buried underneath a pile of clothes and books and the next time you're ordered to clean you'll kick them, along with the clothes, under your bed only to be discovered two years later when you move again. Which is better? The drawer is clearly better because it will be emptied two years hence by process of pouring into a mover's carton and taken to the next house, along with all the unopened boxes from the last move, the new boxes which will be sealed but never opened, the unused heirloom furniture, the spoiled Scandinavian modules.

If they're lucky someone will spot them at that moment and say, That's where those scissors went! and use them for a few hours to cut up boxes. Then they'll disappear again. Punishment.

There's no point in going over the unfairness of her constant, cold accusations in your mind. You do anyway. Three years from now you will drive across town, literally, all the way across town, to the airport where she's going back to college a day earlier than you, drive at top speed, because you found she'd left her wallet in the glove box of the car. You catch her just as she's going through security and she doesn't even say thanks. Later that night she'll call from four states away to ask you to look for her driver's license in the glove box. It's gone. You can't find it. The next time you see her you'll be the sister, still the only sister, but now the sister who stole her drivers license. You'll be that sister to the end of your days, but the modifiers will increase. The sister who spies on her doings to report to your parents. The sister who wasn't around to share the brunt of your grandfather's lechery. The sister who wanted her to get an abortion. The sister who sided with her boyfriend. The sister who forgets your nephew's birthdays. The sister who threw her out of your apartment when she had nowhere to go but to cold friends. At New

Year's. The sister who never shared blankets or turned out the light. The sister whose hand she grabbed like a feral animal when the laparoscope went in, whose hand she dropped like a dead fish when the doctor said, All done! The sister she hasn't heard from in . . . how long is it now? Five years?

You stand in the doorway of her room. Two years ago you would've wrecked it, throwing the stuffed animals around, making your mother make you clean up and then wash your mouth out with soap. But you've learned subtlety, the stuffed animals are gone and she's left the house. It's bravado. When she makes a statement, when she casts down her challenge, she has to walk away to indicate its solidity, its immutability. You can't find the scissors. Stupid bitch. You say it aloud. And heft the scissors in your hand.

Her room is neat. There's a series of photographs in cheap Walgreen's frames hanging in rows on one wall documenting the last five years of her life. In chronological order from left to right, bottom to top. Friends, in order of whom she unloaded first, leaning into the sights, grinning hectically. You have a different set of images in your mind: the same friends, the same faces, but not grinning, rather looking bewildered, asking you, on whichever porch you had that year, why she's so angry with them, why they can't come in, why she says she's not home when they know she is.

Her thinking is so obvious. She is neat. She is organized. Everything is where she can find it. And where she can find it is always where everyone else can find it as well. She has no concept of the pleasure of mess organization, of being able to hold your palm down in the air over a pile of papers and say, Don't touch this mess! I know where everything is. Disorder distresses her.

Suddenly love increases your body, fixing your stare to the wall of faces. You go to the pantry and put the scissors back in the drawer. When she comes back she may check, but she won't let you see her checking. And she'll find them there. And she'll think she's won.

One Afternoon

Dorian Sanae Merina

She closes the door before
the engine dies
her purse her eyeglasses
cadena de amor
in afternoon light

She crosses the gravel driveway
peers through the birdshit
on the window
from her lips she will tell me
of earthquake Island
damage to church walls and water pipes
from her lips she will remind me
to remind her
to get the Kit Kats chocolate bars
not King-Size but Regular
three for ninety-nine cents
and later
will pass them to my hands
with crushed tomatoes
soft peaches
and my father's mail

She calls Batanas but can't get through
the operator says something
about the government and water pipes
She locates Eloy in Manila and gets the news
warns me of volcanoes
and expensive mangoes
at the store

You better go soon, Auntie says
after we pick her up from the sidewalk

on the way to church
Why, will it be covered in lava, I laugh
with no water pipes?
You never know, she says from behind
her dark sunglasses
This afternoon started out cool
and now
I can't remember which car I'm riding in
there have been so many

At this
Grandma pushes the button on her armrest
all the doors click unlocked
we drive in silence

This Is My First Time

Victoria Namkung

Basics

Name:	Victoria
Age:	23
Education:	Graduate school
Ethnicity:	Korean, Irish, Asian American, hapa, mixed race, etc.
Religion:	Protestant and Jewish, but not really practicing anything
Occupation:	University instructor, journalist, booking agent, clothing designer
Area Code:	310
Hair:	Brown usually
Eyes:	Brown always
Cigarettes:	Sometimes
Booze:	Sometimes
Drugs:	Sometimes
Self Love:	Usually

Tip of the Iceberg

Last Great Book I Read: *A Heartbreaking Work of Staggering Genius* by Dave Eggers. I cried at the preface. His sentences are phenomenal.

Favorite On Screen Sex Scene: This is so cheesy, but honest: Drew Barrymore and Tom Skeritt in *Poison Ivy*. She's like this 15-year old runaway bad ass and he's her friend's father. I was excited at the time.

Song That Puts Me in the Mood: Music does not arouse me. I love some music, but am not passionate enough about a song to actually become sexual.

Five Items I Cannot Live Without: Water, Palm Pilot, Family, Touch, Voice

In My Bedroom You'll Find: Simple modern stuff. No stuffed animals. No photo collages of sorority days. No "I'm a girl therefore I need to have 500 pillows on my bed."

Most Humbling Moment: Thinking of a title for this ad

Why You Should Get to Know Me: I think I'm fairly intelligent, socially aware, I'm easily amused by interesting people, unimpressed with people who use big words, and can be witty if necessary. I also care greatly about my family and close friends. I know when to be selfish and when to give.

You Should Be

Gender:	Male
Age:	24-34 (negotiable depending on the circumstances)
Education:	At least some college (negotiable depending on circumstances)
Ethnicity:	No preference—White men seem to prefer me most, then Black, Latino, Native American, and lastly Asian
Religion:	My boyfriend in 8th grade told me I was going to Hell
Cigarettes:	Sometimes, Never
Booze:	Sometimes
Drugs:	Sometimes, Never
Self Love:	Sometimes, Usually, Often, etc.

More On What I'm Looking For: You should not use phrases like "24-7" or "hey bro." Be emotionally available. You should have accomplished one of your dreams by now. Follow through with your goals. If you're Asian, don't have a hapa fetish. If you're white, don't have a hapa or Asian fetish. If you expect me to cook Korean food you'll be disappointed. Be willing to hear me complain about things. Be able to wear nice clothes when necessary. Be able to go to a concert or my office Christmas party. Accept that parts of me want to save the world while others get excited about new makeup or Gucci shoes. Make me laugh.

That Look

Taro O'Sullivan

I took my kids to the state fair this summer. My kids love the animals, and the rides. One of the joys that life brings to parents is doing something that puts a smile on your child's face. We do the best we can. Sometimes our best is enough and sometimes we fall short. When we fall short, it is perhaps the most difficult thing that we face as a parent. Some parents were able to take their children to the fair for the first time, while others were having to tell their children that they couldn't spend as much this year as last year. For the parents who were able to do more this year, the look of pride was evident, but for the others, well, it just wasn't as nice. I know both looks. All parents do.

At one of those hair-raising, white-knuckle rocket ships that my maniacal children wanted to ride, I saw something. These rides have restrictions like minimum height, age, no heart problems, no pregnant women, etc. An older man, a grandfather, and his teenage grandson were being turned away from this ride. They looked cute. They wore similar clothes and looked like a carbon copy of the other. I could feel the excitement when the young man awoke hours before the day was to begin, no longer able to contain the anticipation of going to the fair with his grandfather. It had been planned for weeks. I know that look.

The young man walked away, visibly upset, cursing, and shouting. The grandfather was trying to maintain his composure. He was older, wiser and saw the bigger picture. You see, he brought his grandson to the fair and nothing was going to ruin this day. Just beyond the pair, I saw a sign that stated in large, bold letters: COMBINED WEIGHT NOT TO EXCEED 300 lbs. I don't think they saw themselves as being large. I had forgotten as well. They just looked happy to be enjoying the day, as I was with my children. We all know that look.

Large people are discriminated at the movies, on airplanes, and on carnival rides. It is easy to dismiss it. We have all the right excuses. Insurance reasons, engineering reasons, dietary reasons, and health reasons. This young large boy experienced something that he will remember for the rest of his life. It will haunt him years from now. Just when he thought that it was finally behind him, it will come back. With the full force of all the emotions he was experiencing today. This type of hurt does that. Sadly, I too know that look.

The young girls waiting at the front of the line were giggling. That is what young girls do. No one else seemed to notice. No one else seemed to care. Perhaps some turned away because it was too painful to see, or maybe because it could easily have been them. This boy didn't care that he was sweating profusely, his face flushed, and cussing loudly so that everyone in his immediate vicinity could hear him. He was too hurt to be embarrassed.

Some people are spared this sort of humiliation. This process disintegrates your self-esteem and a sense of self. It happens to people who are different. In the playground, at school, or in the neighborhood, someone yells something at you, and then others join in. Maybe it is about your size, or your color, or the house you live in, or something equally personal which you have no control over. It is something you never quite get over. When I was four, I was teased for the first time for being half white. Kids threw rocks with their obscenities. As a parent, you hope it doesn't happen to your child.

The grandfather was consoling him. I could not hear him, but it was as if he was saying "now, now, it's ok, everything will be fine, let's go on a different ride." You knew the rest of the day just wasn't going to be like planned. The grandfather was still smiling somehow. It must have happened to him before. He had that look.

It is the same look you have when your take your four-year-old son fishing, and he catches his first trout. One of the landmark days for fathers, filled with pride. It is the same smile that you try to maintain when some people start shouting racial obscenities at you and your perfect son on a perfect day. It is the smile that will turn into tears later, but for now, you have to be strong. I know that look.

It makes you wonder why. There just isn't anything you can say. I am not large, but that day, I sure felt like somehow I understood. For one brief moment, that grandfather and I, we shared that look.

Hapa

Taro O'Sullivan

The first time I heard this term was in 1974 when someone asked me if I was a "Hapa." The woman who asked me was from Hawaii, and she explained to me that I was a "Hapa Haole," meaning half White. I had forgotten that I was White. Growing up in Japan in the 60s, I was definitely a White person. I heard the "Yankee go home" and all the other anti-Western terms leveled at me as a child. I was a "half breed."

In Japan, as it was in most other conquered or occupied post-war Asian country, being half American, French, Australian, or English carried with it, a stigma all its own. To the Asian folks, Hapas are a reminder of the outside influences within their homogenous society. All too often as a result of losing a war, or having a war fought on your soil. In Japan, I was a Yankee. I was reminded everyday by the neighborhood kids. I remember growing up thinking that I was an American.

The first American I met in the States was the customs-immigration officer at the airport, who glanced back and forth between my U.S. passport and my face, as he said, "O'Sullivan, are you Japanese or Chinese?" I used to dream of being Japanese. There were hours of name-calling by the kids about being a "half-breed" and the fights against kids that always seemed to outnumber me just to be denied my Japanese heritage by the Japanese kids. I was finally Japanese. I had to leave Japan to be Japanese, and I could no longer enjoy being Japanese, but I was Japanese just the same! Hapas get used to this type of irony.

I have since compared experiences with other Hapas and the parallel is too close to be coincidence. All the "Brown Boys" that I hang around with nowadays grew up in Asia as children. They were all born sometime in the 1950s, and immigrated here in the early part of the 70s. In Asia, to be a Hapa was considered to be dirty somehow. We were like a reminder of an unpleasant event. In the typical Asian way, we were part of the culture, though at the very bottom of the food chain to be sure, but at least they claimed us as a necessary evil. My ethnic "cousin" Tio Polo (he is Uncle Polo to my kids) talked of the movie theatres in Indonesia. The White folks sat in front of the screens, in suits, at tables, in the heat. Hapas sat behind the screen. In the shade, with a picnic, eating, laughing, and staying cool, but behind the screen. We just did not really belong.

Here, we are always seen for our non-White attributes. Folks constantly question I why I don't have an accent. Why do I have an Irish last name? You get used to it after a while. You start to come up with humorous answers to these and other questions. "I was too young to go through the Asian Language Centers where they teach you to speak like Charlie Chan before you can leave Asia," or "O'Sullivan is a Japanese name, similar to O'Hara" and so forth. Some people would get mad at me for having a smart mouth. Somehow, I don't think they ask these questions to their white friends.

When we arrived in the States, we were not accepted by our cousins who immigrated many generations ago. These cousins kept the blood lines pure. Although they were second and third generation Americans by now, somehow they saw us as not part of their group. We spoke the language for one thing, and we didn't quite look like they did. We look kind of mixed, kind of…odd. In the early 70s, there were so few of us here. We didn't know there were other Hapas around. There was no Hapa clubs. So we tried to integrate.

In those days, we were just dark enough to suit the fancy of quasi-liberal White girls who were looking for an excuse to rebel against their conservative "daddies." They would approach us, slowly at first, as if we were some wild animals, and ask us questions. A Hapa friend recounts his encounters with one such woman who took him home to meet dad in one of those unnamed small towns in the Central Valley. One look from the dad, and her mission would be accomplished. The "daddy" would see my Brown friend, and feel the rage rising in the pit of his stomach. The visit would be cut short somehow, the appropriate excuses made, and they would head back to the university, but first, she would proclaim, "We showed him, didn't we?"

I wonder how our parents would have reacted had they known what we went through. Our full-blooded cousins wouldn't even get invited to these homes; they were somehow too ethnic. We were merely an exotic curiosity. We were just dark enough. My first experience was with a White girl who had asked me to go to a dance. When we got there, her recently dumped boyfriend greeted us with this glare. Anyone would have done, but a "Brown Boy" drove the knife in just a little deeper. She never asked me out again.

All my Hapa friends are older now. I listen to these stories as we reminisce about those days of innocence. It is funny; we are all divorced now. We all divorced White women. We joke that we are in a fraternity of sorts, a club, of divorced Hapas. We, in our individual ways, lived out the scene of Sidney Poitier's *Guess Who's Coming to Dinner?* Only, we didn't marry the rich girl in the end.

Some Hapas wanted so badly to be accepted by someone, anyone. They needed this. When you are half Black, you self-segregate with your Black brothers and sisters, and within that framework, you have to deal with your Whiteness. My Hapa Black friends often experience this sort of "you're not black enough" phenomenon. But in the end, the Black community accepted them. With the "Brown Boys," that was not to be. In the first place, there were very few Asian Americans here to begin with. I never met an Asian American in the high school I attended. In college, I remember meeting one Chinese American student who came in on the last tennis scholarship awarded by the university. He was Asian American, but somehow, he was American.

There were some advantages of being Hapa as well. There used to be a lot of scholarship money available if you were Hapa. I remember a recruiter came around from a large university. He came to ask me if I wanted to enroll in his large, brand new, shinny institution, free of charge, instead of the small university I was attending, where I learned that I was a Hapa-Haole. The large university was considered to be more prestigious. We Hapas went through all sorts of funny detours in our attempt to gain acceptance from our peers. Years later, I graduated from a small liberal arts college after all.

I spoke at an annual scholarship dinner recently for a large Asian American organization and was surprised that about half of the recipients were Hapas. It was so nice to see that Hapas were finally accepted. A few years ago, this particular organization wouldn't even give me the time of day, and now, I was the keynote speaker at their annual event with nearly half the recipients being Hapas. The younger generations of Hapas are strong and bold. They have a certain self-confidence that my generation of Hapas lacked. If anything, they have an advantage over their non-Hapa Asian American cousins. They lack the stigma of being Asian.

This is not to say that these new generations of Hapas feel like they belong. I have heard from younger Hapas that they are constantly being asked about just what they are ethnically. Why is it that people need to know? What difference does it really make? I suppose it is the Hapa cross to bear, the questions and the stares.

When Hapas have children, they become my friend who wasn't Asian enough. They become quarter Asian, and sometimes, that isn't Asian enough for many things. They don't really look all that Asian. They just have these angry Hapa dads who insist on raising them as Asians. They live a weird life compared to their peers in school. They eat freaky things compared to their schoolmates.

Theoretically, Hapa is the way to becoming "American." When an immigrant comes to the United States, they mark their arrival and integration into this society when the first marriage takes place between Americans and the immigrants. This union produces the Hapa child. Usually, if they are of European stock, they become part of the topography rather quickly. When we came from Asia, we were considered foreigners. We still are for the most part. No one is quite sure how long it takes to become American, rather than Asian American. Some of us remain Asians by choice to be sure, but even if we wanted otherwise, we were never given the choice of calling ourselves American. The choice is already made for us because of our appearance.

Pan Am, CNN, fiber optics, and satellites have made this world a small place to live in. This sort of "Global Village" concept of the world no is longer a mere academic theory. It is here today. Ideas, people, and commerce flow from Asia and back. As long as this mechanism is alive, we cannot stop Hapas. There will be unions between the continents. Such unions will produce children who will demand due process, equal rights, and so forth.

Hapas are the future, and as with anything ahead of its time, there are difficulties that are associated with being Hapa. The world is currently less than 11% White, and that figure is diminishing. Hapas on the other hand, are on the rise. In the future, we will all look like my brown cousins. We will not be White, Asian, African-American or Latino. We will be a little of this, a little of that, or as the folks in the islands always said, "hapa this and hapa that." There are folks from both sides who do not want to see this happen.

However, we are here and will not go quietly into the sunset just because we don't get invited to the party. We will not be silent when we don't get our share of the American dream. We will seek justice and get it. In the end, we too will get invited, eventually.

My Name Is Forver Burnt...

Amal Rana

she gave me a *chambeli* plant
a love gift
it was
to remind me of that place
where i once lived
to quench a tiny bit of longing
that unleashes itself in my heart
now and then

now and then
i think of you
when the *chambeli* flowers first
begin to bloom
i think of you
when their scent explodes upon
the latticed windows of my memory
i think of you
when i run the delicate white petals
gently down a lover's sleeping curves
i think of you

mysterious undefinable land
like you
i am full of contradictions
loving you
with a red tinge of anger and
bitterness
red like the sand hills
upon which i rolled
laughing and screaming with joy
i have that picture still
i am standing with my arms spread out
attempting to embrace your
elusive beauty

that day i took home a handful of your
rich dry grains
wanting to preserve a piece of you
forever
preparing in advance for the departure
that was inevitable

you knew before i did that we would
have to part
i was born of you
i was born in you
under your luminescent skies
and blistering desert winds
but i could not stay and be free
to live in the ways that you had taught me

the day i left i swore i would return soon
to taste your arid heat
your thickly fragrant nights
to visit your ancient hills in medina
and to slice deep into your salty waters in
jeddah
i swore i would carry your truth
to the outside world
so that they too could see that you were
much more than
rich oil sheiks and silently veiled women
you were a land of old blood, pagan goddesses
and *jinn*
a land that bred me to be resilient and indestructible
to dig deep into the most hostile of soils
in order to find water to feed my soul
a land upon which my name is forever burnt
deep below the ever shifting sands

Published in *Your Voice Tastes Like Home: Immigrant Women Write*

You Sound Like an Ethnic Studies Major

Tony Robles

The brown girl sitting
in front of me
is beautiful

the sun is showing its face
for both of us

lunchtime in the financial district

she eats a vegetable sandwich

...and nuts

we talk about our
brown ness
and she insists
i'm darker than she is

we're about the same

no use debating

she's smart
majored in psychology

i tell her
i learned more
cleaning toilets
than i did in school

she smiles
between bites of
alfalfa sprouts and cheese
and says

"you're funny"

i tell her

"don't patronize me"

she continues to
take small bites:

"You're angry
calm down
you're overreacting"

and

"What's wrong with seeing an
Asian girl with a white
guy?"

and she's really
chewing
chewing
chewing

i bite back
a little

and she says:
"You sound like an ethnic studies major"

looks down
at how
brown
i am

goes back
to her
bag
of nuts

Outdone (Part 2)

Tony Robles

My critic says i'm a phony

says i write the same old
tired poems about
being
Pilipino

she shakes her head and
says:

"You don't even speak Tagalog!
You've never been to the Phillipines!
You look Mexican...sound white.
You ain't foolin' me!"

i guess she's right

she's Laotian
and she's more Pilipino than me

has more Pilipino friends
eats more Pilipino food
knows more Pilipino words
and watches
the Filipino channel
on tv

brings me
mangoes in a plastic
shopping bag
and i write Pilipino poems
to make her forget
i look Mexican
and sound white

but i ain't foolin'
her

only
myself

The Exorcist

Freedom Allah Siyam

i've been through hell and back
in my own rendition
not a victim hood tournament
or urban fiction
not too many war stories to trade
but i'm striving to analyze sexist ideologies i entertain
through suffering comes life
right
thinking
refined my understanding
of the patriarchal ringside
neocolonial pugilist
searching for postwar remnants
of humanity that exist in that void
in the soular plexus of man
i've spent five years exorcising demons
took'em off my square
gained sight beyond sight
sword of omens got my pineal gland open
and now i cee equality
and the potential predator within
the perpetuator of sin
disciple of jinn
who can commodify
exploit and export women
for the purpose of entertaining
twisted desires to see the
spiritual reproductive system
as an expression of perversion
sadistic inclination
which is the embryo of
a colonial mindstate to
keep miseducation a reaility
through their crops and seeds

or understanding
who will be blinded by a binary logic
which cloaks inequalities and allows
the continuation of
white supremacist capitalist patriarchy
i ask myself:
what happened to our woman warriors
what happened to the brothas
that used to support her
kept a bond with her
respected her
who used to love her

An Unwilling Bodhisatva

Alberto Vajrabukka

It's not right, but it's ok. Joe stopped cycling through the channels and decided that Whitney Houston would keep him company for the next four and a half minutes. Joe hunkered down in the sofa, cross-legged, and soles up. He pushed his spoon into the cookies and cream, turning it ponderously.

This night shouldn't be any different, he thought. On appearances it was all still the same. He had his cable channels, his trusty pillow, and the Haagen-Dazs. Tonight though, he couldn't make his usual bedtime call to Erol. No, this weekend they actually occupied the same area and zip codes. And yet he was still left alone with Whitney. Joe turned his spoon some more. Around him the darkness swirled and congealed. Joe would pray tonight.

Since he was a kid, Joe prayed before going to sleep, in the manner his mom had showed him some twenty or so years ago. He'd reach into the night and pluck his star, so he'd never have to sleep alone. As he held it close to his heart, he'd offer sweet blessings for his family, for their health, happiness, and safety.

Since falling in love with Erol, Joe included Erol in these blessings. He would stare at his star, and set his heart into orbit around it. And Joe believed that 600 miles away, Erol could hear his whispers, and that their hearts turned as one.

"Umm, babe...I...kinda messed up...."

Since the night his heart stopped, and his lola appeared to him in the glow of starshine, Joe included himself in these blessings. She moved to where he lay, a broken shadow on the bed, and wiped his tears as her lips quivered and tongue danced, It was more of a hum than whispers that rose from this woman, a harmonic wave that crescendoed and sheared the darkness in two. This was the woman for whom English was too precise to contain the brightness of her stories, so it was only practical for telling him to "eat eat" or "open the light." To him, the language she shared with his mom and her other daughters had been one of recipes, gossip and secrets, such as the secret of the stars.

He began to include himself because he began to remember and understand. He remembered his father's throaty laughter and strange female faces in his house, faces that weren't warm and radiant like his mother's. He remembered paternal fists damming the flow of matrilineal fables.

And he also remembered his own smile, the kind brought on by the easy silent joy of sunshine on white Hanes tighty-whities during a previous relationship that also stretched itself over phone lines and airfares. Secrets flowed through his veins, and they now made themselves known to him. This was the blood of his mother, and her mother as well. And Joe understood its stirrings.

From that night on, he gripped his star in his palms, close to his cheek for warmth. He prayed for it to push back the darkness so he could breathe, for it to bring sleep swiftly and easily.

The front door creaked open just as Whitney cocked an eyebrow and smiled another high note. Erol seemed startled to find Joe still awake.

"Still up baby? Is everything alright?"

Joe glanced over at Whitney and turned his spoon in the soft ice cream a few times. He let go of the spoon and slowly put his hand up to Erol. The air was almost firm and palpable to his open palm. As Joe raised his hand in gesture, the TV flickered brightly into commercials, the darkness almost recoiling in astonishment. Joe looked at Erol, almost through him really, and half-smiled.

"Yeah. It's all ok."

Let The Pen Rest Awhile

Alberto Vajrabukka

What is nirvana?
I know not where it lies.
But you
here
speaking of a niece's first recital,
the new computer at work,
and that new piece you're choreographing.

No mantras.
Just a smile
floats on these lips.

No jatakas.
But tomorrow
our confidantes will hear tales
of tonight.

No mudras.
Just your open palm
against the hilt of my hip
as our bodies join.

Our motions crack lightning
splitting the seams of our shadows.

My Quiet Revolution

Lisa Valencia-Svensson

There was a time when
     i never questioned race
     the colours that moved across
     my father's face in anger
     were those of the shadows
     behind my mother's eyes

There was a time when
     cultures blended together as one
     the foods on the table
     the languages in the air
     all served to mold me into a single whole

Now it's time for revisioning
     lines once so straight
     now burn crooked paths in my mind
     faces grow apart in difference as
     skin gains a power we can barely define

Now is the time for my quiet revolution
     i will speak the divisions engraved in my soul
     the race lines that crisscross my body
     i will shape them mold them
     weave them into a tapestry truly my own

Anong Sagot? (*What Response?*)

Lisa Valencia-Svensson

How did the men from Spain
    once react to our
    easy sensuality
    that flowed like the night
    through the ribbons of air
    that weave along the shores of our tender island home?

They crashed down upon us
    forcing wine and bread down our throats
    hanging our triumphs on a cross
    fashioned of wood which they stole from our
    ever lush forests of green

They dressed us in robes
    pressed stiff and white
    to mold us into their own nightmares
    they taught us to bleed for love
    drained us stiff and white
    so they would no longer be alone

And they showed us the way
    to turn our joy into shame
    naming us indios and heathen
    as they knelt us at their alter of pain

And how now will my own white father react
    to the news that his brown daughter
    is gay?

Must Be the Chopsticks

Anthony Yuen

A Wednesday night in early August in San Francisco's Japantown and I'm meeting with three female friends for dinner at a noodle place on Buchanan. Things are going fine from the moment we walk in until the moment we sit down (about a whole 10 seconds). Instantly, I'm transported to that strange world where all the hapa people I know instantly become about 300% more Asian than I am, ordering several dishes of gyuzo and ramen while I'm still having trouble reading the menu. Japanese or Korean or Chinese is spoken (it doesn't matter which one 'cause in this instance they're all the same) to the server and all eyes turn to me to see what I'm going to order. Flustered, I flip through the menu like a drowning man clutching for a life vest. The server goes away and things get a bit better; people I know are back to normal, at least until the food arrives, then it starts all over again, and gets worse.

Big bowls of ramen noodles make their way to the table, one makes its way in front of me. Each has chopsticks and a soup spoon laid out in front of it. Simple enough, until I try to eat it. How do I eat it? Looking around, I see my friends effortlessly taking the noodles with their chopsticks and placing them in their spoons in just the right amount so as to fill the spoon, then dipping it into the broth, and bringing it to their lips to enjoy. My efforts are rewarded with too many noodles, most of which stubbornly cling to the rest of the noodles inside the bowl. Bits and pieces of the soup splash around, leaving my face and my napkin wet with broth brought upon by my clumsiness. I look around again—same graceful motions by everyone else, same fucking clumsiness on my part. My face begins to heat up, and I feel like crying, like when you're a little kid in school and everyone answers a question right until they come to you, and then you get it wrong, and you just start crying for no reason. It's only a question, right? But you've failed in some way, couldn't keep up with your peers. Failed.

I feel culturally inadequate. Ghosts of my cultural loneliness spring up again. Depression sets in as I put down the chopsticks and the spoon and stare into space, thinking maybe if I don't look at it it'll all go away. All eyes turn to me—I'm having problems. Must be with the chopsticks, they say. One friend makes several attempts to ask the server for a fork, attempts which only embarrass me further, probably because I'm the only one who knows what I am feeling. A fork is brought to the table and sits in front of me, as if to say that it's good that I tried and now I can eat the soup. But that's presuming that I want to eat the soup. What if I don't want to eat the soup? What if I don't really want to eat anything in Japantown? What if I were to say that I'd have preferred something more familiar and less Asian to eat? Would that make me different? Could I truly call myself a "mixed race Asian American"?

Attention from the three turns closer to me. It's inviting on one hand, 'cause I want to explain what it is I'm feeling, but devastating on the other, 'cause this is something so personal that can't be explained easily. I'd have to go back to England in Manchester, sitting in Yang Sing for dim sum, and feeling that cultural loneliness for the first time, feeling that I can talk the talk, but I couldn't walk the walk. How can I call myself Chinese when I hardly know anything about being Chinese? Sure, I know the history, the issues, and all that; but that's all from school. I could go take Mandarin lessons, and work for some Chinese organization, and spend all my time trying to make up for something I didn't receive when I was growing up. But the dark realization speaks up, reminding me that you can't substitute for culture. Language, food, customs, it's all something you grow up with. Yes, you can learn those later in life, but it's just not the same, and sometimes I wonder if I'm just kidding myself in thinking about even trying to do all these things, just so I can feel *more* Chinese.

I want to run away. Leave the restaurant, go somewhere where I don't have to think about this, somewhere where fleeting glimpses of how others have culture don't remind me of how little I have. I want to go somewhere where my father doesn't leave my mother, where I get to talk to my German grandparents while they're still alive, and where I have family besides my brother and sister, father and mother. I want to have a spot where my friends don't make racist jokes when I know they really don't mean it, where little kids in France don't put on blackface to do some jazz number, and where foreign tourists don't confuse the "dangerous" part of town as the "non-white" part of town.

Poof. The meal is over, and a full bowl of noodles sits in front of me. A reminder of how far I have to go and how small I feel. Even after the bill is paid and we're out of the restaurant, walking down Post Street towards my friend's car, I still feel the burning sting to my psyche, the need to drop the weighty tears from my eyes, and the need to feel something other than the profound loneliness I feel nowadays. I think that I can tell my friend about all this, that she would understand, but like so many times before, that doesn't happen. I wait for her to ask about it. That's all I'm waiting for, her, anyone, just to ask, and I'll tell them everything. But no one ever does.

"#8," by Michael Tora Speier

2006

Editors' note (2006)

James Lawrence Ardeña and Brandy Liên Worrall

All Mixed Up is the third and final installment of what has become known as the "Mixed Up Trilogy," a series of chapbooks bringing together Hapa (mixed race Asian) writers, artists, and performance artists. The first chapbook, *mixed up*, was published in 2000 for a reading in Los Angeles sponsored by the long-time Asian American arts organization, Aisarema. Because the response to the chapbook and reading was so positive, we decided to do another chapbook and commit to producing a trilogy of collections. In 2000, we published the second installment, *Too mixed up*, which mapped a larger geography~and therefore, a more diverse experiential lens~as we collected works from contributors in San Diego, San Francisco, Seattle, Pennsylvania, Canada, and Japan. The second chapbook also received an enthusiastic response, and like the first chapbook, all copies were sold out.

It has been six years since the publication of the last chapbook. During the production of the first two chapbooks, we were graduate students in Asian American Studies at UCLA, which afforded us the time and support needed to engage in this project. However, after graduating from UCLA and going our separate ways, it became more difficult to find the opportunity to complete the trilogy. As grown-ups with jobs, children, and other responsibilities~and as editors living in two different cities~our project, unfortunately, was forced to wait. But we did not give up. And it is perhaps because of the waiting that we are able to offer the most diverse volume to date.

Our contributors hail from Vancouver, Los Angeles, New York, San Francisco, Seattle, the Philippines, and Pennsylvania. Unintended themes have arisen out of this volume: food as investigation of history and identity; plants as an expression of hybridity and "invasion"; legacies of migration and miscegenation; and the debunking of expected roles, among others.

We also believe that experience and distance have allowed us to gain perspective on the Hapa experience and this project. We have changed during the past six years, and so has the scope of the chapbook project.

For those who have not had the opportunity to read the first two chap-books, this sentiment will not resonate with their experience in reading this volume. However, we are planning to offer all three volumes in one printed collection, entitled *Completely Mixed Up*, and in addition to all the works published over the course of seven years, we will also include new works by Hapa writers and artists. This volume is forthcoming in 2007. So despite all the differences among the three volumes, one thing remains: the spirit of the Mixed Up project lives on!

We would like to thank all those who have helped us during the production of this third volume, *All Mixed Up*. Michael Tora Speier and Debora O offered invaluable advice on and connections to the Hapa community in Vancouver. Powell Street Festival also lent its support in terms of planning events in the Vancouver area. Others have helped in the organizing of future events in Los Angeles and New York, and we thank them for their support.

Even though this is the last chapter in the Mixed Up journey, we hope to continue the dialogue that was started in 1999/2000~and the discussions that have come before and led up to that moment. In this age of increasing globalization and migrations, the Hapa experience is called upon even more as the model and the ideal for what should happen when we can all get along. This notion, as celebratory as it is, remains problematic in its essentializing of racial, ethnic, cultural, and individual identity~just as the "tragic mullato" stereotype is a troublesome construct with its claim that people of mixed race heritage are identity and cultural victims in limbo, never quite being able to find a place in the world. We hope that this final volume, like the other two, will debunk these notions and the kinds of messages they send. This volume speaks to our heterogeneity, our diversity and difference—the reality that there is no one true ideal identity, nor should there be; that Hapas aren't the answer to the world's ills. Instead, the contributors to this volume are individuals who offer their expressions about the world that will nevertheless continue to ascribe labels and name them for something they may not be, and in these individual expressions, Hapas will undoubtedly name themselves.

Upon Returns

James Lawrence Ardeña

A brush strokes three lines of barbed wire
Just out of finger tips touch
They are~cold
They~vibrate in Santa Ana winds
And separate me from the trees
Of Los Feliz hills and
Cascade mountains
They~cause the nerve endings of outstretched fingertips
To become worn
Left raw~exposed to be ignited
It is hot outside
Move slowly

Nestled atop the hills lies an observatory
To search out stars hidden
From the lights of East Hollywood
Peering in between the second and third strings of barbs
I imagine being there~seeing 1200 miles in all directions
But in particular
To the north and southeast
But sometimes two eyes searching see nothing at all
And beneath my feet
The earth is cool
And moist

Yellow orange rust visions flow freely from yesterday
On to particulate board canvases
I cut vigorously.
Remembering stories and mythologies
that my family and I in the states are all alone
And there are no more.

And love be bonded through letters I receive on my doorstep
The results of many searches thoughout the years
I hear of the namesakes~ancestors I share
Carlito, Ruel, Zacharias, Paulo, Aina in Kuala Lumpur,
Rogelio in Bacolod

It is Magin who confirms what my cousins and I have come to believe
Through the years
When he writes that indeed
Our relatives are gifted in the arts
That, is in our blood
It is thick and unyeilding
Its secrets die too quickly

My cousins remain younger than I
And my inspirations
Day is writing again in her book
Somewhere in between Emmanuel and Isaiah
Life beats 26 rhythms to record a release
And a warriors RSNL is unleashed

Other hospital visits evoke childhood terrors
I am afraid to sleep in my own bed again
And awake crying, for the first time.
Sometimes it is hard to forget
Quickly.

I turn to remember,
Slowly lifting the old wood laminate Pioneer turntable
Slide the arm to the beginning grooves
Which crackle and hiss
At the needles return.

The vision of a 12 inch vinyl single
And Alperts RISE becomes tangible.
Tito Boy follows the music through the doorway.
As long as I can remember, he has always had one glass eye.

And now, he is dancing
Intimately
Alone.

His eyes remain closed,
As his hands caress his small round stomach in circular motions.
Stretching taut his red shirt in reverie
And memories of the seventies,
Who with his wife he danced,
Who in the other room instinctively begins to move her waist
Thickened over the years
In-sync to his.
Her ashy wrinkled ankles lift tsinellas from the floor
And replace them
In time.

Her eyes close
and she stirs the Arroz Caldo
She had been preparing.
She too remembers
And it is beautiful.
It is wonderfully-beautiful.

Anger Is a Gift

Sumiko Braun

He looked confused. He glanced me over suspiciously and asked, "Why are you so angry?"

You want to know why I'm so angry?

I'm angry because when I type "Asian woman" into google, most of the sites that come up are porn and mail-order bride sites.

I'm angry because I come across forms that still don't let me check more than one box and I'm forced to deny my mixed blood heritage.

I'm angry because if I met the woman of my dreams and wanted to marry her here in the grand 'ole U.S. of A., I couldn't.

I'm angry because my grandfather locked himself up in his van with a BBQ and suffocated himself to death when I was only ten, the same man who was driven to a life of gangs and drugs because he was alienated as a Japanese American.

I'm angry because during WWII my family was attacked on two fronts: imprisoned in concentration camps here and murdered in the bombing of Hiroshima there.

I'm angry because a black man on Hollywood Boulevard stopped my sister and me to ask if we could speak English, and being 5th generation American and half white doesn't mean shit when our faces and our skin still look foreign.

I'm angry because someone I thought I could trust raped me, and it took me three years to admit it to myself or anyone else.

I'm angry because I'm not the only one.

I'm angry because 75% of the world's poverty happen to be women.

I'm angry because with all the resources and technology that we have today that anyone is still in poverty.

I'm angry because I remember being 16 reading an article in my school newspaper that blamed me for the proliferation of AIDS because I started my high school's gay-straight alliance.

I'm angry because Gwen Araujo, a teenage transsexual Latina, was brutally murdered for only one reason and that reason was hate.

I'm angry because she is not alone.

I'm angry because I can't sit on the sidelines when there are people out there who are convinced that racism, sexism, homophobia, transphobia, classism, ageism don't exist.

I'm angry because there are so many people out there who aren't.

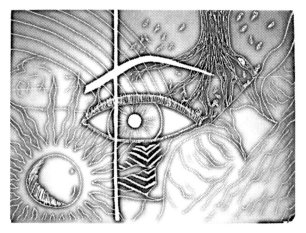

"Watchtowers" by Sumiko Braun

Soul Food

Margaret Gallagher

Some of the most beloved recipes are those that have been passed down through the generations. But in the case of my mom's family, the kitchen secrets nearly skipped a generation.

My mother was born in the sweltering heat of Indonesia. The daughter of a diplomat, neither she nor her three sisters ever had to set in the kitchen. An army of servants turned out sumptuous meals of turmeric-scented rice, elaborately chopped gado gado, and dark, luscious curries flavoured with lemon grass and kaffir lime. My mother tempted us with tales of endless chicken satay and mountains of delicate sweets made with freshly shaved coconut and palm sugar. And then she'd make us a nice tuna casserole.

You see, my mom had to teach herself to cook when she married my father, an American professor. As a young wife, she learned from popular magazines, such as Good Housekeeping and Ladies Home Journal. Neither of which offered much guidance when it came to recreating the food of her childhood. And my grandmother wasn't much help either.

"Your grandma was like a delicate flower," Mom always tells me. "She grew up in palace." Which isn't an exaggeration. My grandmother's wealthy Chinese family had long ago taken over a former royal home in the east Javanese town of Kediri. To this day, villagers come to pay their respects to a long-dead prince and princess buried in the backyard.

The family home had a vast kitchen, but my grandmother was kept far away from its bustle. "It was a different time," says my mother. "And your great-grandmother was very fierce, very strict." She wouldn't let Grandma go near a rice pot or frying pan, lest she scar her tiny perfect hands. My grandmother had no clue in the kitchen. But all that changed with the fall of Sukarno.

President Sukarno was Indonesia's first leader. He rose to power when the fledgling nation broke from Dutch colonial rule in 1945. My

125

grandfather, a lowly journalist with friends in high places, became an "Ambassador Extraordinary and Plenipotentiary" under Sukarno. This suited his wife's fancy tastes just fine. But in 1967, a coup toppled Sukarno and threw the nation into chaos. The Chinese community bore the brunt of a wave of violence. My grandfather was serving abroad at the time, and the family dared not return home. They lost almost everything.

Suddenly, at age 55, my long-sheltered grandmother found herself without servants for the first time in her life. She'd never walked down a street by herself, let alone go to a grocery store. She didn't even know how to cook rice. But among her remaining possessions was a small brittle book with yellowed pages entitled *"Atoeran Masak Vegetarisch"*~A Vegetarian Cookbook. It was published by her mother~my great-grandmother~the same stern woman who had worked so hard to keep her only daughter from the fires of kitchen.

My grandma had carted the thin volume around the world as a reminder of home, but also as a reminder of where she had come from.

On the front cover, a serene goddess floats upon on the blushing pink petals of a giant lotus~foreshadowing the Buddhist principles inside. The opening page reads *"Ini Kitab berisi roepa roepa recept memasak makanan dan sajoeran jang semoanja diatoer tidak pakee barang barang jang berasal mem-bounoh djeewah baik sekali boaet kaoem"*~"This book has 150 recipes, all were created without killing a soul...this food is very good for your spirit."

Grandma was born into a long line of Buddhists, but she convert-ed to Catholicism after a difficult pregnancy forced her to surrender her vegetarian ways and take up meat. But she stayed connected to her tangled family roots through her mother's recipes.

Reading the words of her long-dead mother, my grandma taught herself to cook in a London kitchen. At the same time, on the other side of the ocean, my mother was learning the ropes from Betty Crocker. But there must have been the occasional exchange of lessons, because gradually, fragrant Indonesian dishes began to appear on our dinner table. But only for special occasions. It really can take an army to prepare some of those recipes. And perhaps, the flavours were a too painful reminder of world left behind.

My grandmother never returned to Indonesia, never visited her beloved childhood home again. But her cooking improved over the years. I think her mother would have been proud. When Grandma passed away, my mom discovered the precious cookbook tucked amongst the spice jars. My grandmother's notes are gracefully pencilled in besides some of her favorite dishes.

Mom passed the cookbook on to me for safekeeping a few years ago. I can't really understand the language, and even my mother has to work at deciphering the archaic colonial spelling. Together we've manage to translate and cook one dish-tofu and eggs and rosy, coconut chili sauce. It was remarkably delicious. And when the two of us sat down to eat, we were not alone.

Penoelis ini kitab Hoedjien „T A N"-Java.

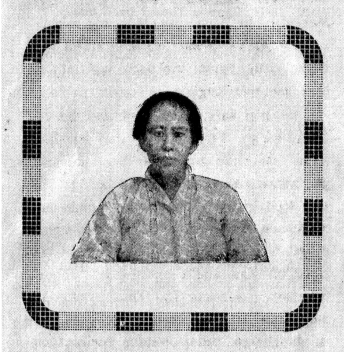

Saia moeat gambar pengarangnja ini Kitab jang soeda mejakinken 20 tahoen lebi, jaitoe Hoedjien „T A N" jang hidoep dengen familie Tjiak Djaij, maka apa jang ditoetoerken disini betoel soeda dengen pengalamannja sendiri.

Moedah-moedahan ini Kitab bergoena bagi siapa jang memakainja.

— Boekhandel —
TAN KHOEN SWIE - Kediri.

A peek inside my great-grandmother's cookbook shows her picture and an author's note.

Tarzan

Sherlyn Jimenez

> *Some experiences may have never been ours, may never have happened.*
> *But remembering makes them real.*

I see men huddled together in the middle of the night. Three hollow blocks surround a fire pushing upwards toward a blackened wok. I can almost hear drunken voices. Someone tells me, a snake, maybe two or three. It's been skinned, cut into bite-size pieces. They add whole peppercorns, some vinegar, flattened garlic and finally, soy sauce. Bottles of beer reflect the fire, send flickers of light beyond the gathering.

The night moves on. They've eaten, and the bottles are emptied out. The voices are interrupted with long silences. A man wakes up from sleep and starts to undulate across the ground of pebbles, stray branches, and dried leaves. He hisses, darts his tongue in and out, and the others laugh, find it all amusing. They go home, leave him behind. When the sun falls on him, he finds he is still voiceless, can't lift his body off the ground. His tongue involuntarily pushes out of his mouth, trying, trying to sense heat.

***

I have a special rooster. His comb is unlike any other. It curls like red flowers in bloom. He has learned my voice, always comes when I call. Then he disappears, never comes even though I promise to feed him with freshly husked rice. My mother tells me, he must have gone away. She is cooking dinner.

***

Tarzan is his name. A big, shaggy dog with mostly white fur and occasional black spots. He loves to lie in the dirt but when I call him, throw unripe star-apples for him to fetch, he bounces off into a run. He would go anywhere to fetch what I've thrown, even to the water holes full of water hyacinths. He comes back dripping wet, root tangled into his fur, but triumphant with the starapple in his mouth.

My aunt's fiancé visits. My mother goes to the market and buys live catfish and carp while I gather firewood for grilling. An uncle pulls out his gun. I had seen him making bullets from melted metal, perfectly round silver pellets that he placed in cold water so they would solidify.

We had another dog before. She was wild. When strangers came to visit, she growled at them and chased them out to the street, threatening to bite them. But Tarzan isn't like that. He lies down to be petted by anyone and drools happily when he is being stroked. Our previous dog understood. She ran and ran. They had to chase her all over the fields even after the first and second shot. Tarzan comes at once when he is called. I am in my parents' room trying not to cry. One loud shot.

My mother serves *adobo*. I spit out the whole peppercorn before I accidentally bite into its bitter-hot center. The meat is tender, slightly sweet from the cane vinegar my great-aunt has aged. I have forgotten how to move food down my throat.

A Grandmother's Request

Sherlyn Jimenez

I grip your thin unswollen hands
when pain arrives
you see
       my eyes wrinkled shut
           my mouth fastened to my gums
                knuckles bony white
I'm past caring
whether my shrunken breasts
show through the hospital gown
when I rock what morphine
cannot wrench away

What's he doing here
sitting on my bed
Tell your grandfather
I'm not ready yet

I want to go home
       rub coconut oil on my hair
       drink Sanka in the mornings

but my eyebrows stand stiff
and your grandfather is waiting...

                            When

I've left
I will wear a white sack
over my head and visit
you in your sleep
I will pull
at your clothes
digging
for warmth
you must help me
return

131

Walking with the Dead

Sherlyn Jimenez

I heard they slept through the fire while their baby sister crawled out. Two boys, distant relatives on my father's side. I imagined a roasting pig stuffed with sweet rice and coconut milk, its charcoaled skin crumbling off.

One of my first friends was only six when she drowned with her younger brother. Lungs come to believe water is air. Did she have bangs and missing teeth or was that me afraid to smile? I think her name started with M.

A bamboo shoot among bamboos. Hedged by people in dark clothes and white cotton bands on their forehead, I made my way to the corner of a room, climbing atop a chair to see. They were like dolls, the mother and baby rouged and perfumed in formal clothes. Even the baby wore lipstick.

...

I am walking with my grandfather, my five-year old hand enclosed in his, our feet thick with dust and scalps hot to the touch. The sweat on his muddied t-shirt mixes with the smell of the lake and water hyacinths. He is promising me a nickel for being good. The road is narrow and cracked, fringed with yellowing grass. Up ahead, it turns to liquid haze. The purple-gray mountain, an old woman in repose, waits for us.

Wake before the road ends, my grandmother tells me. Don't walk with the dead.

Apocalyptic Pollinations

Kelty Miyoshi McKinnon

.ly growing in strength and number

"Legions of alien invaders are silently creeping into the
United States and quickly taking over...this tide of inva-
sive aliens poses one of the greatest threats to the United
States. . ."

While not out of character to the current U.S. administration's
paranoid accusations, this statement comes not from the Department of
Homeland Security, but from the National Park Service's public website.
Prophesying disaster if the enemies are not destroyed, the NPS states that
"Invasive plants are one of the greatest threats to the natural ecosystems of
the United States and are destroying America's natural history and identity."[1] In 1999, then President Bill Clinton passed Executive Order 13112
which established the National Invasive Species Council of America. At
the inaugural meeting, co-chair and Interior Secretary Bill Babbitt advo-
cated for the passing of a government approved "White List," a limited
list of approved species that called for the extermination of all unapproved
species existing in the United States. Those species deemed "safe" for import,

possession and transport were limited to an estimated 0.25% of the earth's biota, the remaining 99.75% considered "contraband, with penalties for possession and mandated extermination."

The imposition of a list of those that belong and those that do not asserts a kind of eugenicist order on an invaded land, drawing a clear boundary between what is "American" and what is "other." The miniscule quarter of one percent is deemed the moral majority that manifests America's natural identity: the progenital material of America's genus loci. The belief that, like the Garden of Eden, the United States is Natural and Pure and needs to be sequestered from the rest of the world in order to maintain its purity is a common one, echoed in the nostalgic rhetoric of environmental organizations and governmental agencies alike. It isn't and never has been plausible to seal borders and freeze genetic drift, so to prevent the propagation of the 99.75% noxious and impure while protecting a 'pure race' of particularly American plants under globalized conditions seems particularly absurd. The issue should not be whether environmental degradation is moral, but how it is addressed and portrayed. Standard policy assumes that ". . .exotic species are presumed guilty until proven innocent."[2] The implication is that invasive plants are immoral and politicized, indeed that they are "unnatural." Likewise, there is the assertion that this earnest environmental rhetoric is apolitical and moral.

The NPS assertion that space is being stolen and identity subsumed reveals a fundamental belief that "place" is defined and understood as an assertion of boundaries and of difference, and that isolationism is the key to maintaining identity. Invasive plants magnify that a site is only considered culturally (or ecologically) significant when it is unique--when it embodies difference. Genus Loci is described as the distinctive atmosphere or pervading spirit of a particular place, and locates meaning as innate, divine and independent. A unique genus loci is considered a prerequisite to the authenticity, or aura, of the site. To blur the boundaries is to lose identity. The characteristic rapid, infinite reproduction of invasive plants cancels this notion of originality, enveloping space in an undifferentiated, pollinating miasma. Replicated hundreds of times, each copy of the mother plant resists demarcated limits, creating a generic condition that is neither solid nor liquid, a vague terrain formless, placeless and drifting.

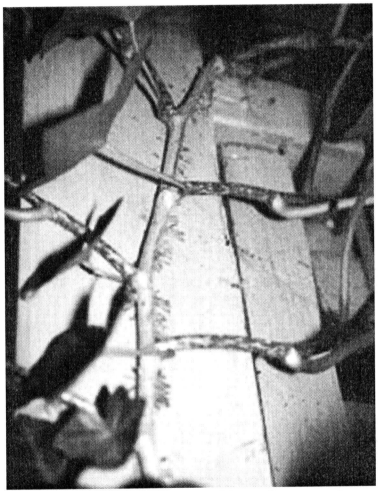

We are living in a cultural moment where the anxieties of globalization are feeding sweet nationalisms and bitter xenophobia. We rate Ivy 3 out of 5 for exoticism.

In IVY League, a web based collaboration with New York-based new media artist Jillian McDonald, our research into invasive species focused on Hedera helix, commonly known as English Ivy. This plant has simultaneously been glorified for its abilities to rapidly anchor erosive soils and filter polluted air, and vilified as an invasive plant which can rapidly dominate native ecosystems, outcompeting other plants for nutrients, sunlight and air and eventually choking out any growth but its own. An attack on the hyperbole that surrounds Hedera helix, the website documents web-based ivy research, revealing conflicted, bizarre and oft times militant forms of nature worship. Recent rhetoric surrounding native vs. invasive plants is concurrent with notions of hybridizing identities and nationalisms due to the forces of globalisation. In all biological life, "immigrants and foreigners" tend to be the scapegoats for local problems. Invasive species are constantly blamed for the changing "degraded" landscape, camoflouging the role that localized irresponsible land use patterns have played in large scale environmental degradation.

The IVY League webpage is a hypertextual tangled vine of knowledge that explores the similarities between the rhetoric of the war against invasive plants and the war against terror that is espoused by environmental groups, the mass media and governmental agencies. Under the conditions of globalisation, global cities such as Vancouver and New York are havens for invasive plants, where they thrive in almost any condition, creating lush green oases in the concrete jungle. A hypertextual garden manual, the website also offers conflicting directives for the propagation and eradication of English Ivy. IVY League raises the notion of a global and a virtual garden, where Hedera helix tangles issues of transculturation, globalisation, colonialism, the placelessness of contemporary urbanisms, and the privatization of the public realm. Invasive plants are a rude interruption to the nostalgic reverie that a unique place is a discreet and isolated unit, reminding us that globalisation makes it even more impossible to hermetically seal borders, that political and geographic boundaries are rarely aligned, and that we are deeply implicated in, not separate from, ecological process. Invasive plants are rendered the memento mori of contemporary life, constantly present, peppering our gardens with the solemn, sublime reminder "Et in Arcadia Ego"~"Even in Paradise There am I."[3]

136

1. nps.gov/plants/pubs/actionagenda/apwg/apwgaction.pdf

2. *Natural Areas News*, Vol.3, No.4, Autumn 1999.

3. An art historical reference to the paintings "Et In Arcadia Ego" c. 1621-1623 by Guercino (Galleria Corsini) and others by Poussin containing the element of drama and surprise on the part of shepherds that encounter the tomb with this inscription. In Poussin's second version of "Et In Arcadia Ego" c. 1630, the element of drama and surprise on the part of the shepherds is eliminated–instead displaying pensive contemplation.

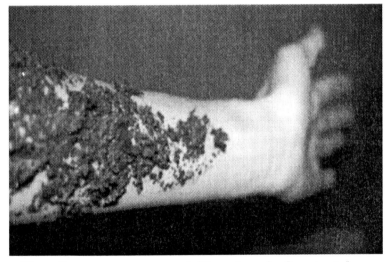

The leaves are antibacterial, anti-
rheumatic, antiseptic, antispasmodic,
astringent, cathartic, diaphoretic,
emetic, emmenagogue, stimulant,
sudorific, vasoconstrictor, vaso-
dilator and vermifuge.

The Bean Tree

Trina Mendiola Estanislao

The bean tree didn't want to grow here
it was used to the land of heavy sticky air
washed clean by warm monsoons clear
skies then revealing the harsh beat of the sun god's hair.

It shuddered in this land of cold beaches
winters cold, cold hands, snot running cold
but it was here and so as a baby reaches
for a finger it can hold

The bean let loose a root or two
touching water and air and earth
absorbing the soil-shock, pushing through
drenching, asking, widening its girth
to the explosion of a yellow leaf quivering
stolid, forced, in a land of white shivering.

All I Have to Show

Rashaan Alexis Meneses

All I have to show for my culture(s)
is the color of my skin,
the shape of my eyes,
the small frame of my body.
No foreign tongue to speak:
Visayan, Español, or Pangasinan,
just plain English.
No exotic birthplaces to tell of
about some far and distant land.
Just a hyphenated American,
the Filipina and Chicana
loosely dangling,
threatening to fall off at the eye of the beholder.

All I have is what is here before you;
what's presented to me, handed down
by the many different people
who compose this mosaic
of my ancestry, my heritage.
I thread these things together
as dissimilar and incongruent
or as harmonious as they may be.

If I let this existence speak for itself,
allowing the many different parts to breathe
and give movement,
unwilling to be tacked down
by preconceived notions and misplaced ideals.
All the seams showing,
some parts missing,
other parts overlapping,
sometimes in a disheveled mess.

I will not be pinned down.
No consonants or vowels can bind me.
They cannot contain all that I am.
All I'm capable of being.

Where the Asphalt Meets Concrete

Dorian Sanae Merina

> *All living humans are related to a single woman who lived*
> *roughly 150,000 years ago.* *

a shadow of water
dampens
the curling script of graffiti

a swirling necklace
of smooth-abdomened ants
carrying blond eggs
on their backs
the plump jaws of larvae
undulating

green tufts of grass
shoulder concrete
exhaling in small shatterings
the day's weightlessness

the sky
revolving face
of an enraged
and tender lover
promises a flashing echo
and wind

when the rain comes again
you will remember
a certain origin
a canopy of molecules and mist
you will forget to want yourself
a different shade a different shape
instead
another bed

of injury and faith
a quiet quiet some
thing
no stronger than a leaf
taking shape

gingko leaves gather
in the undefined border
of the gutter
two petals softly arc
around a bundle
of filmsy-skin stamen
a car rushes by and
they shake
still

their small red mouths
darkening as they dry

*from *National Geographic Magazine*, March 2006

Culture Jam

Shyamala Moorty

He flew from India to the U.S.,
with only $26 and a student visa

She hitchhiked from Colorado to CA,
on a whim

He was getting
a doctorate in philosophy

And she had just joined
a spiritual commune

When they met

He liked her openness and thought
she looked sort of Indian

She dreamed they were
the answer to the war in Vietnam

She would cut
photographs of their faces in half
and paste them together
half hers/half his
half West/half East.

THEY

SE...

PA...   RA...

TED

But a child remained.

"Immigrant Pride" by Shyamala Moorty and Kashyap Trivedi

"Urban Artifact" by Shyamala Moorty

Black nor White

edited by Kashyap Trivedi

Shyamala Moorty

When she was a child (pink or blue?)
People often asked "where are you from?" (foreign or friend?)
She claimed, "I'm 1/2 Indian, and 1/2 Cuban, Dutch, Greek and
English" (pure-bred or mutt?)
       Until she discovered her grandfather was adopted,
           and might actually be Welsh (fact or fiction?)

When she was a teenager,
she thought she was white (mind or matter?)
Her friends dug her tan, and said
she'd make a great blond (real or fake?)
She craved Barbie blue eyes,
fed up with boring brown (diamond or stone?)
       She flaunted her second-hand Guess jeans
           But they never fit just right (clone or clown?)

She arrived at college, hungry for friends (geek or slut?)
She attempted to fill the empty spaces (dick or clit?)
Finally, the Indians took her in (Asian or American?)
       She looked like them,
           so they assumed she was (black nor white)

She basked in Bindis and Bollywood (Madhuri or Madonna?)
But was controlled by
colonialisms and communalisms (tradition or tragedy?)
She didn't feel Indian on the inside (self or other?)
       But soon she learned,
           "I am my skin" (truth or maya*?)

* Maya means illusion in Sanskrit

Threat Condition Alpha

for Sonja, without whom I might have stayed asleep.

Mark Nakada

The power of the taifuu is absolute now. It owns the outdoors of Okinawa, where the street wild cats take cover in caves filled with decomposing WWII ordinance, and the poor bones of dead Ryukyuan mothers, their children still waking in nightmare terror. Where the cicada's endless droning song is even drowned out, where the howl and whistle through the barred windows of every cement fortress house threatens to tear the roof off, to expose those inside to yet another overwhelming force, always pressing down, things crashing around outside, things pushed over by another culprit in the night, while the rain falls sideways, bullets climbing in through the cracks of closed windows and dripping in under tile roofs, pulling TV antennae listening for storm updates. How many meters per second is the wind? How far offshore is the eye of the storm? How long will the streets be deserted and the trees strain against their roots and the flash of lightning soundlessly flickering as some insane photograph briefly glancing through the blackness exposing the howling, the wind pushing linoleum up as some habu crawling beneath the floor seeking entrance. Its chill breath coming up through the tatami mat softly against the bodies of its prisoners...no escape. Okinawa is awash in things larger than itself, unnatural forces turning Her upside down, dependant upon them for water, to drink, to bathe. The taifuu brings life.

Seiji gets up and looking out the window at his first taifuu, thinking he'll be lucky to go outside without being blown away. "What a day for it," looking by candlelight into the mirror at the bandana he would have worn on his head into battle today. Plans for the peace demo are ruined. Turning on the TV, Seiji clicks past an infomercial with large-breasted white women riding exercise machines, Japanese voices dubbed over their strangely moving mouths. Channel 8 is a talk show with hoards of people hosting on stage, an all-female audience giggling at the humiliation of two guests from Africa, touching their hair, commenting on their strange clothing, the woman's probable breast size, hosts screaming and jumping back and falling down laughing. Channel 10 a man and wife being taken away in a police car, faces digitally blurred, flock of reporters aiming telephoto lenses trying to catch the essence of shame, the money shot. This couple poisoned her parents' curry-rice hoping to collect on the insurance. Channel 12, NHK news shows the spray-paint outline of a body, rather, not the outlines, but a stick figure with a circle for the head, the essence of the body, its inner structure, marked on pavement after a marine's drunken hit-and-run. Shots of the kid's funeral, high-school girls lined up in uniform, holding her picture, looking for a last glimpse of their friend's coffin. Channel 6 is in English. Tropical Cyclone coded warning in the lower left corner of the screen on American Forces Network reads TC-1E: Tropical Cyclone Status One-Emergency. "All Department of Defense employees please remain inside until you receive the TC-AC all clear signal." Now a commercial about the importance of OPSEC for servicemen and their families who ought not discuss their (or their father's) missions and threatening Operational Security. After the recent bombings in Kenya, all bases now operating under Threat Condition Alpha.

Today was the day of protest. The protest delayed by rain. Seiji slumps back into the vinyl couch, waiting for AFN to give the go-ahead signal to the small group of demonstrators. Meanwhile it is morning. The mail and newspapers are being delivered, small children go to school. People are moving on, disregarding the TC-codes because they never thought to bother with Channel 6. Seiji wants to be local, but the screaming wind outside is still scaring his shit out. Rainwater and an aluminum can sliding uphill past the throbbing window clank. If he were local, he'd be outside.

Goya Chanpuru

for Michael Tora Speier

Mark Nakada

Izumi Misaki district of Naha City capital, we go to a small run
down tin-roofed izakaya for goya chanpuru, local bitter vegetable stir-fry.
Variety show TV noise of the owners' living room spills through a wide
open doorway blending public/private space. We sit on tatami mats, realizing the restaurant doubles as the family home. Squat ancient obaasan with
hearing aids leans over a low table in front of the TV prepping vegetables.
She pays no attention though i'm sure not many gaijin come in here. Her
daughter, the server/cook, takes our order in Japanese after asking us the
usual questions and disappears into the public/private kitchen.

The usual questions, when traveling with other gaijin, are:
1. "Are you Americans?" 2. "You're not gunjin?" 3. "You *live* in Okinawa?"
The usual responses are:
1. "I thought you were military." 2. "Sensei ka! Sugoi!" 3. Better treatment.

We settle in and are ignored by regular customers after some nearly
undetectable glances. Being ignored here can be a compliment. It *does* get
worse.

Before the food comes i begin to feel eyes on me, but this is ever-
present, ever nagging. I've learned from constant exposure to shrug it off,
so that i almost never react. That's when the old woman, a customer, comes
over: "You are halfu."

She isn't asking a question. Many old women in Okinawa, especially in the south, in stores or on the street know this. They sometimes
approach to talk, breaking code of silence and gaijin kowai. "I have a halfu
daughter and two grandchildren," she says in thick Okinawa-ben. So many
elderly women were abandoned with halfu kids by their GI boyfriends during WWII, Korea and Vietnam. They, more than anyone else here, recognize a halfu because their own children were born and denied both American and Japanese citizenship. What passport does the null-citizen carry?

"My daughter went to the U.S. with her husband. I met my two grandchildren once when they were babies, but I don't know them. You speak good nihongo, nee! Won't you translate something for me?"

So many Okinawans ask me to teach them inglish so i usually have to say a politely vague "yes" in the Japanese way that means "no" but she doesn't want lessons. The woman stands up on the tatami mat, doesn't bow, and waddles out of the restaurant. The server brings our chanpuru and shakes her head at me saying "sorry that woman is always annoying" and "pay no attention."

Goya looks like a short stout cucumber with deep green smallpox. Its bitter flesh is sliced into thin rings and tossed with sprouts, tofu, carrots and cubes of spam over a gas-flame stove. A proud local dish that most kids react to like spinach or Brussels sprouts here.

When we are nearly finished eating, the old woman returns carrying what looks like a Christmas card. I'd promised to read for her but didn't really expect her back. She clutches the card in both hands like treasure and hands it to me with a gruff "Onegaishimasu, nee." I wipe my hands with a napkin and receive the card in both hands to show respect. I see it is a New Years greeting card in inglish from '96. Inside is a photograph of a young family, a marine officer in dress uniform, a hapa woman and their two children. I explain that the card says "Happy New Year Mother" and that the girl, Jennifer, is 13 and the boy, Jordan, is 6. They live in Delaware or New Hampshire or one of those states you tend to forget. No other information is given. A wide smile comes across her face and she takes the card back quickly and caresses the photo, staring. "Thank you," she says getting up. "You good boy," tear in Obaachan's eye with a pat on my head, her grandson's surrogate head eating izumi misaki goya finally coming back.

Wandering out to street level noise of the TV public/private kitchen gas fuming taxi drivers blazing by honking post-war. Halfu grandson stand-in izakaya hologramming war-babies messenger translation. Obaachan no contact with the GI's leaving first her, then taking her daughter back to Delaware New Hampshire states you tend to forget. Obaachan those kids love you though you couldn't remember their American names or exact ages never seen them. They'd love you because i love lost Obaachan's too. Bet she makes a mean chanpuru and would be proud when i liked it. Halfu okinawa sansei sensei induction thinking everyone else here resembles family not predicting i too might be recognized for long lost family resemblances.

Was it Obaachan i saw in my photo, or me in hers?

Hapa Mapa

Debora O

Exhibited at Powell Street Festival in Vancouver, BC, as part of the "All Over the Map" show curated by Michael Tora Speier, July 31-August 8, 2002, Gallery 83

Mapping the mixed communities of old and new worlds is an impossible task. This is especially true since conventional maps legitimate traditional notions of the nation and its geo-political boundaries. Such maps have little if nothing to do with the reality of mixed peoples' multiple cultural affinities or with the shifting notions of homeland for cultures and communities in transit or in diaspora.

"The Hapa Mapa" is an imaginary map that challenges notions of discrete and permanent origins. Here there, are no fixed genealogies to divide human culture and to produce "difference" according to arbitrary definitions of blood, race, or religion (which are then used as essential markers of a people as a whole). By breaking up the symmetry of "the world map" into puzzle pieces, the Hapa Mapa invites an interactive disturbing of the visual and territorial restrictions to the way we look at our world. As we take apart and remake the map, we become increasingly aware of the constructed nature of territorial ownership and the ideology of protection and aggression that it necessitates.

This map can never fully represent all the personal and political moments of cross-culture and trans-culture--this is the irony of trying to encapsulate the complexity of identity through fixed names on a one-dimensional surface (colonial ideology in a nutshell!). When this map was exhibited at the "All Over the Map" show, I asked guests to interact with it by adding their own personal or mythological knowledge of homelands that are racially, culturally, and religiously mixed. At the end of the exhibit there were many such additions that spoke to both fantasy/legend and personal family history, as well as to documented, historical communities of mixed peoples. The participatory nature of the project made it a fun learning experience and a subversive opportunity to re-write personal and national histories.

This project aimed to make visible those lives that are pushed to the "impure" peripheries of nation states and nationality. It also tried to recognize the real presence of these mixed communities and their need for presence and belonging--they are what haunts, disrupts, and makes possible any conclusive representation of the world according to racial and national lines.

Despite what history books tell us, many if not all cultures are impure and mixed. I believe that in this is the root of culture itself. And while the convention of mapping speaks to a fixity and ownership of place and identity that a mixed experience has rarely claimed, the Hapa Mapa tries to show that the history and experiences of mixed race peoples are not devoid of place and landscape.

Homespace

Debora O

the brocade of these walls
used to run
          slick

with the grease
of untempered talk

red
      running into

green
      running into

yellow

colours
of the old world
reflected in a new   but distant

flag

revolution
and
eggrolls

both consumed
at this table

both soaked
in its own
      red cloak

revolution
and
red smarties

rolled into
morning newspapers
                    delivering

small hands

today
yes,

            today

yeh yeh

i wake to find myself
asleep

on the red leaf
of another country's
autumn.

Millennium

Debora O

I. becoming morning

the laughter of warm bellies   tittering.

she chooses
the
tray
of
blueberry

with only
one square
missing

children~

              quiet,

                   noisy,

everything.

hearts large enough
to hold
our constellations

and a tottering dog
standing still
in this wind
              pivoting its head
for a leg moving

out
      and
back

on the other side
of this glass pane

holding back the waltz
                    of a hapa child
                                    watching

boy and bagel
slowly

climbing crescendo

of
we   were   that   once
                              before

quiet diet
of bagels
for a hapa boy

eyes big
wrist held tight
in the air

not yet seeing
but seen

II. hapa child

briny currents
sweep the delta
            between hollow eyes
who dares write your name?

parents listless
air tightened

               an anonymity scripted:
               'don't draw attention'

fear and shame
hidden

hidden~

the vinyl skin of these booths
betrays the silence of broken lineages

a shattered familial
familiar with

               staring, smiling
               seductively empty faces

a freedom born,
not gained

i rush to hold

               this tiny fistful of salt
               you bring me

night winds
blowing
will scatter this mineral
down a coast of bloodied encounters

together we will whisper a legacy
               longer than lineage
and possibilities,
     older than freedom.

Supplication

Debora O

I. diaspora dissertation

does it speak of
of the new year?

brought in
improvised

with the help of shopkeepers

on Main
     who smirk at
               attempts to stay connected
when the connection was lost
long ago.

     fleeting gestures of hope.

biting into a new year bun

unsure of the timing
     always the timing

as in what comes before   and after

forget the now
'cause it feels awkward
walking the thin line between

     honouring

          +

               sacrilege

afraid to offend the ghosts
that watch
in fear   of betrayal.

158

II. mother/tongue

she watches me struggle to form the words

there is delight
                    and amusement
in this game

I struggle to hear
                    through broken syntax
the mystery uncovered.

flesh of flesh
blood of blood

only our tongues do not move
in unison

stumbling upon the divide of language   again.

I take shelter
in these grafted sentences

one language occupying another

looking across the silence

for longings
                    grown thick with absence.

Highlights from "High(bridi)Tea"

Haruko Okano and Fred Wah

"High(bridi)Tea" was an interdisciplinary collaborative installation/performance between Fred Wah and Haruko Okano. The focus of this audience interactive project was a combination of storytelling based on personal experiences growing up as cultural hybrids and racialized language. The visual component of the project consisted of 26 place settings at which the two artists offered stories interspersed with servings of black tea and white bread. The bread was screen printed with words provided by Fred Wah. The words were printed with mould spores so that within a week the mould would spread, covering the entire slice of bread. The accompanying jingles were provided by Fred and were screen printed in black ink onto napkins made of fungus.

The fungus is cultivated in a solution of black tea and sugar. The fungus plates are documentation of the struggle for nutrients between the fungus and the contaminating mould. Each plate is darker, recording the mould's gradual take-over of the surface while the fungus culture sank to the bottom of the tank where it continued to grow. The installation was created by Haruko Okano. The performance changed with each of the 5 productions mounted between 1998 and 2005.

Notes on the performance props

26 racialized words and jingles, created in 1998 at the Banff Centre for the Arts by Fred Wah.

Waiter's Bill Pad created in 1999 by Haruko Okano

26 Poems and images superimposed over Oxford Dictionary definitions under the letter "M".

Diamond Grill Menu, created in 1998 by Fred Wah.
High(bridi)Tea single setting and tea setting image by Haruko Okano

Collaborative installation created by Haruko Okano using Kombucha Fungus for plates and napkins. Words on the bread and jingles on the napkins contributed by Fred Wah silkscreen printed with mould spores and black ink.

The performance combines personal narrative and the serving of tea. Performance begins as soon as 26 members of the audience sit at the table(s).

162

igh Muck—
a—
muck
tips
don't run
amuck

He tears into one of the Baker Street nickel millionaires who picks up a tip from a booth that hasn't been cleaned yet. We all know the tip's there; it's at least a bill because you can see it sticking out from under a plate. As the guy's looking through the menu my dad goes up to him and says jesus christ Murphy what do you think you're doing lifting the girls' tips. They work hard for that money and you got more'n you know what to do with. You think you're such a high muckamuck. You never leave tips yourself and here you are stealing small change. I want you to get out of here and don't come into this cafe again. The guy leaves, cursing at my dad saying he doesn't know why anybody'd wanna eat this chink food anyway. He never does come back. A pipsqueak trying to be high muckamuck.

am
the im—
before
migration

Entreés

Manzo Nagano	18.87
Lucky Jim	18.92
Komagata Maru	19.14
Karin Erickson	19.22
Aquitania	19.47
Paper Son	19.51
Doug Collins	2¢
(only in season)	
Fujian	19.99

O MALE ENEMY ALIENS
NOTICE

Under date of February 2nd, 1942, the Honourable the Minister of National Defence with the concurrence of the Minister of Justice gave public notice defining an area of British Columbia, as described below, to be a protected area after the 31st day of January, 1942; that is to say, that area of the Province of British Columbia, including all islands, east of a line described hereunder:—

Commencing at boundary point No. 7 on the International Boundary between the Dominion of Canada and Alaska, thence following the line of the "Cascade Mountains" as defined by paragraph 2 of Section 24 of the Interpretation Act of British Columbia, being Chapter 1 of the Revised...

Naku... Beby

Uetto

1.

Over spilt milk,
he remembers
freedom.

3. That no Enemy Alien shall have in his possession or use, while in such protected area, any camera, radio transmitter, radio shortwave receiving set, firearm, ammunition, or explosive.

S.T. WOOD (Commissioner)
Royal Canadian Mounted Police
OTTAWA, February 7, 1942.
TO BE POSTED IN A CONSPICUOUS PLACE

lugh bridi tea

left margin (rotated): mew-tin-l n open rebellion against authority

right margin (rotated): mew-tayt v. to undergo or cause to undergo mutation.

center margin (rotated): mew-til-ate v. to injure, or disfigure by cutting off an important part

far right margin (rotated): make v. to perform (an action etc) make war,

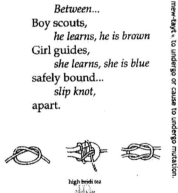

Loppu

Between...
Boy scouts,
he learns, he is brown
Girl guides,
she learns, she is blue
safely bound...
slip knot,
apart.

high bridi tea

63

f
ake
die
fusion
fuss
w/ foreign—
icity

Slopwater Zoup........85
Cream of Socks........85
Underwear (Clear)..95
Cold 'N Sweet..........75
(Summer only)

g
raze
the inte—
gaze
the gap

Happatizers

Opium Cocktail............................... .10.45
Gambler's Relish...................................1.60
Chili Jili...2.35
Half Past Pickles..................................1.65
Scott McFarlane Medley....................1.50
Muttered Tongue..................................1.70

*Then he did what he had learned
to do so well in such instances, he
turned it into a joke, a kind of self-
putdown that he knew these white
guys liked to hear...*

Dekki

The floor boards
whisper secrets.

But
Even as you tiptoe,
I hear...

We...to Lemon Creek

high bridi tea

mutter. to speak or utter in a low, unclear tone

to utter subdued grumbles. muttering, muttered words.

mute adj. silent, refraining from speaking, not exressed in words. *In mute admiration*

Dolosu

Under where
no body sees.

Wear, hides
desire.

high brich tea

(of a letter) not pronounced, such as the e in voice is mute. to deaden or muffle the sound of…(of colour) subdued

kick
splits

I'm just a baby, maybe six months (.5%)old. One of my aunts is holding me on her knee. Sitting on the ground in front of us are her two daughters, 50% Scottish. Another aunt, the one who grew up in China with my father, sits on the step with her first two children around her. They are 75% Chinese. There is another little 75% girl cousin, the daughter of another 50% aunt who married a 100% full-blooded Chinaman (full-blooded, from China even). At the back of the black-and-white photograph is my oldest boy cousin; he's 25% Chinese. His mother married a Scot from North Battleford and his sisters married Italians from Trail. So there, spread out on the stoop of a house in Swift Current, Saskatchewan, we have our own little western Canadian multicultural stock exchange.

make good. to become successful, or prosperous, make good the loss. pay compensation

mis-teeka. an aura of mystery or mystical power.

We banked our hopes,
one coin at a time.

Silver lined clouds,

Shiluba-Go

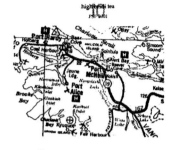

Aratobe

Grasping the name
with our tongues

We make the place
our home

moo-tah-tees   moo-tan-deess
[things]

when the necessary alterations of details has been made. (in comparing

Choice Grill Stakes & Chops	
Tied Tongue	15.45
Mixee Grill	11.60
Rented Muscle	12.35
Half Heart	13.65
Skin—Under—Gaze	9.50
Split Pidgin Aux Champignon	14.70
Peas & Canned Toes	8.75
(by the Pound)	
Breaded Native Top Sirloin	16.00
Back Talk	6.50

Jargon
's split
tongue

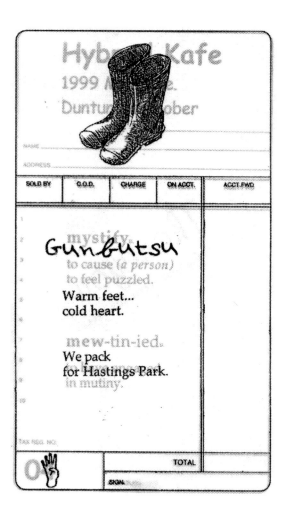

Hyb... Kafe
1999 ...
Duntu... ober

NAME
ADDRESS

SOLD BY	C.O.D.	CHARGE	ON ACCT.	ACCT. FWD.

mystify.
Gunbutsu
to cause *(a person)*
to feel puzzled.

Warm feet...
cold heart.

mew-tin-ied.
We pack
for Hastings Park.
in mutiny.

TAX REG. NO.

TOTAL

SIGN.

166

Banbaizolai

a feeling

The smell of broken dreams,
of wounds dressed...

uneasiness.

then redressed.

m u m *adj.*

(*informal*)
silent,
say nothing
about this.

"She America"

Stevii Paden

Names
Opinions
A mouth full of mush
Secret messages

I can't speak
I can't speak
Vietnamese

Vietnamese
I'm not one of them
I'm not the same
"She America"
they say

      (cue the hysterical laughter)

I'm an American baby
I'm an alien around my family
I can't breathe the same air they do
The way they spell things out—
      I choke on that too

In this place I can't stay!
Who knows what the hell to say?

Hapa Big Board

Michael Tora Speier

Hapa Big Board is an interactive sculpture in the shape of a giant skateboard filled with kids activities, original art, writing, audio, resources and articles all created by, and centered around the theme of, multiracial individuals, families and their communities.

The hefty but portable Hapa Big Board exhibit sports 12 drawers and many secret compartments; the deck is strong enough for a whole family to stand on, large enough for a small class of kids to use as a workstation table, and tall enough to act as a mini stage for a 2-person surf punk band! Created in 2000, the project is about people of all ages and backgrounds "shredding" the boundaries of where we live.

Photo by www.jenniferstrangphotography.com, design by John Endo Greenaway, Big Wave Design, for Hapa-palooza Festival, Vancouver

Excerpts from Nectarine River: the tale of a mixed race surfer

Michael Tora Speier

Through text and 35 original paintings, *Nectarine River* is a contemporary surfer dudesque reimagining of the centuries' old Japanese folktale Momotaro (AKA Peachboy):

A precursor to Michael's Hapa Big Board multiracial giant interactive skateboard project, *Nectarine River* brings mixed ethnicity to the center of a once xenophobic story about a country under invasion from outside demons.

Where the child warrior Momotaro was a hero who protected his homeland, the updated character of Hapa the Kid Surfer rides a big offshore wave that carries him all the way upriver to meet the stern personality at the heart of the homeland itself. Think Joseph Conrad with more "awesomes" and "gnarlies" thrown in to attract a younger set. The purpose is to explore our cultural landscape~one of shifting boundaries and many many historical interweavings.

Story Excerpt
Nectarines, fiery colored fruit!

River, carrier of reflections...

Did you know, ages ago, nectarines came from the branches of peach trees? Wha? Is that true?? Through many peach and nectarine trees flows Nectarine River, a short drive from surf's up Beaches. Upstream, growing along the river shore are tall and wide condos, busy people places.

In Nectarine Villa a dad cradles newborn baby...then passes sleepy "hot potato" to mom. Bzzzzz!! All the relatives pour in~dads are Jewish and kind of noisy...moms are Japanese...and kind of noisy. Big family squish-a-thon...

Everyone waiting on baby's eyes to open, aunties uncles grampies grannies
and cousins peering,

> "Awww Look At The Baby!
> The looks are the mother's, the looks
> are the father's,
> the left eye's Asian
> the right is Caucasian,

> "The nose is Romanian
> the teeth are Canadian,
> those thumbs are gargantuan.
> An Okinawan bellybutton
> & tickly feet with intuition~
> this kid's gonna be a jazz musician!"

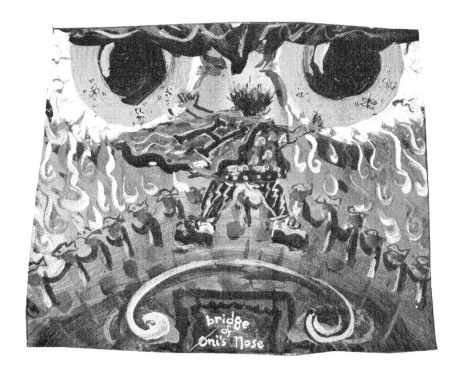

(Cousins' chorus):

> "See it's a baby! All babies are born
>> whole and brand new,
>> no pinch of this nor dash of that,
>> no half-and-half, no mixed up knish!
>> Baby is hapa! And a hapa baby's all Hapa,
>> a nectarine kind of child, a very peachy blossom...Awesome
> Hapa, Awesome!"

***

Baby crawls, toddles and gets way bigger, a pretend super hero:
> Hapa the Kid Surfer!

Polkadot whale hiccups and Hapa kid surfs upstream on Nectarine River past tall trees...thunderclouds...prehistoric creatures?!...around barns and through ice cream factories,
past skyscrapers and billboards...
way into the foothills, stopping at the ankle of Oni Mountain where Hapa remembers lives a large, grumpy demon.

Ahead, dual flames from a dark pair of caverns...
Wait a minute! They're two big nostrils of Oni, the crankiest mountain demon of them all.

Oni belches fire,
  "AEORRrupfh!
  I ate too many spicy people today, Gurrrrrrr Urrrrrrrrrrr!
  WHAAT urr YOUUUU?"

Michael Tora Speier

NEW WORLD PICNIC (Diasporic Finger Foods)

I am descended from diasporic lineages on both sides, a common North American story. My immediate family left the U.S. for more peaceful Canada when I was six. My grandparents were first generation American-born children of diasporic families. They came from Hungary, Romania and Japan. Their movement reflects the trial and hardship of their abandoned homelands. Born in North America, I cannot quite imagine what they went through to arrive here and begin new lives.

For Jewish people, there are foods that ritualize and remember their diasporic history. My New World Picnic honours these diasporic roots. Here, the idea of picnic is lured toward other sources, shedding the myth of picnics impressed upon us by images of lackadaisical European aristocracy and their puny lapdog airs.

In my short (and unresearched) history of picnics, their origin, at least in western consciousness, as television verifies, was with Victorian classes of privilege and immovable wealth getting together to shmooz, snuffle pate and offer one another dilettante advice on love. The ruling class gave way to a busier, aspiring leisure class who picnicked next to classic cars, on fine English linen, popping champagne, toasting their richesse and pairing up like diamonds. In the sad 60s, Elvis reigned; and in the 70s, this evolved into beach barbeques of the white middle class. At that time, in Canada, hotdogs, jello ambrosia (orange or green jello molded w/marshmallows and fruit cocktail in it) and sprite, with adolescent groping after dark, were widespread.

New World Picnic comes from another tree of gathering altogether. The temporary changing site of the picnic is for remembering the movement informing our histories. The foods are offerings to the basic ingredients of our lives—our dream to be safe and rooted, and to belong where we have chosen, among people, to settle.

This is a picnic about tracing paths toward home. Your picnic basket should be lightweight, insulated and sturdy enough to cross a desert. The dishware of heirloom quality. An umbrella will really be a godsend if you can carry it. If you live in Canada or the northern U.S., try this in winter using inflatable cushions and goretex picnic blankets. The best sites are high passes offering views of the valley below. If it snows you don't need to bring ice for drinks! Bon chance!

Baby Octopus Salad

I grew up in Canada where hockey is a national addiction. I kicked the habit after a million blank hours of fascination. If someone throws an octopus on the ice during the Stanley Cup Playoffs, it symbolizes the 8 games a team needed to win the trophy before the 60s expansion era. This is an appalling waste of a beautiful creature's life and I used to have conflicted feelings like I must choose between food (roots) and hockey (new world). This is a salad of my mixed boyhood loyalties:

Thaw a 2 lb. box frozen baby octopus (found in Asian supermarkets)
tsp. coriander seeds
Juice of 1 small lemon
Juice of 1 small lime
1 red shallot (or Tbsp. chopped red onion)
1 Tbsp. olive oil
1 tsp. vinegar
1 tsp. brown sugar
1 tsp. fish sauce (Chinese supermarket)
1/4 red bell pepper, slivered
1 sprig coriander, chopped
Dashes: worchestershire
        ketchup or Vietnamese hot sauce
        ground black pepper
        curry powder
        mustard powder
        salt or garlic salt
3 dry chillis

Gut heads, remove beaks and eyes, cut each one into 2 or 3
pieces and parboil until the meat turns reddish and curls (no
longer than 2 minutes!)
Drain and cool in a bowl.

JAPANESE-JEWISH ATTRACTION,
an interracial salad
Asparagus, avocado, red onion w/ black sesame dressing

A recipe of familial tastes which, like myself, begins at (but prefers leap out of) my parents' mutual attraction in the early 1960s. A Berkeley-born product of that time, I am confused by certain assumptions veiling that significant wave of mixed-race love children. For instance, mixed race marriages do not, for me, equal the triumph of love over racial disharmony; nor do I feel I am the product of a "miscegenation". Nor am I responsible to solve either of these models. I am specifically here to add dilemmas not only to historical cultural boundaries but also, to the contemporary ideals and belief systems of people struggling to place themselves, and me, in their inhospitable design; I remind that world I am not a fraction of who they think I am.

My mixed race experience is a river of unique and shared yearnings, a setting I get to thoroughly crash and explore. It is easy to be cloaked in names of others: Eurasian; halfbreed; mulatto; mestizo; watered down; faded; (invisible). As an antidote, I desire my own mixing, exercising my soul's sense of self re-creation: infusion; spiral; hybrid; risotto; freestyle laps in the gene pool; nectarine; double helix; constellation...

Interracial Salad

1 bunch crispy asparagus
1 unoppressed avocado
1/2 tiny red onion, sliced into thin rings
5 leaves butter lettuce
1 large green onion, slivered into 3" lengths, chilled in cold water
3 Tbsp. black sesame seeds (get at Asian supermarkets)
1/4 C vegetable oil
1 tsp. black sesame oil (Asian supermarkets, can substitute plain
    sesame oil)
Juice of 1/4 lemon
1 tsp. rice vinegar
1 tsp. Japanese soy sauce
1 tsp. sugar
3 cloves garlic
1 sprig coriander
dashes: dry minced garlic, optional (get at Vietnamese Grocery)
        dry mustard
        red wine vinegar
        worchestershire

        sea salt & ground black pepper

Cut tough ends off asparagus. Steam washed asparagus until tender but not mushy about 3 minutes. Set aside to cool. Arrange whole or halved over lettuce leaves (I prefer whole, in one parallel clump, like green paintbrushes desiring ink).

Toast sesame seeds for a few minutes in a pan on low heat. In a medium-sized grinder or suribachi, grind black sesame fine as dust. Try food processor if too tiring a grind. Add garlic cloves and grind more, using slow addition of oil to loosen and smooth the mixture. Combine this with the rest of the seasoning ingredients except the optional dry garlic. The consistency should be very thick, but pourable, like crude oil!

Pit and slice avocado and, with red onion, arrange over or beside asparagus. If the salad is going to sit for awhile, squeeze lemon on avocado to keep from oxidizing brown.

Pour dressing across salad in one artful sweep. Garnish with green onion, coriander and dry garlic sprinkles. For spicier tastes, you can sliver a chilli pepper on top and grind more black pepper...

A Coming Out Poem

Claire Tran

you taught me to show love through food.
offerings of
cool and warm,
crisp and smooth,
sweet and spicy.

i am a good daughter, dad.
after a long anti-war march,
i share with her my 2 dollar bánh mì.
we exchange crisp, warm bites,
and talk politics between chewing.

in our little yellow house,
you carefully prepared bowls
balancing cool, crisp cucumber,
with steamy, hot fish and rice.
one for each child.

at the same time as brother makes rice soup with his soy sauce,
sister picks at her fish and I eat all the cucumbers first,
you explain our history through talk story.

i am a good daughter, dad.
in my own kitchen,
i pat a mixture of flour, sugar, butter, and macadamia nuts
into a pie pan.
I blend the baked brilliantly purple ube into a creamy mixture,
and I top it off with a coconut cream sauce,
cool and sweet like she is.

in our hot kitchen, on our tiny stove,
you lightly shake the pan,
spreading the bánh xèo mixture evenly,
until it cooks crisp and mung beans melt inside.
each of these yellow half moons makes us smile.

I am a good daughter, dad.
I make warm noodle soup now,
and I build a mountain of mint leaf, basil, limes, and chilis,
but I make vegetarian broth just for her.

you still roll dozens of egg rolls for all your co-workers,
turn the local fisherman's fresh fish into crispy flavorful fishcakes,
and invite the neighbors over for hot steamy crab.

dad there's something i've been trying to tell you.
there's something i need you to know.
there's something i want you to know.
i love like you do.

bánh mì: Vietnamese sandwich

bánh xèo: Vietnamese crepe

Completely Mixed Up

2007-2015

Encapsulation

Neil Aitken

There is always something that refuses to be contained. Small matters,
like fall-how it appears suddenly in the margins of our world, say

in the torn edges of a love letter (an unnamed city of desire buried
in its blue-inked scrawl), or the river gravel scattered at your feet,

or whatever the wind wraps around a wrought iron angel at dusk.
Something eludes our description of the world and its objects.

The birds casting their long fat shadows across the last traces of light,
even rain, or the leaves in the fallow field caught between fire and gutter.

Here, another line forms, a procession of constants, a conduit of sorts
that carries what it does not consider, the watery grey sky,

the now-brittle veins of summer. The earth overflows with the memory
of itself and every incarnation of the dead. Layer after layer.

Husk after husk. One life bleeds into another. Inside, the stones
are fitted so precisely that not even a blade can find a home.

It's not that we do not know the order of the world and its unmaking.
There are methods here, secrets to be held. Things we should remember

and pass on, by one name or another. We set our ears to the coldest wall,
listen to the night like an old trawler sounding its way through the deep.

Beneath us, the sharp bones of ships, the incessant thrum of waves.

First published in *Ostrich Review*

Float

Neil Aitken

-a fundamental type used to define numbers with fractional parts

Like a bell, or rather the sound of it opening,
a silence that having tolled speaks again

suspended between states of incompleteness~
a point traversing a numbered landscape.

This country of small infinities is what we do
with what remains: bits of window panes,

refracted light, what gathers in the torn leaves
from the dimming edge of the red fields

grown dark. Say what you will, the body is no more
than the moon, a white trouser button in a pool

of gasoline, a halo of ash and flame
ascending the ladder of night.

First published in *Radar Poetry*

Frankenstein's Creature Bids Farewell to its Maker

Neil Aitken

What ever was I to you, but a ghost-a phantom of dissembled lives,
not yours, not mine, but stolen, part and parcel from the grave?

And now, when it comes to this, you lie, silent, set as a corpse,
cold and pale upon the unlit pyre, the kindling readied to catch flame,

and me, left at last alone, unburdened of every name you branded
upon my brow, unwilling to gaze and see someone other than yourself

mirrored in my ghastly soul that strains within this hulking frame.
I was always *your* creature, *your* demon-twin and shackle-mate,

but now, against the dark and final night, the vast unbroken howling
wind, I reject it all. This role is not mine to play, but yours.

I refuse to live a life defined by others stories, their mythic fears,
their need for a shadow to call their own, to cast themselves in light.

Who wishes to live as the antagonist always? I am the terrible master
of my fate, my face the beauty that I own. I will not remonstrate,

but claim the title of *monster* to my very core, for here, in the white
nothing of this domain, this deafening blankness of frigid space,

I sign my name, my secret name, across the horizon's line, I write myself anew,
and make whatever legend that trails behind me, mine. I will show

that in me resides a million more selves than you could ever know.
I contain multitudes. I am the silence you dare not hold.

For I am large and have many worlds endlessly turning within my soul-
and in my mind, have lived, and loved, and died a thousand thousand times.

Your story ends here, a final spark, then smoke that ascends into the void,
but mine grows bolder with each telling, consumes the heart, plays the stage,

stumbles onward, a grand machine, unstoppable, unbreakable,
a god that bleeds in text and unspeakable dreams, that rises every morning,

and makes itself write.

First published in *Free Monster Poems* (Hyacinth Girl Press 2015)

Break

Neil Aitken

The days circle round and round, unstoppable, until the office
seems like a hard country, your ergonomic chair, a poor conveyance

to the land of sleep. No one stops you when you slip out from behind
your desk to wander the half-lit halls after hours with arms and hands

swinging in an intricate and imaginary gun ballet of exhaustion
and poor taste. Something fails in such moments, your body

no longer wholly yours, inhabited instead by some stuttering shadow
of motion unwillingly bound to the world of intangible labor.

The hour is late and you have already left what remains of yourself
in the draining sink, in the bathroom mirror that refuses your gaze.

Everything is on the verge of disappearing, you think. Everything
moves toward the raw edge of time where anxious factories loom

like great trees in a storm about to break. The end is almost here,
you sense it on the horizon–how it hangs over you, heavy, faceless,

like the imminent demise of a star whose last brilliant flare
will arrive long after the earth has gone its own way into the dark,

and whatever was you and the life you lived will have slipped free
of the wheel at last, and found some sort of respite from samsara,

from this continual remaking, this constant arising and going forth
into the broad and echoing world patiently awaiting its destruction.

In your waking dreams, you see your father as a young man
on a hillside with a shovel and rake, clearing a path to hold back a fire.

How simple it seems, his task always at hand, crafting a middle way
between what would consume us and what would leave us be.

First published in *Eleven Eleven*

Operator

Neil Aitken

Someone receives the call, patches it through to the outside world,
sitting in a small box behind mirrors, he signals a mechanical arm,

shifts pieces in the candlelit dimness behind a labyrinth of false gears
and pulleys. Elsewhere, a head nods, a hand made of wood and metal gestures.

The unseen labor of the mind turns over and over till someone new steps in.
Here, always a series of workers taking their place between what we want to see

and what the machine can give us. This performance. This act that transcends
what we think we know about the face of the other. There is no breath here,

and yet we listen to its hands spelling out answers to our questions.
Even now, we take this word into our ears to mean something else.

A cross, a road, a star, a slash that cuts a body into pieces.
Sometimes a pipe. Sometimes a sign that collides two worlds

and takes only what is common between them. If not reality,
then this shared dream of a body not quite like our own,

or a mind, waking, that emerges out of the symphony of steel
and brass, that somehow begins to sing an old familiar song.

First published in *diode*

Long

Neil Aitken

-a fundamental type for declaring long integers

As long as possible, the story continues, while there is breath
    in the iron-lunged moon, while the stars inch onward

in their slow unremitting deaths, the night unspooling
    the horizon's dark line, while the cicadas call from the edge

of the earth, while there is room enough to receive, while there is rain,
    the parking lots forming oceans, the alleys rivers,

the old lady on the corner in her bed of papers, a cocoon
    spun out of every breath she exhales, her face rough with words

and dates, the photographs of strangers–tonight, the streets all fold
    into one, their names meaningless–and here,

everything fits inside this hole I have carved in my chest,
    the space where I let the wind sound the strange song

that I carry with me, that says everything and nothing
    about who I am, and who I forgot to be.

First published in *Ostrich Review*

Afar

Kevin Minh Allen

red light blinks
red light sweats

on leave
on fire

wake mother
blame father

rise of dust
show of hands

blood is blood
until it's yours

drown misdeeds
deliver ocean

warm milk
button eyes

widen gaze
open palms

sheltered light
upending night

home away
heart afar

Some Resemblance

Kevin Minh Allen

They say you have your mother's nose and her ears,
although you have no Mother.

They say you have your father's eyes and his chin,
although you have no Father.

Truth is, no one knows what you look like.
Instead, they tell a story about a life you do not live.

Faces in the photo album smile back
as if they know you better than you could ever know yourself.

Always the quiet surprise in a plain brown wrapper.
There you are with a nod and a smile, dutifully mum.

Yet, you were never that quiet.
We remember you speaking about a plane that never lands.

We remember you slumbering underneath the paw of a stone lion.
Your warm breath never left our mirrors.

We remember your Father on patrol in another village over.
We remember your Mother naming you after her father.

You have never been finished.
You will always have more to show us.

Nature's song: for brandy

James Lawrence Ardeña

Don't bring those here she said

Click
crystal eyes click~open
when you stand her up straight
Black thick lashes glued above them~close
when you lie her down
Glass clear ovals
before symmetrical pupils
Peer through translucent pains
Beyond soft blades stain memories
Or White tupperware bowls
Which can hold three cantaloupes or
Perhaps four chopped chickens

During 2:15 recess
near the jungle gym
The lao girl, who sits 4 desks back
And three rows across
Asked what I'd bring tomorrow for
Family food heritage day
I'm gonna bring lumpia I told her
They won't like them.
Everyone in my family loves lumpia
Nobody else here is asian
My pa isn't and he does
Just don't bring those here she said.

ma awoke early that morning
She had everything
The wrappers, the pork, ground beef
Carrots, onions, water chestnuts
diced into tiny perfect cubes
She rolled each one herself

Fingers dipped in a cloudy bowl of water
Sweat glistened off her cheekbone
moistened each one
rolled tightly~then sealed

Dark brown crisps rolled gently in bubbling golden oil
And with each new entry rising grease spatters
Burning her hand
But it remains
Unmoving over the pan
Clenching soiled chopsticks
in which to coax each
to just the right color

Is that her mom I hear behind me
At exactly 10:36 that heritage day
Mrs. Braxton opened the classroom door
Ma's there - standing with her bowl
Lined with paper towels
to soak up the excess
and delivering them crisp and hot

Everyone brought something
That heritiage day
Cupcakes
Cookies
A pie
More cookies
Potato chips, a loaf of bread
The lao girl brought the real good cupcakes
You know the chocolate ones
With the squiggly white line of frosting down the middle
Those went first
Some of us didn't get none

When it was all over I looked to the bowl
No one had touched them

Not even the teacher
They just sat there
and became cold

the lao girl, followed me home
Yelling across the street
"I tow you! I tow you!"
if she hadn't I woulda eaten them all
or ditched them in the grass along the way
but I couldn't
and so I didn't

the door slapped shut behind me
her attention turned to me
"they like? they like?"
she asked quickly in succession
she noticed my arms were tired
her eyes grew heavy
I swear a little glossy
She turned
Looked out the window
Across the fields
towards school, the town, and the rest of it

I just waited
And waited

Till her eyes broke
Shifted
Focused on the tupperware again
Stretched out her hand
Took it
Placed it on the table
And lied down

Memories in Blue

Sandy Sue Benitez

I thought of you, mom
as I walked into the Riverview,
warm and dark as your womb
adorned with silk umbrellas
in sapphire and golden hues
which hung delicately
from beaded threads of love

The walls were lined
with thick, tawny bamboo,
palms and Angel fish mingled
emerald-green tablecloths
adorned black lacquer tables
as candle flames
danced with memories

Buddha sat alone
in quiet contemplation,
his golden skin
radiant in the dim light,
I remember watching mom pray
to you while kneeling,
her blue and white stone pendant
dangling on a silver baht chain,
do you remember mom too?

Soon the meal arrived
the scent of exotic spices
mint, cilantro, ginger, and lemongrass
seduced my nostrils
I knew that I was home again
familiarity growled in my stomach

Pass the shrimp phad thai please
extra crushed peanuts,
papaya salad soaked
in lime and fish sauce,
make it three stars,
chicken satay in peanut sauce
a side dish of cucumber salad,
it was all too much and yet
never quite enough,
hell, make them all three stars,
you haven't lived
until you've eaten a star

I dined, I devoured
savoring every bite
my tongue was on fire
more water please,
mom was laughing
behind a bamboo screen,
take it easy baby,
or was she laughing

in a dream I remember you mom
I remember you loved blue

Siam Rose

Sandy Sue Benitez

The abalone handle
inscribed Siam Rose
rests gently in my palm
as I hold the mirror close
to my fair isle skin
and a face whose features
suggest Amerasian

Dark almond eyes pierce their
way into reflections of golden
temples and Buddhist monks
praying in fire-orange robes

Scent of incense burns away
ancient Thai prayers
drifting up into the sky
only to dissipate and rain down
on the dusty streets of Bangkok
cleansing the city of foreign
dirt and immorality

I think of the GI in olive drab
stumbling his way into
a side-street family bar
to drown his homesickness
in Budweiser

Then she appears
strutting around in slinky silk
and 3" heels, a debutante in heat
walking over to the lonely GI
who glances at her
trying to look unimpressed

in that I-don't-care-who-you-are
kind of way

But he does care
fumbles with his wallet
trying to remember how much love
he brought with him

and what to name me.

Grey Pearl

Sandy Sue Benitez

She was born with Thai chilies
coursing through her veins.
Spicy blood. Dark, almond
eyes the color of burnt rice.

Her mama smiled at the little girl
with a sense of awe and confusion.
What to make of the porcelain
skin, brown hair, and nose flat

as a button mushroom. White
nurses huddled around her,
studying every nuance, every
limb, birthmark, fingers and toes,

like mad geneticists attempting
to decipher the DNA of some rare
creature. Meanwhile, her daddy
stood near the edge of the bed

snapping photos. Vanilla fingers
trembling in excitement as he tried
to steady the camera. The first
few photos were blurry. Inkblots.

Mama and the nurses agreed.
But he disagreed. Saw her quite
clearly. There, behind the black
and white~a soft grey pearl.

Wondering Home

Tamiko Beyer

Lost in the flurry of visas.
Asylum stamp's resounding thud.
Untether the paper sheaves. Ask:

Is this the moment you claim freedom?

Island of your birth, lanky as a young boy's limbs.
Spot of land, equatorial
majesty. You know its cool, set buildings and lush, blunt hills

detest your bloom, how your heart
loves. Cannot name you, cannot
treasure the gorgeous bird you have become~

body not body   crossing borders
in flight under a dark sun. Past the iconic lady, her
torch burning. You claim

no country, no country claims you

but this: a Brooklyn apartment, white walls,
and hanging maps of your desires. Contorted
into odd shapes of longing

you offer yourself to the city's throbbing center. Subway
rattles. Buildings constructed
skeleton to glass fleshed under your skilled eye.

How to write the passage of your body
into memory long as the unfurling
sky? The noodles your mother made. Hot broth.

Ceiling fan's lazy spin. Remember
dust suspended in sunlight,
ask: Is home this number on the door?

The way your key fits into the lock?

First published in *The Collagist*

In Which Hana Learns a New Word

Tamiko Beyer

> there was a door
> > shut
> a peach and a frog
> > a lonely boy and a lonely girl

A ravine a creek a darkening sky Hana finds a friend a frog green
        skin slick its throat's soft underside trembling like raindrop
porous skin absorbing water from air like a mouth taking in and taking in
        Noah leaves the model B52   touches the ravenous skin
strokes the quivering throat   squeezes too hard~

Soon miracle skin turns gray and hot Hana sobbing with the frog's papery
body cupped in her palms feels her father's hand
        stroke her tangled hair once

*

Once a house
on a cul-de-sac wide
windows and a palm
tree When the mother left
not to return
grime coated the windows
The children whose faces looked
more like each others'
than their parents'
experienced
many things

      water-fall   free fall   fallout

They fold a piece of red silk staple it shut and bury it in the back yard

      There was a window
                shut
      TV and packaged soup

*

Noah swears Hana to secrecy They kneel at the TV the preacher sweats
        and hollers his congregation chattering syllables of holy
Hana and Noah shake on the shag rug pray
        ma mam amama ma mamamama mamamam ama ma am

Their father yells from upstairs to stop making a racket and change
        the goddamn channel

        There is a father
                        shut
        a story and a storm

*

At school the other children have glowing cheeks eat mother-
            made sandwiches do not know the story
of the peach boy   Noah comes home
            with nosebleeds and scratched arms   He makes Hana swear secret
Midnight in the back yard bare patch where red silk and the dead
            frog are buried Noah picks up a stick
scratches the ground Hana watches letters form

                    J   A   P

That's what Mom is Noah spits on the earth rubs hard at the letters with
            the sole of his sneaker *Jap* Hana says   The word disappears
tastes like chestnuts tastes like iron

*

Mother, elsewhere
slices
a peach
juices run down
her wrist   thin
sugared trail

*

Father   home   turns
in his sleep
          frogs gasp and children
shake on dusty carpet

We look more like each other than we look like ourselves

Tamiko Beyer

I carry a word in my walls. Or two,
to share. What I was once sure of,
I am no longer. I've lost the feeling of being

a small girl putting on a dress
that will never be that clean again. I lost
a doll's face to the teeth of a dog.

I am a lifetime of mediated language.
I found my body, its song of coming,
and it frightened me in its softness.

On the blue plate, the egg hardens~
its solid white, its yolk eye.
Having lived too many moments

to name individually, we become bodies
in motion, circumscribing
responsibility. To touch

is to become responsible.
To say is to become entwined.
Incantations mark a threshold—

step into, become with. Remember
with me the strange light that seeped
under the typhoon shutters three decades ago.

I give you a narrow street and a concrete wall,
inscribed, signified. I carry a stone
in my pocket. Or two, to share.

First published in *Tuepelo Quarterly*, Issue 6, 2015

Gravity

Excerpts from the play, which has toured to Catifesta in Guyana, Trinidad, and Montreal

Tricia Collins

In 1834, the slaves who had been taken from Africa to the colonies of Britain were set free...The resulting reduction in the labour force caused the sugar plantation owners to search for replacement workers. They obtained large numbers of labourers from Madeira (Portugal), India, and China–each bound by a contract of indenture. The first batch of Chinese landed in Georgetown, British Guiana in 1853, and for the next few years all were men, most being taken forcibly. Chinese women began arriving in 1860, but in small numbers. The ships traveled by way of Singapore and Cape Town, arriving at Georgetown after a journey of between 70 and 177 days.

~ *Cane Reapers*, Trev Sue-A-Quan

Characters:

The Girl from China ~ Born in a village in China. Shipped to Guyana in 1879 at the age of 15.

Josephine ~ A true Guyanese. Ageless as a ghost trapped in the falls. She died at age 33, the same age that Jesus died. She looks down at people still alive and follows her daughter's life.

Maya ~ 27 years old. Lives in Canada and is a student completing her PhD in Environmental Engineering.

All characters are to be played by the same person making use of different dialects and video projection. The timeline of the characters is set in 1879, 1941, and then in 1969, respectively.

Scene 1

There are wooden crates, piles of boxes, sacks, and darkness. A long white tissue hangs from the sky. Rain is pouring down a windowpane. Maya is up late at night scribbling and writing, editing pages in her thesis. She wears intense glasses and tensely rifles through her pile of papers, crosses out replaces words. This is a week before her thesis defense. She whispers the words of her proof, moving through the details with precision. She walks slowly her thesis in a circle, whispering and drawing the centrifuge on the floor. Pulses of her thoughts appear and fade through the rain in projection, the design of her thesis the centrifuge, the rain, the Kaieteur falls, the rain, the ocean, the rain. Maya has created her thesis on the floor, around her she is re-writing history gesturally and vocally, she has put everything into this work, this is her whole life. The projection then bursts into violent ocean turbulence. We hear and see a storm of water crashing, the cacophony of an angry ocean. The following words are projected:

The Pacific Ocean, 1879
Somewhere between Hong Kong and Singapore

When Time and Tide wait for no one...

Scene 2

The words disappear as lights come up on The Girl from China who sits in a box.
The Girl is trapped in the belly of a ship. She is pushed about by the pull of the ocean.
She has a small satchel from which she withdraws a needle and colourful thread.
She continues to embroider a Feng Huang, a mythical Chinese Phoenix, onto a pair
of traditional Chinese slippers. The ship groans, and she is flung onto her side. She
recovers her posture and continues to sew. She spreads a burlap sack and sits on it.
Voices of men hollering outside.

> The Girl: There are many of them out there. Large men.
> The barbarians. You've heard about them I'm sure. They
> have big round eyes and very pale skin. I saw some before
> they sealed the top down on my box. They look a little
> funny I think. They should eat more meat and then may-
> be they won't be so pale on their faces. Mama said "Be
> careful of the Barbarians for they like to eat young girls
> who do not do what they are told. They find the meat is
> that much sweeter. Their barbarian religion teaches them
> to eat god-flesh and also to nibble on naughty girls." I am
> much too skinny now for them to want to eat me. Not
> much meat on my bones now that it has been so long rid-
> ing these waves, rolling and rolling, up and down.

The box rocks and she is flung across it, she gets up and sits again.

> The men from the ship come at night. The orders were
> placed long before. From across the seas. The men are
> fast. You scream but no sound comes out of your mouth.
> You lay awake at night and count the small marks on
> the ceiling. 88 small marks and then, heavy feet in the
> hallway. You clutch your satchel. A needle pierces the
> skin. You see the blood but don't feel a thing. No feeling
> of the needle in your flesh, just the look of your blood
> dripping, no feeling of the large arms sliding under the
> sheets under your back. How can it be so quiet, so dark?
> My mouth quiet, the doors so quiet. No snoring tonight.

The resounding echo of a heartbeat.

Only this sounding.

She touches her heart.

And this.

She touches her head.

I taste the cloth in my mouth and the dust on the back of
my throat. They use a very dusty rag. I don't like to drool
or spit, but a rag that big makes you drool whether you
want it or not. In the bouncing rickshaw and down the
windy road, so quiet even now, slow motion everywhere
on the way to the sea. The night is more pitch dark with
the burlap bag against your eyes. I've had the bag ever
since. I use it to prevent slivers. You must be very careful
of the slivers. I found a large one in the middle of my
hand days ago or weeks ago. I bundle up the burlap bag
and sit on it to keep from finding more wooden slivers in
other places. The cloth isn't as rough as I've worn it in.
As rough as the belly of the ship. And now here we are.
My belly hurts now. Too much salt water. It dries me up a
little on the inside.

Magical Feng Huang, Mama let me sew you the night I
was taken. She gave me this satchel. For protection. She
helped me start a few stitches around the edges. Silently,
teaching me, showing me how with her hands, no words.
But you beautiful Feng Huang I embroider all by myself.
I'm so glad you're here with me now.

The girl continues to sew as lights fade.

Scene 3

The projected image of the blustery ocean spins into a tidal whirlpool. The water spins clockwise into a waterfall and we hear the sounds of water falling and crashing. On a separate screen are the projected words:

The Kaieteur Falls
Guyana, South America
The longest single drop of water in the world.

The Kaieteur Falls were named after Kaie
An Amerindian Chief who sacrificed himself into water into air
He died over the edge to save his people from a terrible curse.

Josephine, the woman in the waterfall, is climbing the silks with the waterfall projected onto her. Josephine is a ghost trapped, falling for ages.

> Josephine: Falling is hard work. Because you can't let go, girl. Eh heh. Me had a man in my life. He was *the* man. He name was Cyril and he was perfect. A god. Sorry Lord. He be my first lover and my last lover. Dis man teach me things I can't talk to you about here. Maybe when you're older. You fall in love like that you remember details so clear. You remember da rooms you were in. Da rooms you were loved in. Da first time I see he I know. We were teenagers, he play a cricket match in Georgetown.

Dancehall music begins.

> He move so fast, so beautifully. He move like a river, like water dripping wet all over me. He whine my innocence away. We meet at early morning hours in the shower wet when he just don't leave my mind. And now I remember all the time, the little things like beads of sweat that trace the edge of he face and drip wet onto me lips. So I can taste he salt. I remember lying up on my side, with he lying up on he side around me. I remember *everything* he say, whisper deep into me. My girl, he said he loved me.

214

Here
Hand on head.
Here.
Hand on heart now.
And Here.
Hand on belly. Dancehall music goes out.

But I didn't mean to get stuck up in Kaieteur! You got to
know that. I didn't mean to fall. I here to tell you there
are things you need to know about where you come from.
You listening?

I remember so clear the night we had to stop. My mudda
words burn through me, an icy shudder run up my back.
"Josephine can't be with a brown man. She will do what I
say. When she marries Chinese we all be better off."
So I write he a letter. The first one, I still can hear it.

Dear Cyril,
Thinking of you
Missing you
Pause.
I had that dream again where I am falling, I told you
about it before. When I'm falling forwards and looking
down and everything moves so slow. And I can't see you.
Thinking of you
Missing you
Pause.

The letter goes on. I had to do what was right, what I
was supposed to do for my family. Leave him be. But I
couldn't help it, girl, I flowed after he. I followed and
floated and fell over the edge. I got trapped up here, stuck
in Kaieteur falling.

My heart reaching up, my body racing down. Suspended
in time. Waiting.

Lights fade to black. Josephine slithers off the cloth in darkness.

Scene 4

Rain falls on water. Maya runs through the falling rain and covers her head with jumbled papers. She is hyped and greets people. We are now in defense room at the University of British Columbia, and Maya is a PhD candidate defending her thesis. Maya wears a suit, thick glasses and has a laser pointer. She has a micro-phone in her lapel and drinks from a glass of water. She moves through the follow-ing dialogue at lightening pace.

> Maya: Good evening, everyone. My name is Maya Ho-A-Yun, and tonight I will be defending my thesis "A Centrifugal Water Drainage Model for Developing Nations, A case study: Georgetown, Guyana."

She uses the laser pointer to initiate the development of her centrifuge projected behind her.

> As you know from my thesis, the Dutch then British colo-nization of Guyana built its capital, Georgetown as a port city. Intended as a direct route for export of sugar cane, gold, bauxite and other minerals, Georgetown served as a channel, if you will, to the rest of the British Empire. The central problem left in their wake: Georgetown exists below sea-level. The seawall that encapsulates the city has been up until now, the only barrier keeping Georgetown and the Atlantic Ocean apart.
>
> Recent erosion and cracks in the seawall compromise this protection.

She takes a sip of water.

> Thus the reason I stand before you today. Due to George-town's sub-sea-level status combined with recent natural

catastrophes, the city has become prone to flooding and thus infectious disease.

So, I have reworked the current drainage system.

Video of the elaborate labyrinthine design grows behind her; a wheel entrenched with lines and detail.

Behind me you will see my central design for the centrifuge. This figure is designed to reflect one of several structures to be embedded beneath flood-target zones in Georgetown, Guyana. We would theoretically install several of these centrifuges beneath the heart of the City of Georgetown. So that during intense rain periods rainwater will spill into the centre of the centrifuge, at which point its weight initiates the "spin cycle," if you will. The generators connected to inland waterpower fuel the centrifuge into motion. All the rainwater that fills the centre is forced outwards via circular gravity into flexible polymer piping. As you see here the piping reaches out like the spokes of a wheel. The water then moves into troughs connected to the channels currently present. Water is siphoned back out into the sea, kept in check by the kokers or rather sleuths in these channels.

Are there any questions at this point?

Silence. Lights down.

Scene 5
Sounds and video of ocean turburlence. The following words are projected:

The Atlantic Ocean
Somewhere off the coast of Cape Town

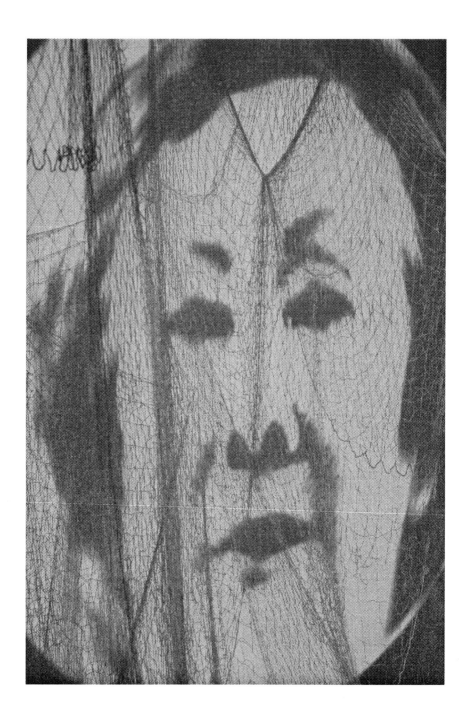

Lights up on The Girl from China in the corner of her box, light hits her face from a broken hole in the crate. She wears an undershirt and mends her own shirt, gives up then picks up her slipper and works the embroidery. Projected is a blown up image of mother hands that help small hands embroider the blue phoenix on The Girl's tiny slipper. The Girl shakes in general.

> The girl: Stop shaking hand. Stop it and stitch steadily. I have to finish the Feng Huang. My family plans a match for my marriage. Mama chose the Loh family because they have a handsome son. That is why our families meet and have tea in the early mornings every month. That is why I work so hard on you little slippers. To show the Lohs what a good wife I can be. But maybe they have changed their minds. Still I will embroider you Feng Huang onto my slipper because you are powerful.

Sound of a heart beating melts into a wing flapping against the sky.

> Great when you fly high above these little things that happen on the earth's surface on the sea's surface. The sky so big and wide a place; but you can stretch the whole length of it with your wings. You are as big as the sea because you are not just a bird but a powerful fish too. Made out of magic.

We hear the sound of a flapping wing speed up to a heartbeat, quick and tense.

> Mama said barbarians bite. She said they are fierce and mean. But I don't think he was a barbarian. He spoke Mandarin, whispered some bad things to me. He smells bad still on me. They should have trapped him in a box. Locked him in a crate not me. They did afterwards, I heard it through the slats. I heard them beat him luckily.

She stitches her slipper.

> Feng Huang, you will come if I call you. I would have
> called you when he first crawled into the box but nothing
> came out of my mouth. There was not a cloth there any
> longer, there was just nothing.

The Girl is frozen still and silent. Lights go to black.

...

Scene 14

*The waterfalls fade in and out lightly. Maya sits atop the Kaieteur Falls she speaks
to the ghost of her mother Josephine.*

> Maya: I hear water falling. I hear nothing else these days.
> I can feel you holding on so tight even though I'm so far
> away. But I'm never really that far away at all, you know,
> I never have been. Even when I tried to crawl as far as
> possible I was right behind you. Stuck. I know that one of
> your hands grips the past and the other grips your invis-
> ible future and you are trapped in the falls. But if you can
> just let go and fall with the generations, and with me, and
> listen to the wind behind swirling around you, you'll be
> free. Limitless. I want you to move again because I hear
> you calling. So, I guess there is nothing else to say, noth-
> ing so important to do but just keep my eyes shut and to
> see you there.

She closes her eyes.

> I can still see you. You're pretty beautiful. This isn't good-
> bye mummy cause I'll be right behind you. Right here,
> wherever.

Lights fade.

Autobiography at 43

Wei Ming Dariotis

Age 43: Happily, greedily, looking down on the fog
returned to my City, cozy
in my little one-bedroom cottage
a book about to come out
a writing partner
a whole community of Critical Mixed Race Studies scholars
people wanting
to share this story with me of being mixed
of being whole.

Things set just the way I like them, a garden,
a life of the mind and a life of the body, rediscovered

an empty heart where my child should be.

My department chair sends an email, Can you
explain your "ancestral lineages" so we can
explain why we should be able to give a "Chinese American" scholarship
to mixed race people who *don't* have a Chinese father?
and I say, Why?
Why are you asking me for this again?
You know who I am.
I am Chinese.
Wei Ming is
Chinese.
It is my mother who makes me Chinese
through her Chinese labor, her Chinese milk, her Chinese myths, her Chinese whispers, her Chinese tears, her Chinese love-pinches, her Chinese chin, her Chinese skin, her Chinese scorn, her Chinese love for all things Japanese~and for Korean and Thai soap operas~her Chinese desire to email Bush junior when he was President to tell him how much he sucked, her Chinese need to bite policemen, her Chinese mother's admonition, Don't get married, marriage is a bad deal for women.
No fucking "explanation" necessary.

Age 33: Clock ticking down and heart broken I stumbled
thinking I had the perfect plan
into the arms of a broken man
and gave years away, and my body became
a frozen wasteland in the hotlands
of tired West Oakland and fragrant Alameda
and one year became five and my uterus
was tested and dyed blue

and I was asked to forgive my father
and I asked myself why I had trapped myself in anger
and I knew I was holding on like a gambler keeps going
too much invested to stop now
and my husband asked, Why do you seem different, so sparkling?
and I said, I want a divorce.

Age 23: A Master of English literature, and angry as fuck at what it took
or what was taken from me to get that degree
and my mother sent me away that summer
to Uncle's place in Bangkok, where Sunday was for brunches with
my handsome, womanizing grandfather, my Goong-goong,
smiling and eating, smiling
and eating
just one of the Eurasian generation of the Chan Clan
finally being there, finally being on the Chinese side
being seen as Indian in Vietnam,
as Thai in Thailand

and as a member of the ghetto of over-privileged Asians in
Santa Barbara, where I was privileged
to bring down diversity on the wings
of my full ride
where I asked my white multicultural lit professor,
Do you even know any Black people?
and he said, I don't have to know them,
I can read about them.

Age 13: How many times have I read
The Lord of the Rings by now? happily, greedily
reading everything and encouraged to do so
since 4th grade happily, greedily
encouraged since leaving public school.
By 13 a firm B-cup with long dark hair,
did those 40-year-old men really think I was in my 20s or did they really
just not care?

Age 3: Flying free! Flying up on United, SFO to Sea-Tac
the innocent adult who sits beside me
not knowing he will be regaled
captive audience for 2 whole hours
with my ENTIRE life story from birth in Australia
to the dera in India
to Yia-yia's house on Dogwood Lane
to Santa Cruz and my pronouncement,
"We should leave him."
His kidnapping me, and then, finally freed
up to San Francisco, the City of my belonging
where my mother and I
stood back to back against the world
a mother and her little girl.

At birth: My mother tells me
she hovered
above her own body untethered from 33 hours of laboring.
Dying, she heard the nurse call out, Come back! Come back! Your daughter-
she needs you.

White Snake Woman in San Francisco

Wei Ming Dariotis

> *had you not seen her*
> *become a white snake she would have*
> *loved you*
> *writhed with you*
> *born you*
> *sneaky snake children*
> *happy happy happy*

I kick off the black '70s-style platform pumps
~so much like the ones she once wore
delivering drinks to Mr. Nakamura, Yamada-san, or Mr. Kawasaki;
everyone wanted Sally-chan (so exotic!) the only Chinese girl
at Kabuki in J-town~
barefoot toes aching I stumble to the hot shower just like at dawn

> *she became more snake than woman, her woman-heart*
> *shifting in her body, like her woman-skin*
> *becoming snake skin*
> *not gone, but transformed*
> *lead into gold*
> *snake-heart worth more than woman-heart*
> *that white snake-skin her best armor*

soap to water just this side of scalding as I wake myself from dreams of her
lost last face
her mouth open in that horrible terrified "O"
I had to
tell her; I had to give her permission
I was three years old/and then I was forty

> *a series of coordinates matched up point to point*
> *out of this I create myself into a universe*
> *a constellation a matter of perspective*
> *call it "White Snake Woman Galaxy": myself*
> *galactic white snake body entwined snake to snake*

with my lover
in a sea in a bed of stars

I don't remember which theater, but I think
the one on the edge of North Beach
near Union Street, because we lived there for a year or so.
She would take me to
movies she remembered from Hong Kong–she'd skip lunch for a week
save every penny and spend
all day Saturdays in the theater
escaping home, escaping her mother's cigarettes
and frustrated slaps.
And here now she'd bring me with her, trying to
connect to something lost or pushed away
trying to make me Chinese through
visual and aural stimulation–as a vegetarian, I couldn't be
transformed /*my whiteness*
shifted/ by language or by food

> *the sound of her white snake body unfurling*
> *snapped like a war pennant*
> *angry in the wind*

every night the same dream, and even during daylight waking
her mouth
that "O"
her lost eyes

> *you were never supposed to witness*
> *her transformation–men don't understand*
> *there are mysteries they cannot master*
> *she was always happy with him,*
> *but it couldn't stay that way*
> *she wasn't human, and the gods don't like it*
> *and what would their children be–human, or snake?*
> *could she risk asking him that? asking him to love her*
> *in her true form?*

my father never touched her again
after the two days of birthing me
he was young I think, barely 21, so do I forgive him?
for dragging her to Australia so he could avoid the draft?
forcing her to be vegetarian in Australia in 1969?
commenting on breasts~young tits old tits perky tits saggy tits~until
my mother got some new ones?
for being a white man?
for telling me that~hypothetically~should any child
of his be queer he would feel
well he wouldn't want any child of his to experience
that kind
of discrimination: girl child. not. white.
my queerness visible only when I want it to be, not marking my
visible brown woman body

> my transformation unwitnessed
> my skin sloughs end to end making galaxies
> of stars spinning and spinning
> and planets plummeting past
> and people
> people to live on them

Anti-imperialist grrl raising a hapa feminist boy: a peminist mom's progress

For Zacarias Jose Roberto, a.k.a. Stinson[1]

> *Melinda Luisa de Jesús*

Motherhood was something rejected
at first.
I resisted being reduced to just
my body, mere biology~
my nature, as my dad called it
my duty, according to my mother.
Any cow can have a calf! was my retort.
I wanted the room of my own
I had so much to learn.

Then, at 40, motherhood humbled me profoundly
I have never loved my brown body more
As I grew and then birthed my son early, at 34 weeks
no drugs
Stinson unaware, feeling nothing
Secure in his watersack until the last moment.
Clasping his tiny fingers and toes
I was in awe of him
So beautiful, so fragile.

"But he's so white!" his dad's mother couldn't help exclaiming
when she saw the first pictures
"We're sure he'll brown up right away!" his dad answered.
And so, on my baby's very first day
The lines are drawn.

I miss the simplicity of pregnancy
The baby swimming inside me
Of me, of my own body,

protected.
This little boy has my face
But his light skin means that somehow
He can't really be mine.
The difference between our skin colors
Is the only thing people can see.

We always thought of you as white!
Stinson's grandmother told me some 15 years ago
Like it was the highest compliment she could ever give me~
> Because somehow I had overcome my tiresome cultural baggage?
> Because I'd somehow managed to emulate my colonizers and fully
> deracinate myself?

I bristled with the ridiculous absurdity of it
Caught between my class privilege and my brown-ness
What could I say?

I'm so damn white the racist neighborhood kids tried to burn down our house.
Twice.
I'm so damn white my siblings tried to lighten their faces with baby powder
before we went to school.
I'm so damn white my 5th grade nickname was "The Oriental Coffee Bean."
I'm so damn white I created a note system in 4th grade
where I was fucking Scarlet O'Hara!
I'm so damn white I was never taught Tagalog or Ilocano-languages
my parents spoke.
I'm so damn white my dad told me that there was no culture in the Philippines
until the Spanish arrived
~and I believed him.
I'm so damned white I learned to swallow my confusion and my anger, eat it down,
pounds and pounds
> *of heartache.*

I was so deracinated I was in graduate school when I finally learned the
history of my own people
Of our resistance
Of my family's role in Philippine independence

Of our colonial mentality
And suddenly my childhood made sense~
And my journey into my own history and identity began.

Decolonization
Is the legacy
I must pass along to my son
As I raise him deep in the belly of the imperialist beast
To resist erasure and whitewashing
To know his roots
Claiming Pin@yhood is our greatest gift and challenge

My mom's slow slide into the darkness of Alzheimer's drives this urgency.
She's the last tie to our homeland
She, who taught Filipino literature, Tagalog and Philippine folkdance~
        things she denied me and my siblings because we didn't "need them"
Her memories, our family history, slip away
And the mom I once knew disintegrates before my very eyes.
As she travels backwards, away from us,
Will Ilocano and Tagalog become her final languages, just like Grandma?
None of us will be able to reach her
And I can only watch, horrified,
as that long, frayed thread snaps...

But what will Stinson need?
He can pass, the mestizo dream~
And still
He seeks reassurance from me:
"We have the same skin, mom, right? The same hair.
I look like you!"
Yes, you do, son.
We have the same love for books and music and dance
For bibibingka and pinsec,
Polvoron, adobo, and fried rice.
The same energy and emotions,
(To the chagrin of your father!)

I've surrounded you with books about the Philippines,
about Filipino American culture
But I worry~will it be enough?
Can it be enough?
What do I have to give you except
My writing
This family history
My own story of becoming Pinay.[2]

I want you to feel proud to be Pinoy
In your own place and time
In your own way.

And so we walk this road together,
holding hands
Our journeys so different
Yet forever intertwined.

1. This poem was originally published in "Asian American Mothering as Feminist Decolonizing Reproductive Labor: Four Meditations on Raising Hapa Boys," by Melinda Luisa de Jesús, Patti Duncan, Reshmi Dutt-Ballerstadt, and Linda Pierce Allen, *Mothering in East Asian Communities: Politics and Practices*, edited by Patti Duncan and Gina Wong (Demeter Press, 2014).

2. "Pinay" is the Filipino American term for Filipino women. "Pinoy" is the term for Filipino men.

Debris or Dead Bodies (Typhoon Haiyan)

Cheryl Deptowicz-Diaz

I don't know whether to start with silence,
or start with rage.

Should I tell you about the debris
or the dead bodies?

Should I complain about every newsflash
or rejoice in bits of information?

Should I tell you about the calm in the eye of the storm
or about the wrath of horrors in the outer rainbands?

Should I recount the digging of mass graves
or recount the tragedy of surviving?

Should I memorialize the ineptitude of elected leaders
or memorialize the power of the people-consoling, comforting, sharing?

Should I describe the sky's falling thunderous waters
or describe the blistering heat of the sun?

Do you want to hear the wailing cries of hunger
or hear the quiet tears of a grieving mother?

Do you want to feel the wet raw sewage around your ankles
or feel the emptiness of distant helplessness?

Do you want the blood and gore
or do you want the hope and more?

I can take the time to describe the howling winds and falling rooftops
or I can take the time to describe the helping hand and the falling pride.

I can give examples of the failures and weaknesses of the human heart
or examples of the successes and strength of a community.

Should I tell you about the destruction, devastation, and desperation
or I can tell you about relief, respite, and reconstruction?

Do you want credit and glory
or do you want results and victory?

I shall tell you about a people,
rising from the clutters of debris and dead bodies.

My True Success (Superstorm Sandy)

Cheryl Deptowicz-Diaz

I tell you, my Diego, what Ralph or Bessie said in the poem, "Success,"
Success is to have laughed often and much...
To win the respect of intelligent people and love of little children
To endure the betrayal of false friends
To find the best in others
To leave the world a bit better

I tell you this, my Diego, so you can go read the rest of that poem.
I want that "success" for you, my boy.

I want for you a world where you will know racism
Not because you experienced it or saw it with your own eyes,
but because you read about it in history books.

I want for you to never know the word, feminism,
Not because you grow up to be a machista,
but because you live equally among all people, women and men.

I want for you to never have to know homophobia,
Not because I'm worried you may be gay, or even phobic,
But because being one will no longer be a pundit's tool.

I want for you to never have to toil long hours
Not because you are lazy,
but because the hours are shared and the work divided amongst all.

I'd like to think that I am strong enough now, and forever will be
To make the right decisions for you.

I'd like to think that these arms are well-built,
Will always be strong enough to carry you when you tire of your play
Gentle enough to point the way when you have lost your way.
Soft enough to serve as your pillow at the end of the long day.
Sturdy enough to wrap around you,

Hold on tightly and protect you, always protect you,
Whether it be from an oncoming superstorm about to flood our home
Or from the howling winds about to blow off our roof
From rats coming out of drainstorms
From messages of emergency funds and celebrity fundraisers
From mobs fighting over food shortages and fuel rations
From despair of people ravaged by war and poverty

The superstorm of life will come again
And the eye of the storm will grow strength again
Ready to pummel our coasts and trigger blackouts.
Blackouts of electricity and blackouts of the mind.

But, keep your wits about you, my son.
Your papa and I are old, and we will not be forever around.
Be kind. Be patient. Be wise.
Be kind enough to share what you have
Be patient enough to discuss solutions
Be wise enough to know when it's time to pick up the gun

Be brave. Be strong.
Be brave to take a stand.
Be strong in your heart and strong in your mind.

I'd like to think that we are preparing you well
Preparing you for the necessary death of this world.

Keep your wits about you, my son.
Hold on to the laughter we have taught you.
Hold on to the love we have given/do give you.

Listen to others
Hold off on judgment, analyze first.
Don't judge, but understand.

May your tears be of laughter
If they be of sorrow, may they be brief, and worth the shedding.

234

May you love, and love deeply
and may that person, place or thing be deserving of your heart.

May your heart beat
With excitement, with exhilaration, with passion, with love,
with sweet surrender
As my heart has beat for your Papa
so much so that it has created you, my son,
my sweet, sweet Mexi-Pino child,
my true success.

The Fairest Blooms

Cheryl Deptowicz-Diaz

The evening breeze joins me
through the wide-opened bedroom windows.
Its soft caresses, rare during this summer's heat wave,
are a welcome treat.
Where...have you been?

It is the first time in months
that I hear...silence
It is pierced only occasionally
by the sounds of my dogs lazily stretching in the distant living room.
I am alone.

The sun has just tucked in for the night,
yielding the open sky to a waxing crescent moon.
The full moon and all her glory is promised in about 9 days.
I am hopeful for the promise of new beginnings.
For now, the evening sky is lit a soft blue.

The humming of the ceiling-fan above
pushes my hair front and back,
slowly, wispily, softly.

It is the first time in months
where there is only me and
my own breathing-deep and labored.
Other breaths are out running errands.

I venture to see the person
I am without them.
Who is this woman without husband and child?

Across my desk—where the week's battles were fought,
Hearts analyzed, threats assessed, deals negotiated,
worries allayed, plans drafted, and tears fell and
gathered away for safekeeping—were my bouquet of flowers.

At week's start, the purple blooms stood tall, stems sturdy and bright green,
neatly arranged, held up by rocks in clear, fresh water.
Now, Friday, the green stems are wilted, doubled over.
Brown water has stolen the perfumed smell.
The sepals have opened allowing the petals to loosely fall one by one.
Yellow dusts from the anthers are strewn over papers and telephone messages.

The evocative bouquet.
So pretty. So tired.
Dutifully a few stems hold up fair-looking blooms
Holding on to finish out the rest of the week.

Like Most Things

Lance Dougherty

Light. Life. Like.
A brightening indiglo on the wristwatch of the possible
Or the impossible, improbable, but mostly disposable

Let us read and write for the post modern era
Reacting to pre-script nuances with post-script novelties
Forgetting which pre led us to post, and missing the lines between

We scratch the record and sniff the sounds
Backpedaling on bent needles and skipped beats
Basking in the blend of old rhythms and dancing them new

May they mutter haikus with an extra syllable
Paint the beautiful in pencil and eraser for the sake of susceptibility
The disruption of the classical in an attempt to rework old world

I am, we are, you will, be the discrepancies
A shake away from changing the whole etch-a-sketch
Like most things

Mixed

Andrea Duke

I'm mixed
>An ethnic mix
>Representing the 2 divided groups of my high school
>White and yellow

I'm mixed
>Like the looks I get when people meet me
>Like their responses
>>What they say
>>How they act
>>What they don't say

I'm mixed
>On my thoughts
>On what I want
>On what I think should be

I'm mixed
>In a melting pot
>Or in a mosaic
>In whatever I choose to accept and believe this day

I'm mixed
>And mingling
>And so are the messages I'm getting tonight

Thoughts and Glances

Andrea Duke

Stop staring at me. STOP.
I know I look different.
I know you look confused
Trying to figure me out.

Now the question comes.

Half Chinese. Half ummmm....British.

I know what you're thinking next.

No, that doesn't mean half Chinese, half Canadian.

4th generation Chinese. 3rd generation British.

Yes, perhaps more Canadian than you.
My Chinese side~we built the railroad,
We brought this country together.

No, I've never had a problem crossing the border.

Iceberg

Angela Martinez Dy

Ay naku[1]
I've lost
the word

when you speak
with multiple tongues
a forgotten word
is a loss.

it is the sun
swept fast behind
an ominous cloud.

it is a sewing needle
missing its mark,
drawing blood instead.

it is ice-cold unexpected.

your language
is the music
of which you are composed,
so its loss is laryngitis,
a symphony with pages missing,
three part harmony
sin soprano.

a worn-down sock,
the big toe
newly popped through.

a stopped clock,
a slipped condom ~
little losses
of control

that leave you
shaken, unsure
if you are still steering
your own ship.

AY, AY
naku.

I've just lost
the word.

it's on the tip
of my tongue.

if I show you,
will you help me
scrape it off?

I'll save it
till the weather's warm
and there's no more talk
of icebergs.

1. Common expression in Tagalog (Filipino), used to convey exasperation or surprise.

Tribu

Angela Martinez Dy

> *There is a pulse in my veins*
> *that throbs with the story of my homeland.*
> *If I wait too long, it will split me open*
> *for now it's just a hairline fracture*

I. *Gutom* - Hunger

We met on the roadside
a band of homeless Filipinos
roaming the earth
searching for its center
and our own as well
We called out our emptiness
heard a faraway answer in our native tongues
"*Nakikinig ka ba sa akin*"?
Yes
Tao Natin ~ Our People
I am listening

I know my people by their hunger.

We met on the roadside, caught by the look
in each others' eye ~ the look that said
"I was meant for more than this"

I know you by the sound your stomach makes
when you are given a plateful of rice
It looks like a dreamy cloud
for you to rest your cares upon

I know, too,
that your cares are heavy
They begin with the weight
of your distance from home

Home: an island nation across a growing ocean
where the income levels of neighbors be disparate as ever
where desperate poor construct for themselves
villages of cardboard and of metal
Hoovervilles~only~Filipino style:
naked toddlers playing in the heat
of an afternoon sun, beating down
on the brows of brown bodies. *tsinelas* slap
on the ground, *sandos* float on clotheslines, ragged and thin.
Old men sit in the mornings, drinking in doorways
framed with cardboard and steel. The weight
of the world bears down on their shoulders,
though they've never been able
to name it distinctly.

I inhale
the weighted air.

II. Diaspora - The Growl of a Ghost

I have heard my people groan
under the third world's weight
seen us running
only to stay in last place
of Southeast Asia's Western-made rat race

brown women's bodies become fodder
bit of cash to bare skin by the skin
of their teeth ~ they are gleaming

in foreign lands
more slowly cook
in the heat
cleaning millionaire's homes
and powdering rich babies' bottoms
while their own young broods cry for mama

A diaspora sounds
like the growl of a ghost
It looks like trade winds
scattering seeds. It smells
like sorrow, spilling over ~
it tastes like metal, the steel of a gun or a
sword pulled from its sheath
sadly, late ~ too late to defend
from the splitting / open
our cavities gutted
and guttural
like the ancestral rage that rises in my throat
sometimes a groan but low, lower now
the growl of a ghost

we're making money off our skin
by the skin of our teeth
we are gleaming

and then there's me

a distended, pale lower branch of the family tree
with Amerikan luxury running laps around me

I will not rest here
but I will dream

III. Tribu

our tribe is no barren field
or human cogs for a machine.

our tribe is warm and sun-browned
organic, not organized, grown and fertilized
with sweat and tears ~ never futile ~

our tribe is in the thick mixed skin
that is distinctly
Filipina

in it is the seat of humanity

our tribe is no barren field
or human cogs for a machine

we are loud and laughing
we want to make room for you
as you pass us on the street but
we take up the whole damn sidewalk
the whole damn walk
all the walk
my tribe is all walk (tho we like the talk)

our tribe is made of small concentric circles
circles joined at the hip
our tribe is hip
our tribe is hungry
our tribe is restless and wandering,
just like the rest of us,
more or less

I am hungry and wondering
        (lest the rest of us wander)
when we may happen upon
our homeland

Secret Domestics

Hillary LP Eason

Here is the plight of the modern woman:
hanging up coats means organizing shoes,
returning all your necklaces to their boxy homes,
shelving the books you left out on purpose
because you knew you wouldn't read them if they
weren't in plain sight. The language
of things can't be heard as well in order:
your backpack on the floor says you
made it out of bed, your sweater has breath
where he pushed it aside. So they
layer and layer, like slices of the rock
you rode past out in Flagstaff with the Hoovers
the summer before Debra left for good,
where the record of lost seas
watched your bicycles on the cliff.

Laundry folded is love. Folding laundry is like
waking up next to someone
on a morning with snow and no plans. My clothes
blanket the carpet like slush on a Monday,
their arms and legs spread open as though
they want us to be together. The pages
of my daily calendar lay, cast off,
on my desk, where they keep
my company like a secret, saying nothing
about the fact that I am living in a palimpsest.
Trying not to read too much
into the unopened Bible on my floor.

Here is what we want,
all the people who never stop asking:
maybe wine, a few books. And a house
with walls we can paint whenever we feel it.
Where not every hole requires filler.
Where we know how it feels
to forget about breathing.

Notes for a Biography of Rosette Phan

Hillary LP Eason

1. <u>Scene</u>: Her daughter looks for the house on Cong Ly Street. There are no houses there, she is told. No one lives there anymore.
2. <u>Scene</u>: New apartment, "retirement community," money behind the picture frames.
3. Last time she visited the author's house, utilized past military training to conscript author's fourteen-year-old brother into a daily routine involving delivery of Fig Newmans. Two cookies, three PM, zero excuses accepted.
4. Met author's Uncle Andrew's father at Club Unique, where she had the French chef who fried frogs' legs in butter.
5. <u>Quote from son</u>: "She saw the writing on the wall."
6. <u>Not a quote from son</u>: she got married to escape.
7. <u>List, in order</u>: Grandfather, Daddy Ray, Ton Ton (descended from Wyatt Earp, once friends with Daddy Ray).
   a. *Grandfather*: sang "Les Feuilles Mortes" like an angel, still visits in dreams
   b. *Daddy Ray*: made chipped beef in the mornings
   c. *Ton Ton*: taught author's father how to shoot
8. IBM stock she owned in the sixties was stored in Swiss bank accounts. Like the Nazis.
9. Now it's evenly distributed among casinos out West.
10. When author sees her father's youngest siblings, the aforementioned Uncle Andrew and his sister Aunt Tammy, she can now only see them as children on a road trip. Sitting quietly in the lobby, or a hotel room if they were good.
    a. Hungry.
    b. Not knowing that she had lost all the money.
11. Was once v. stylish, though her pants now scale to her collapsing breasts.
    a. <u>Picture</u>: smiling, in the creek, outside of Bến Tre.
       i. Wearing those gauchos that look like the author's.
    b. Check on pronunciation. No one understands it when author says "Bến Tre."
12. Did not misunderstand author's mother. Rather, did not like her.
13. Her skin is the softest author has ever known. What is her secret?

Bru Children

Hillary LP Eason

Souvenir

Hillary LP Eason

Sesshu Foster

game 20

is all about talking about hawaii. it probably involves going to hawaii, but not for you. it is when the talk turns to hawaii. the talk is about hawaii for an hour or more. you have dinner and what can you eat. who do you know in the islands? do you know so and so? yes i know so & so, he/she is/was my neighbor! who else do you know? yes, i worked with this or that person. did you know so & so died? yes, he/she died this or that year. yes, he/she was important in the sovereignty movement, for indigenous rights and the recovery of a certain geographical area, a valley. discussion of local history related to the military, world war 2. i have some of this plant from that valley, actually, growing at home; it's important for such and such a ceremony. i'll have to give you some. you can grow it from a cutting. did you know that it's good for dealing with ghosts? yes, ghosts. which island do you go to? now it's your turn to talk about hawaii.

game 21

At that time, she said she no longer had any interest in white men.
At that point, she told me she was no longer sleeping with men.
Some hair you shave, some you cut and brush, some you ignore.
I thought she was kind of old to be still sucking her thumb.
The woman had a four or five year old boy sitting on her lap nursing at the breast.
At some point, you decided not to give panhandlers any change, except for homeless women.
She told me she always acknowledged the homeless as human beings and to try to give them something.
She said recently one of them screamed abuse at her and threatened her.
With the attention to detail intrinsic to applying make-up.
He said, he just woke up sick one day and decided that was enough.
After the last visit, she told me that she'd never let him in the house again.
They stopped writing to each other.

They stopped talking to each other.

Too old for children.

He said, at that age they get too big to spank.

She said to me, I'm too old for that kind of bullshit.

She said, she's old enough to make her own decisions now.

He said, there won't be a woman for me now.

It doesn't matter, he said to himself.

After awhile, she had a lot of cats.

She said that the way she found out whether or not she was compatible with a potential roommate was by sleeping with them, but when I suggested I might simply sleep on the porch tonight given how late the hour, she said that that would not be possible, so I spent the night on the street, and, a year later, saw her 'roommate needed' notices posted again on campus.

One day, he stopped eating, and dad was the only one there, waiting with him till the end.

After a certain point, I stopped giving money to the party.

After a couple years, I said I would no longer participate.

She told me, you don't have to get the dishes that clean.

game 27

The photographer died last week. His daughter and I were working on an exhibit of his work. When she found him, he could no longer stand; he had a terrible pain in his belly. It took about six hours. The drug they gave him to keep his heart going (after it stopped) wore off. He was no longer conscious. They buried his ashes Thursday afternoon at Rose Hills. I stood under a canopy with the family and looked across at the bare earth of the hillside opposite, where a tractor small in the distance went up and down the hill in the glare of the afternoon, breaking the ground into furrows. I remembered Nacho swimming at Redondo Beach, in his eighties, beyond the breakers, beyond all of us. Sometimes the life guards would call him back. The priest, distaff in-law from Guadalajara, was speaking of sin and Christ.

The little tractor went up and back, a long way off across the broken ground.

game 29

I noted the cast on one foot, *otherwise not a single visible scar* she smiled pretty as ever the girl who'd thrown herself drunk off the freeway overpass onto the 605, Vietnamita with black hair she tucked behind her ear with a nervous chuckle ("My father didn't want me to have a boyfriend." "How are you getting along with your father now?" "Better.") ("That girl's getting a reputation," somebody a lot like her would later say.)

*From World Ball Notebook by Sesshu Foster (San Francisco: City Lights Books, 2009)

Twenty-five

Shamala Gallagher

Alone on my birthday I find
I am happy.

It is not
the glee froth
of panic.

Or the black
joy from wasted
life.

It is new
but barely different
from boredom.

I can see now
how people live
whole childhoods
like this,
not wondering.

My number
has a weight
like a small
plum.

I have learned
how to clean
my house.

I have a
cat.

For years
no one
to my face
has called me worthless.

I have a love
though I think
he will die
before me.

My cat I can scoop
in my arms
and will die.

I will lose
all I love
later.

Now
I am happy.

I am proud
enough
of my body
which
will writhe
into something
knotted.

Out in
the world
bodies
have writhed
and knotted
a trillion
times. They
writhe
now.

But I live
in a safe
room
and it strains
my eyes
to look.

On my birthday
I find
I am happy.

Ziggy

John Endo Greenaway

Karen and Me

John Endo Greenaway

Tsunami

Catherine Irwin

I am a body of no returns,
a collect call
a body for Miwako's Asian Connection,
where East meets West
in the Grand Imperial Ballroom
at the Holiday Inn.

The invitation said, "Come as you are."
so I dressed in barbed wire
your basic kimono pattern from Simplicity's
Oriental Collection
Made in America
Guaranteed to Last.

I tie the wire to
curve with my hips,
my groove of gray mesh
wrapped around my waist,
cinched by a large bow
at the small of my back.

I stretch my eyes with prosthetics,
pack my face in powdered snow,
squeeze my lips to melt them red.
As I glide through the door on heels
held up by convex hips,
Miwako cries, "Give them a show!"
I supply each spark that flies~
an alabaster pose
an edge of an ear
felt by no one
but a man's breath,
his whisper, Me, My, Mine.

I am his little bird,
a shimmy up his spine,
undone by strobe lights.
With a twist of barbed wire,
I become that rumble, that shock wave
almost but not quite.

Akeldema (*Field of Blood*)

Installation Piece about the One Drop Rule

Catherine Irwin

Only my mother understood, as she began
ripping her clothes into rags.
She steps into the void and scrubs,
fills the space of the body with her rags
soaked in water and warm vinegar.
I watch her reflection approach my body,
the laying of her hands against hands, chest and forehead.

Her sweat rises to meet a substance no longer
flesh but a silent image from an era,
where a piece of cloth could mean
something really happened,
something really lived.

As the blood washes over me,
men and women enter the hall.
Longing for the missing piece of themselves,
they kneel, sit and stand at awkward angles to touch
to enter this installation of blood-soiled memory,
like thorns piercing the skin and eyes of broken glass.

Clustered now in small circles, they become
the black-tie guests whispering quietly
about the quality of guilt in the vintage red.
Patrons of the arts, they analyze me from all angles
as if waiting for a sign to rip
my body from out of its grave.

Looking for myself in *Akeldema*,
I watch the way my mother tells his mother
it was not yet time,
as they tried to wash the blackness from our bodies
and make small talk,

until their own bodies gave way to forsaken sorrow.

Rising from the blood
that chased me to the edge of the earth,
I burst open and spill out
like a scrimmage of red and yellow leaves.
Believing I've escaped death,
I watch my skin speak its way into substance.

Papers & Porridge

Michelle Tang Jackson

My grandfather is porridge and newspapers, with whiskered face calm from morning prayer and Tai Chi. I smile, pouring more hot water into his mug. On KROQ, Brad Nowell croons Jerry Garcia and I instinctively reach to turn the volume down. Gong-Gong points to his hearing aid and laughs. He says God blessed him with deafness so he didn't have to hear the women gossip. We smile at each other and dip large spoons into steaming bowls of congee.

Gong-Gong pens his daily thoughts into little notebooks he buys at the drugstore. I write along with him—on legal pads and the backs of takeout menus. His letters are perfect, straight and graceful as bamboo stems. Mine leap all over, like street performers at the pier. We write at our little half-circle table, lit by kitchen light.

He is a poet. We have the same hands.

After grandmother dies, we stay with him. Through the walls, we can hear him singing childhood songs in his bedroom. Of course, he's taken his hearing aid out and can't tell how loudly he's singing. I smile though, knowing that he is not too lonely.

I write it all down. I will someday inherit his notebooks.

He and I walk down the hill to Chinatown. Sidewalks plastered in wet newspapers, large families waiting outside dim sum restaurants. I stand a foot taller than he and almost everyone in the store. I ask the shopkeeper for a Sing Tao. He asks laughing, "How old you are?" I blush, my pronunciation is wrong. I stutter, "Bou...zi? The newspaper, not the beer." Grandfather smiles at me and places exact change on the counter. When I offer him the paper, he takes my hand in his. We walk back up the hill with our hands, the same hands, folded together like a pair in morning prayer.

December 7th

Daniel Takeshi Krause

"December 7th, 1941, a date that will live in infamy." Those were the words of President Franklin Delano Roosevelt when he spoke about the Japanese attack on Pearl Harbor. "Always will be remembered the character of the onslaught against us." He said this the day after Japanese forces interrupted a beautiful day on the Hawaiian Island of Oahu to destroy 8 American battleships, and 188 aircraft, and to kill 2,043 American servicemen, and 68 civilians. Other words President Roosevelt used were "dastardly" and "unprovoked." The attack on Pearl Harbor galvanized a nation and overnight united the States against the Empire of Japan. It led directly to the signing of Executive Order 9066 requiring more than 100,000 Japanese Americans to submit themselves for arrest and internment, a fancy word for a cage. It led directly to my infant mother and her parents living at Santa Anita Racetrack, in a horse stall with hay and manure, but no horses. December 7th was indeed a day that would live in infamy, but not just in 1941. Instead it might live in the throbbing of a black eye, stung with tears, or somewhere subtle, somewhere you don't realize it hurts until years later.

But for me, December 7th lives in my freshman year of high school, 1991. A new school, new teachers, new rules and social hierarchy. We big fish of middle school were just starting to see ourselves in a slightly larger pond. But not all changes were difficult. Some were exciting. It was the first year I'd gone out for the soccer team. I'd been well acquainted with the soccer ball by way of my friends, but never went out for the team. I couldn't afford the pair of shoes. When my friends came up with an old pair of cleats for me to inherit, I ran out of reasons not to play. Being on the soccer team was like nothing I'd done before. I cherished it all, straining in practice, learning to work together, training for when we'd do it all for real. And then in the games, holding nothing back, leaving everything on the field for my team. Wins, losses, it didn't matter, the camaraderie was the sweet byproduct of countless afternoons spent together, sweating out the hours as easily as we ran the field.

But really, this isn't the story of my first year on the soccer team. It's the story of December 7th. For me, it's the story of being pulled back from

264

believing that I was only me, not everyone who came before. One more reminder of what living history really means.

Of course that day I went to school and kept my head down. That's just something you learn. You learn to keep especially quiet that day, to watch the clock and wait for each bell to ring you out of class, away from looking around the room for the person who will shoot first. December 7th, a day to walk in groups, a day to be invisible.

And what sweet release, to hear that last bell of the day, calling you out to the soccer field, where the grass is always greener. But again, this is not that story. This is not the story of running the field and shooting on goal. This isn't even the story of failing to defend and losing the game. That story would be just fine on this day. But this is the story of December 7th. This is the story of what it is to be small. What it is to be silent and still.

I'm going to soccer practice. I'm lacing up my shoes, and I'm putting on my team colors. Gathered on the field, we're stretching and running and kicking the banter back and forth. I'm laughing and warming up my muscles for the next few hours' work, until a familiar feeling creeps.

"Hey Daniel, I'm just curious. I don't mean to be racist or anything, but how much of the field can you see anyway?" I'm not really sure what he means. "I mean, with your eyes."

Just a twinge of sourness comes into my mouth, but I swallow the poison, sure I am strong enough to make it disappear. To disappear. "No seriously, is it hard to see the ball? I just wondered. I mean, don't worry, I don't think of you as Japanese. I just wondered." He drops it in the water like chum and the sharks start swirling. Quite suddenly, we are not stretching and running and kicking the banter back and forth. We are circling. Or rather, they are circling, and I am holding very still. "You Jap bastards killed my father, you fucking nip!" I'm sure his dad wasn't at Pearl Harbor that day, wasn't in World War II, his dad is probably now at home drinking Bud Light and watching TV, but yelling in my face is funny. It's getting funnier now, as they're all laughing. They're all laughing at the new game we're playing. And by now I've swallowed too much poison because I'm laughing too,

265

like ashes in my mouth, but no matter how hard I laugh, and no matter how quickly I try to say it's okay, I can't make myself invisible. The grass is wet and cold on my back, and the afternoon sun slides across the field and into my eyes. I'm squintin' up real good now, and they only laugh harder. Then the sun is blocked out by someone's face right over mine, the air is blocked out of my lungs by someone's knees bending my ribs, and hands press my arms into the dirt, sliced on the way down by a thousand blades of unconcerned grass. But they don't cut deep enough and I don't bleed enough, not enough to please them, not enough to pass the poison that's working on me now, infecting me. I'm blinking out the spit that's falling into my face as he yells, only to look and see myself surrounded by a circle of boys, all suddenly much bigger than me, laughing and cheering him on. I see myself reflected in their shining fangs. The poison is too much and my body rejects it, forcing it stinging out through my eyes, and I hate myself a little more. Years later I'll long to go back to this moment to hate them instead, but not now. Now, their faces distort into horrible shapes and impossibly wide smiles as everything breaks apart in my eyes to a swimming, liquid mess. I try to speak, to tell them I wasn't there, that I'm just like them. But hands on my neck jerk the words out of me before I can give them shape and the sounds I make only add to the fun they're having. If they'd only push a little harder I'm sure I could sink underneath the grass. Underneath where it's dark and cool away from the sun, where it's quiet. But their hands are pushing me up at the same time, stabbing into me with claws sharpened on what their parents say. One cut for every car I didn't build, a future scar for each job I didn't steal, a wound for every war I didn't fight, every life I never took.

The rest of the day is, of course, less interesting. I don't remember what homework I did that night, or what I ate for dinner. My father didn't yell and my mother didn't cry because I was too ashamed to tell them. For me, what stands out this year is, lying there on my back, held down by the bony knees of ignorant children, wincing at large toothy screams, gagging on poisoned words and bleeding as fast as I can, I'm quite sure it's the last time I ever tried to think~I was born in California. I was raised in California. My name is Daniel Takeshi Krause, and I'm Japanese American. What's Pearl Harbor got to do with me?

In Shadow

Noemi LaMotte-Serrano

The light plays tricks on the mind, shadows dancing in the mirror, erasing history
and she is fifteen and beautiful.
She stares transfixed for hours as darkness falls, remembrance clouds.
She blinks twice and startles, horrified at the unkempt image that surfaces.
Figures shift and the balance is lost between fiction and madness.
There is a child crying softly somewhere in the distant corner.
She wonders if the neighbor's son has fallen again.
His sobs always seem to interrupt her dreams, sabotaging the calmness of
confusion.
But here, now, the moon is rising.
The child cries louder, closer, his six year old fists pounding hopelessly,
begs, "Mama, please."
Soon the sirens will arrive and he will be left once again in silence and ash,
an abandoned animal licking his wounds on a cold floor
in front of the borrowed Christmas tree he carried behind him for six
blocks and up three flights of stairs.
He wraps himself up in the thought that somewhere, snow is falling.
The earth spins.
This broken child becomes a father who struggles to love without destruction,
to give all of what is not whole.
At times he can not overcome the past and his six year old daughter learns
to bury the words that erupt angrily, poisoned with alcohol and unforgiving.
She hides them somewhere deep inside where later they will become nightmares,
tidal waves in the ocean of her own regret,
heartbreak in the voice of her son who wonders why she is always so angry,
resignation in the eyes of her husband who studies her reflection in the mirror,
searching for softness, reaching out to her across continents and through
the grasps of ghosts who weep in forgotten tongues,
fingertips brushing the fragments of beauty and madness.
But the light has faded
and she has nothing to give but shadows.

Duplicity

Noemi LaMotte-Serrano

There came a day when the tower of freedom and his twin, hypocrisy
were demolished into the dust of unbreathable democracy.
The sun of security was swallowed in ash and debris,
while the moon tripped over burning bloody feet.
The callous acts that callous the palms of souls,
indifference shattered by fingerprints on fragments of what once was whole.
And the whole truth
is a hole uprooted, a mass grave,
where under the flag of salvation entire peoples were slain.
No longer do they lie
Silent.
In the midst of reborn innocence there arises a sleeping giant.
In his demented delusions he truly believes that he is flying.
He is beyond reason or retribution for before birth he knew he would
never be free.
Our safe harbor is gone and now we all must swim this bleeding sea.

I've seen the seeds of demons breathing in the beating of unborn hearts
and false starts. I've walked along shores that breed slivered truth,
where illusion is swallowed down by starving youth.
It slides through throats coated with the absence of inspiration,
becomes puddles of peddled dreams that sleep in stagnation.
And I dream in shades of indignation,
search for truth between media head lines that outline the disintegration.
Shadows cloud the four skies of third worlds where innocence is an affliction,
where rising above becomes revenge becomes suicidal addiction,
where children learn death before learning to walk,
learn to load semi-automatic weapons instead of learning to talk.
where mothers lactate poverty from the naked breasts of hate
and fathers pass down empty fists as generations wait.
I shut the gates
of my familiar freedom to the screams as ancestral dreams were damned to hell.

So now I am dancing for inspiration in between the thin lines of rhythm
and rage.
Chipped fingernails of youth pick seeds of truth from the yellow stained
teeth of the page. And I am amazed
blinded by the beauty I now find in breathing,
weakened by a knowledge so strong it shakes me when I'm sleeping.
Burning to feed this hunger for belief
I journey alone across black skies while the city sleeps.
I've held stars in the broken veins of arms,
silhouettes of shadow whose hearts still beat,
who found the waters of heaven but ventured too deep.
Their silence repeats, "It's never like the first time."

I've kissed the skin where bullets slipped in,
beneath sunburnt skies where the descendents of fallen angels lie,
where faded streets of concrete beaten by passing feet tremble softly, then
slowly sigh, tired of all the blood that seeps from the children who speak
the only truth they've ever known.
   And that truth is blown.
   Tainted with distortion, painted out of proportion,
   conceived in misfortune until it becomes the abortion
   she didn't have.

There is a question that buries itself,
roots deep in accidental uranium and spilled napalm.
A question that flops silently like a poisoned fish,
   baited with democracy,
absent on the shores of Vieques.
There is a question that tunnels blindly through Philippine soil
saturated with hypocrisy and Poly Chlorinated Biphenyl
as forty year old sailors fill hollow adolescent bellies
with the seeds of hopelessness and disease.
There is a question waiting calmly in the jungles of Chiapas,
bearing witness as once again the murder of innocents
is acceptable in the quest for riches.
Corporate exploitation and the extraction of the indigenous
hide behind a mask of development and biological research.

There is a question smothered in the last breath of Ali Awad,
who swallowed Desert Storm leftovers,
  as pacifism became cliché and revolution curdled
  in the stale cups of coffee shop rebellions.
There is a question that seeps out of the holes in toxic waste containers
  of government cover ups and into the pores of unborn infants.
There is a question America must ask itself
before there is no one left to answer.

Anak

Noemi LaMotte-Serrano

Anak. I journey alone and tired through dirt-paved streets and jungle beats To find the rhythm in these four letters. Anak. I trip over misplaced intentions to the steps of tribal dance The abstract pattern of romance In my search for familiarity in alien phonetics. Anak. Becomes this longing deep inside me Because he slaved on a ship amidst the stench of fish heads and broken backs Because she fell asleep watching you wishing she was Mrs. Brady and swallowed her own dreams All the A's you worked so hard for The scholarships, the awards The poverty you put in your back pocket The history of our people you forgot to remind me of The rulers cracking down on brown knuckles When you couldn't find the right word in English It is a word that I can't write A struggle that is not mine I dig deeper Through buried nightmares My fathers drunk voice asking~why can't you be with a filipino boy? I spit the words I swallowed at seventeen~why couldn't you? In dreams it was always my mothers voice that comforted Smooth and steady English though sometimes it touched on notes of sadness that echoed across oceans of blue But my fathers tongue Always angry Over AT&T long distance rates about bad influences and bad grades Always angry that I never found the identity he couldn't give me on my own So I sought out other voices felt comfort in other tongues Never missing my own lost language until I found my son Now I want to give him this word Anak It struggles to reach the surface As I struggle to understand The shadows of my father's heart. Anak Anak I always hated when he called me that. Anak Anak if only I could take those letters back and make them mine. I would give them to you Baby, Son, Mijo come so naturally And you smile. But under the moon, when you lay sleeping I whisper Anak Anak Anak Into your tiny ears And I don't care if I sound awkward. Anak Anak.

Decolonize Your Mind

Marjorie Light

decolonize your mind
reclaim your expression
start your own struggles
find out the intersections
dismantle your oppression
then enter a new dimension
so we can be free
so we can just be

I cherish the indigenous
what they tried to take away from us
the soul survives within
it lies just under my brown skin
within our bodies lie cultural memories
the way things used to be
the way things are supposed to be
I create my own rituals
to connect with the sacred spiritual
the life force that feeds us
they can never take that away from us
so I must bust and I must flow
I must show and make visible my own soul
I live on the borderlands traveling between worlds
as I analyze systems of power they all begin to unfurl
I don't believe in your constructions all your constructions I shatter
I defy labels and boxes I defy the slave master
seeing through the eyes of the snake and the eagle
Filipina feminist growing up with my people
traveling the world collecting beats from my indigenous tribes
keep the music alive cuz its a tool to survive
guerilla warfare its a way of life trained through everyday battle with the
stress and the strife
state apparatus is ready to attack and trap
but I won't let them break this bridge called my back

reclaim what was denied for so many years
step up and wash away all of the fears
be a warrior and take back what is ours
fighting and destroying to take back the power

decolonize your mind
reclaim your expression
start your own struggles
find out the intersections
dismantle your oppression
then enter a new dimension
so we can be free
so we can just be

I'm a woman of color anti-racist feminist
I'm a hip hop scholar ethnomusicologist
I'm a punk rock riot grrrl artist activist
I'm a girl with a mestiza consciousness
I'm the girl waiting at the 180 bus stop
I'm the kid from Northeast L.A. straight out of Eagle Rock
Asian woman with the rhymes that make you go into shock
I stray away from the rest of the flock
I'm the Filipina fresh off the boat
I'm the one who can't pay because she's flat broke
I'm the diva who scores 99 on the magic mic
I'm a woman who fell in love at first sight
yes I'm every woman it's all in me
any mic you want I'll rock it naturally
but I'm not an individual I'm part of a legacy
in the mirror see my ancestor's face looking back at me
much respect to the teachers who come before me
I come with love and peace
hope our numbers only increase
so we can question society critique this institution
deconstruct the theories and start a revolution
its what I want its my desire
take it to the next level take it higher

decolonize your mind
reclaim your expression
start your own struggles
find out the intersections
dismantle your oppression
then enter a new dimension
so we can be free
so we can just be

Political Ambivalence

Cassandra Love

Forget bi. Forget bi-racial, forget bi-sexual, most of all forget social binarisms. Hell, let's even forget multi: multi-racial, multi-sexual, mutlipolarity. It's about time we accept the fact that people are meta-. Meta-racial, meta-sexual, metacategorical.

Prefixes are supposed to clarify the proceeding signifier, the proceeding label, the proceeding connotation contained in every adjective turned noun. Meta- is a prefix we should adopt as our signifier of all that we are not. We are not bound by race; we are not bound by gender; we are not bound by sexuality; we are not bound by anyone but ourselves. Despite what society wants us to believe, it's really not that hard to be perfectly comfortable in obscurity. The strength is in taking what we are not and being ambivalent based on a heightened knowledge, not ignorance.

Who do I mean by we? Well since people are even metalingual it would suffice to say that if you feel like you are included in the "we" then you are. Communication is about getting the message across to those with whom you are trying to communicate; I intend to communicate to those of us willing to listen.

So listen up, we are meta- and ambivalence is our modus operandi. It's not even appropriate to say that we refuse to acknowledge the existence of categories, because without them there is nothing to be meta- about. The categories are there, binarisms exist, lines are drawn.

We are not living in ambivalence in order to destroy them necessarily, but to recognize them. To see them for their necessity, their limitations, but mostly for their irrelevance. Necessary irrelevance, that is what societal constructions are. Necessary for society to function, to give some sort of structure in order for laws and governments to exist. Irrelevant in that individually these categories do not personally inform how we live our lives.

I am a "queer" "bi-racial" "woman" and none of these words encompass who I am. I am me, just as you are you. We are meta-. We are beyond categories not because we are better, but because even if these lines and categories exist forever, we would rather die knowing we were never bound by any of them than succumbing to the limitations of imposed boundaries.

We are the living revolution. We are meta- and we will always exist.

Hasta la victoria siempre.

Motherly Love

Cassandra Love

The beautiful, Manila-born woman
smelled of Tatiana, her favorite perfume.
Her presence was a seven year tease,
a preview for a show that never aired.
I was most attached to her exotic
language and aromatic cuisines.

At first, it wasn't even physical.
She fantasized about
taking away her body.
A foggy gloom fell over the
brightness of her previous vivacity
I lead her through the night
never aware of the age difference,
or the roles that existed between us.
We were merely two women forcing
survival, armed with only each other.
Until she left me in the darkness
to fend for myself.

My Sister's Nightmare

Pia Massie

The suits swinging in unison, the open crack you peer through, hoping not to lock eyes with the killer as he zones the room, honing in on the shrill silence of your fear.

The eye always moves to motion in a still frame. A heartbeat traverses all distance. The suits could be swinging in air, in water or in blood. I would still hear your heartbeat roaring in my ears.

This is your dream and the one way out is when I distract him, when you don't lock eyes with him, when somehow he misses you and turns and mistakes me for something I am not.

Next time, pack the memory of now to the future turn of this dark dream: You have already tackled him; this spoke of the machine~a part replaced over and over again in a hundred equally grimy settings.

Your truly fierce eyes, your scathing words, your brilliant mind can make mincemeat of this evil. Pin him up in the hard light of your power and one day the suits will sink to the floor, empty as dust, tired from the exercise of fear.

Unanswered Questions

Pia Massie

Sometimes in my dreams I see grubby men with strong, cracked hands and dark toques around a barrel of fire, shaking off the chill, seeking a tribe, laughter, a story to tell or get? I lean in but I can't hear: this vision of male bondage is always MOS-without sound. It is in the loam of evening, the edges of memory, the black barrel's bright flickers of history. I don't know if I am scanning/ searching the faces to find my father, my son or locate myself.

All that sweetness flowing down the long hillside of my father's maple trees, running to a huge carboy-resting on planks in the woods, a rising pool of gold. Memories of the warm fall fire, sticky bits of twig crackling in to soft white ash: the fire, the phase change agent, the mercurial passing of a life caught in one moment. There on the fire is my father's grade K syrup, almost black, relished for its lack of refinement. This is what he held back for us, for the family and to prove his communion with the earth that bore those golden trees.

All the sap, the energy of my life flows out with the water from the laundry, the dishes, the bath. Where is the time outside the good soup on the table, the bills paid and beds made, for a mother to write, to think, to breathe?

How do you know he loved you?

He plucked me out of the street holding me so close and ran back to the hospital. I was 5 days old. When we got there, the emergency room nurses had to pry his arms open to wrest-the baby-from his grasp. I was slathered in blood but it turned out when finally I got cleaned up that it was all his. He had gone through the windshield in this first accident, requiring 30 odd stitches in his face. I don't know who told me this story. Not Pop. Ever.

I still have a lifetime of unanswered questions; a few details I would like to get clear. The get-away Cadillac that knifed our VW bug in two-what were they escaping from when they shot through the red light?

My ma, lying in a wreckage of ripped metal and broken glass, what was she thinking there, all alone? Is this love~this fierce, courageous terror that does not know itself~these are the events that shackle one generation to the next.

I cling to this story I lived but don't remember, as proof. I ask you, is this love or fear? My father's father died 5 days before he was born. My uncle, the history writer, once said to me that his greatest cruelty towards his adoring younger brother was to tease him about how their father had never laid eyes on him;

How he was gone before his child appeared.

So plucking me out of the wreckage and sprinting back to the hospital, holding me so close, locking his arms around my spark of life, seems like an urgent dash back in time. I want to call it love. I wish it were a clearer signal. I wish it tasted warm or sweet. I wish it wasn't covered in blood.

Nana is dragging a tree behind her; it tears up the underbrush as she plows forward. A German tugboat who could push a fleet of ocean liners out to sea, she was less than 5 feet tall. She clears the woods around the old house, burning stuff in a big black barrel encrusted with ash and charcoal. I am sorry I can't find the footage for you. It was the purest vision of Nana at her industrial essence. She held you in her arms before she passed on, your great grandmother, triumphant that some part of her, a very bright spark would keep the fire banked.

I used to keep all the chits, the scraps of paper with beautifully crude pencil drawings he made for me, sometimes with a word underneath just in case the image was not
self~assuredly recognizable~speakers was a labeled one, under an image of two boxes. The collection floated in a cigar box; a precious cache of presents never given, IOUs to make me keep looking towards the future.

We didn't have a barrel for burning garbage in the country and I know we weren't allowed to burn garbage in the backyard in Brooklyn. Yet I see myself burning these wisps of my father's creativity, carefully letting each one float and fall in to the fire of my disappointment.

The one gift he gave me one winter was an enormous book, Coleridge's
The Ancient Mariner, with the terrifying Dore etchings. Oh dear Pop,

By thy long grey beard and glittering eye,
Now wherefore stopp'st thou me?

[You] could not speak no more than if,
We had been choked with soot

Like one that on a lonesome road,
Doth walk in fear and dread
And having once turned round walks on,
And turns no more his head.

Happy Thanksgiving. Your favorite holiday, the one that speaks to all pilgrims.
Even though I am exiled from your house, not welcomed at your table, I am
certain in my belief that yes, you have always loved me.

I speak for you where you are silent.

Where Are You From?

Stephen Murphy-Shigematsu

The taxi driver is politely quiet, but I notice that he is eyeing me in the rear view mirror. I have seen that look of curiosity before.

The taxi is cool but smells of tobacco, like the old Japan. We ride through the late afternoon city traffic, dodging the uniformed children on bicycles returning home from school. My grandmother asks about my plans for the evening and the work that I will do in Okinawa.

The driver is still looking at me. Finally he asks the inevitable question: "Where are you from?" shifting his eyes to my grandmother, perhaps hoping she will translate, though we'd been speaking Japanese all along.

I look out the window. "Where are you from?" How can I answer such a simple question? I could say, I was born in Japan. I grew up in the U.S. I live in Japan now. Can I say I'm from both places? Or do I have to say one or the other? Am I homeless, a man without a country? Is the world my home? Could homelessness be my home?

I glance in the rear view mirror. The taxi driver is looking at me waiting for a reply.

I try to dampen his curiosity. "Tokyo," I say curtly.

But he is not easily discouraged, "I mean which country?"

"Country?" I repeat. "Isn't Tokyo in Japan?"

The taxi driver looks at me strangely before laughing. He seems puzzled and dissatisfied by my answer. He must be thinking, how can someone who looks like me be from Japan? But I was born in downtown Tokyo. My family has been here as far back in time as we can trace. My mother, wife, and children are Japanese and I have lived half my life here. I have a Japanese passport, work for a national university, and live in housing for civil servants. Even growing up in America I never forgot that I was from Japan, and can thank my childhood antagonists for reminding me that I was "Made in Japan." So I could say I am from Japan, though some people may think this odd.

But when they get to know me they tell me, "You're American on the outside, but on the inside you are Japanese." Sometimes they go even further and say, "You are more Japanese than the Japanese!" I know they say this as a compliment, but how can a Japanese be more Japanese than the Japanese?

We pass silently through the neighborhood where the house we lived in after the war once stood. My grandparents accepted my American father into their home as the husband of their only daughter and my older sisters and I were born there. I wonder if my grandmother is reminiscing about those times. I hope she's not remembering that painful day we departed on the great ship for America. The three grandchildren she raised were gone, and she told me that she cried every day for two years, alone in the empty house.

I suppose I could just say I'm from America. The taxi driver would nod his head and maybe say that's he what he thought. And in fact living in Japan makes me aware that I am also American as nearly every day, someone talks to me as though they think that's where I'm from, lest I forget.

I suppose I became American that day our ship passed under the Golden Gate Bridge in San Francisco. My father's photo on the piano is a daily reminder of the half of my life spent watching Leave it to Beaver on television, eating McDonalds' hamburgers (before they went global), and rooting for the San Francisco Giants (not the Tokyo Giants). While strangers taunted me with "Jap" or "Chink," my friends claimed that I was as American as they were, as "American as apple pie." They didn't even think of me as Japanese, they assured me. Funny, but I can't remember ever feeling American like they seemed to. I wonder what it feels like.

I know what I look like. I've seen my face in the mirror before. But I don't see Japanese or American–I just see me and my father and mother and other ancestors. I forget that others seem to think I look different until someone reminds me.

Stating that I am Japanese, or that I am American, doesn't seem to satisfy some people. "But what else are you?"" they reply, or counter with a condescending smile, "Okay, but where are you really from?" And it never really pleases me, either, to say that I am just one or the other. I want to assert that I am from both countries. I want to proclaim that I am multi-cultural, multilingual, multinational, transnational, international. I want to shout out that the complexity of my being can't be contained in their boxes that separate. I want to declare that I am a global citizen, intimately connected with all the people on this earth.

But why should I have to reveal so much? I don't even know the taxi driver. I will never see him again. He doesn't need to know who my father and mother were. I don't owe him an explanation of who I am. I don't have to tell him my life story. This may be a teachable moment and it may be my responsibility to educate him but I choose my battles.

My grandmother suddenly interrupts my musings by declaring to the taxi driver, "He's from America."

Her words stun me and protest wells up inside me. I want to say, "Yes, but I'm also Japanese!" But I know that it is futile. My grandmother has known me for fifty years. I want her to declare that I'm Japanese, just like her. But why worry that after all these years that she still regards me as her beloved American grandson? Is her love for me any less because she thinks I am different from her?

"He's from America. That's why his Japanese is a little funny," she explains. I wince. Does she really need to say that? And after all these years, is my Japanese really that funny? It seems I can't disguise myself even in my speech.

"Oh, so that's why; I get it, he's from America! I thought so, because he sounds a little strange," the taxi driver says, a little too insulting and self congratulatory for my taste. He speaks freely as if convinced that I couldn't possibly understand a word he is saying. "Japanese is really a hard language, isn't it!" he declares.

It can't be that hard if you learned it, I am tempted to say, but keep quiet. I don't want to upset him or my grandmother. I am not used to anyone pointing out deficiencies in my language ability, and have been spoiled by constant praise for speaking Japanese so well. It doesn't take much. Just a few words of fluid speech from my mouth, from this face, is enough to elicit that familiar refrain, "My, you speak Japanese so well!" This double-edged comment means that you are regarded as a foreigner because you look different and sound different.

But to me, I am one of many people who may look different and sound different from the majority but are citizens of Japan and therefore Japanese. All citizens must be included in the word Japanese if it is to mean the people of the nation of Japan. We can be from somewhere else and still be Japanese. I even think that some of those who are not legally citizens but have lived here a long time, or their whole lives, could be regarded as Japanese, if that is their wish. Many of us may not "look Japanese" in the eyes of people who think in terms of "Japanese blood." But this is the reality of what Japanese are today ~ an increasingly diverse and multicultural people.

I am often reminded that not everyone thinks the way I do. To my grandmother and the taxi driver, a person is either Japanese or American, one or the other, but not both, and can't be both. Nations have borders and people must fit within their boundaries. For them, Japanese is defined narrowly and does not include those who look different, or who talk or act differently.

After I leave my grandmother at the nursing home, I walk for a while past some now out-of-place inner-city rice paddies, listening to the raucous but soothingly familiar chorus of bugs and frogs. The early evening air is refreshingly a little cooler, but still heavy, hot, and humid. I watch some children playing with firecrackers and sparklers on the riverbank before hailing another taxi to return to the hotel. The driver eyes me in the rear view mirror before asking, "Where are you from?"

You Don't Look Irish

Stephen Murphy-Shigematsu

On the first day of school Mrs. Sullivan, my new teacher, called out my name, "Stephen Murphy" and I raised my hand like she had told us to. She stared at me with a quizzical expression and said sarcastically, "You don't look like a 'Stephen Murphy.'" The other children giggled and I was embarrassed and confused.

I recall this incident, and others like it, every year when I celebrate St. Patrick's Day. This is a day on which I am reminded that my paternal grandparents came from Ireland. And I am also acutely aware that I was born in Japan to a Japanese mother.

I know that many others celebrate their heritage on St. Patrick's Day with mixed emotions. Ryan McCollum, whom others usually think is black or Latino, says, "Growing up, I knew I was Irish even if the rest of the world didn't." Mari Tanaka is also someone who others immediately label-incorrectly: "I guess I look Asian, but I don't feel comfortable with people just assuming that's all I am. Growing up, being Irish has been such a big part of my life."

Many of the growing population of young Americans who claim a multiethnic heritage have Irish roots. But the joys of embracing Irish roots are complicated by the challenges of being multiethnic. Their identity assertions are often met with incredulity and challenged. As Kelly Bates, a mixed-race Irish-American put it, "I always feel this deep kinship with Irish people in Boston, but I don't always feel like they have this kinship with me." There are self-proclaimed Irishmen in the United States who tell multiethnic Irish that we are not Irish. We may also have to deal with the complexity of being Irish but not White, as socially defined. And we may be challenged by those who claim that we are trying to identify as White and rejecting our other ethnic identity. We may have to reassure them that we are not distancing ourselves from our other identity, just embracing our wholeness by claiming all of our heritage.

Challenges may be especially common among those labeled as black, even though Irish and African Americans have much in common. They were once both stigmatized by other Americans and worked and lived in close proximity, but as the Irish "became White," antagonisms grew over labor rights, housing and public school desegregation, expressing themselves as racism. But some multiethnics are mending this rift by telling their stories. Alex Haley, the famed author of the classic African American identity novel, *Roots*, wrote *Queen* about his Irish roots. And President Obama nearly became O'Bama after visiting Ireland and proclaiming his Irish ancestry.

On St. Patrick's Day when I belt out classic songs like "Foggy Dew," I feel a bit Irish. I realize that the difficulty in being Irish is not mine, but is created by racial divisions. I, and other multiethnic Irish, will encounter challenges to our authenticity~"How Irish are you?" But we can empower ourselves and our children by exploring and knowing our Irish family roots, language, and history, to prove our Irishness.

And "the times they are a changing." Signs that the face of Ireland is changing are striking in places like the All Ireland Dancing Championships* where the top dancers included Julia O'Rourke, of Filipino and Irish ancestry and Melanie Valdes, of Cuban and Irish ancestry. In years past they have even included Tokiko Masuda, just like me, Japanese and Irish.

So I'm stepping out of my Japanese identity and making my public debut as an Irishman at the Irish-American Crossroads Festival in San Francisco in March 2015. Fittingly, it's called: "'You don't look Irish!' A Reading and Conversation with Multiracial Writers of Irish Heritage." Because of our physical appearance, being Irish may be an invisible part of our identity. But we are reminders that every Irish person doesn't look like a stereotypical Irishman. Irish come in all colors. And the next time someone says to me or my children, "You don't look like an Irishman," I'll just say, "Well, we are Irish, and this is what we look like, so we must look like Irishmen!"

*http://www.npr.org/blogs/codeswitch/2014/10/27/358107719/irish-dance-steps-up-diversity?utm_campaign=storyshare&utm_source=facebook.com&utm_medium=social&fb_ref=Default

spam maps I

Mark Nakada

Okinawa, April 1945

before) 350,000 American troops invade Okinawa
their navy bombards the island.
four shell bursts for every three square metres of land.
122,000 civilians (20% pop.) killed. survivors dub this shelling "the
typhoon of steel." all homes and buildings destroyed.
people rendered impoverished, apathetic; for several years the land will
lay gutted.

Arline dreaming of a big house in Los Angeles.
her father left her in Kin-Cho when he left for Hawaii.
now gardening for Mr. Baskin and Gordon MacRae in Toluca Lake,
she thinks he cld strike it big with some inheritance from his rich clients.
her only comfort is that hope.

cooked gruel of sago palm before daybreak.
Mr. Afuso gave her imo tempura fried in motor-oil, two bites. (the way he
looked at her.
G.I.'s coming up-island soon, no fires allowed.
hot smoking craters as she emerges from the cave.
neighbourhood landmarks, brick lanes, gardens,
gone.
now navigate by looking to the hills, half-remembered location of the spring
turn left at the rubble hulk of the Yakuba,
past the stench waft of bodyfluids oozing downhill
through cannibal cockroaches
among broken foundations
the Namisato Kuominkan stood here,
maybe.

past a paste of bloody hog carcasses
steaming shattered bones in the shit piles of pig-sties. no smell like it.
not one pig survives. no bird picks over the carrion.

288

a few beetles in the eye-sockets.
the meat staple of the islands, buta,
all gone.
the relief ship *John Owen*, like noah's ark
brings the first 550 Portland pigs 3 years later.

private first class Alden Nakama, Arline's cousin
landed three days ago with the 442nd.
for the all Japanese-American unit,
kicking jerry's ass at Monte Milleto and Anzio was one thing.
invading their parent's homeland is another.
a real killer homecoming!
the Okinawan American boys have their own agonies,
their own missions.
Alden gripping the old photo of Arline, aged 9
tries again to plant a memory of her face in his mind.
they're strangers, and she'll be 16 now.

the squad marches on high alert, two by two into the wastelands
formerly Kin village. most locals hide in fear, snug in their muddy caves
considering suicide. "marines must spear their mothers with bayonets
before signing up!" or so they've been told.

Alden spots Arline, his family, his blood, without even seeing her face.
hunched over filling a jerry can with mud-water from the spring.
he looks at her back, the way she crouches, the outline of her neck and knows.
he breaks rank, running up the mud bank toward her calling "Tomiko!
Tomi-chan!"
her Japanese name.
she knew her cousin might be coming, that he hadn't speared his mother,
that he might come as family first, enemy second.

first contact: averts her eyes as Alden begins touching her emaciated body,
checking for injuries but finding all ribs and bones.
she pulls away as he tries to hold on and collapses screaming, anger panic.
"Iyada! Iyada, mo!"
her brother Shigenobu, a sailor in the Japanese navy killed months before
by Alden's friends. maybe by Alden himself?

he speaks a soft, broken Japanese, trying to calm her.
Arline stands in defiance, no words.
connects both cans of water to the yoke
begins a defiant march up the hill and away.
a moments pause and Alden chases after,
wrestling the yoke away from her as she screams "Mo-ii! Mo-II-YO!"
Alden squats beneath the yoke and will haul it uphill for her.
legs wobbling, he launches up causing the cans to swing
alternating out of balance, stumbling steps, slipping through the mud,
worsening spiraling incredible weight
brings him down face first in the muddy laughter of other young girls
waiting for their water. regular load for Arline, too heavy for a soldier.
Arline prepares to hoist her water and never look back.
Alden watches, semi-prone in the mud
then frantically rustles through his combat pack saying "wait, just wait! I
have food."
now kneeling he bows, face close to mud and both hands produce shaking
K-rations
outstretched arms offering above his head no looking.
not a pause,   but a realization.
he feels it ripped from his fingers.
as he looks up she already has the tin of Spam opened,
scooping with two fingers filling her face, they lock teary eyes as she
gorges herself
with worthless pork shoulder.
spiced ham falling from her lips, laughing and crying.
first meat in weeks.
like she never knew before. before Alden came home.

spam maps II

Mark Nakada

gift of the rescuer:
a"Typhoon of Steel"
rescuer's gift: military rations of bullets and pork
callit "emergency relief supplies"
callit "Lend-Lease Act"

peace offering: spiced ham   imperial fuel

from alden to arline
   a peace offering
    the bait and switch
cursed gift
cost of acceptance

here in the grocery lineup
impossible dreams of
musubi   ewa
    chanpuru   kin-cho
        loco moco   hilo

spam on the counter
clerk's judging glance   the white
reciting recipes   trash stigma
friend's gagging throat

separated families
      kikokushijyo role reversals   John Owen's ark
       shinseki ironies   landed too late

spam maps III

Mark Nakada

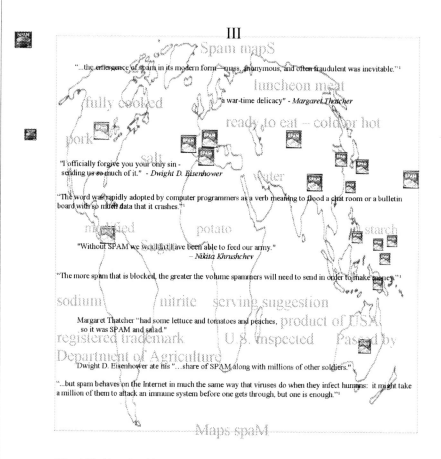

[1] From Michael Specter's article "Damn Spam: The losing war on junk e-mail" in *The New Yorker*, August 6, 2007.

"spam maps I, II, III" were originally published in *West Coast Line* 71, Vol. 45, No. 3 (Fall 2011).

Old Man

Lynda Nakashima

Corn

Lynda Nakashima

Watermelon

Lynda Nakashima

Ichiban

Lynda Nakashima

YOUR GOOD LISTENING SKILLS WILL
OPEN MANY DOORS TO YOU.

Kabocha

Lynda Nakashima

YOU ARE PROMPTED TO SET NEW
GOALS & DISCOVER NEW DESIRES.

Ice Cones

Lynda Nakashima

Chromatic

Debora O

Chromatic /krɔ̀(Ω)'matik/ *n. & a.* LME.
[Fr. *chromatique* or L *chromaticus* f. Gk
khrṑmatikos, f. *khrṑma*, -mat- colour: see –
IC.] A *n. f* 1. A person who preserves his
'colour'; a person who is dyed-in-the-wool.
As in 1979, when, barefoot and pyjamaed,
I stood toe-deep in salmon-red shag – the
colour of my mother's maiden dreams – in
a room where lawn mowers echoed their
late evening presence, accounted for in
the slow, billowing dance of sheer, white
curtains, eclipsing all other colour which
wrestled, like me, for reflection against
spectre walls: inside these multiple chrome
legs, the marrow of another country. 4. In
pl. (treated as *sing*). The science of colour.
L18. Because, despite the surface calm,
all is not white; and among the dustless
shelves lie our sticky fingerprints – rusty,
stubborn evidence that, yes, we live here;
the dryness permeating the walls of my insides until they spill out on early morning
sheets (nose *bleed*), the moist fear of anger
(à *sneeze*), spilling out pollen and grass; dis-
placed and taking root, we climb these glass
pyres: prisms of light, trapped – my body (à
stumble) – learns to exceed itself.

Mixed Spices

Genevieve Erin O'Brien

Mixed Spices is an attempt to gastronomically represent the culture of mixed race people. The artist endeavors to translate the ethnic and cultural heritages of mixed race people into unique flavor and spice combinations. While some are general mixes~"Mex-irean" a combination of Mexican and Korean spices or "Blackinese"~Black and Chinese flavors, one can commission their own personalized mix, for example the Perski~Persian and Polish ~or "Chimacan"~Chinese and Jamaican.

Vietnamese Suitcase

Genevieve Erin O'Brien

As a mixed race Vietnamese American, my body and my existence often feels like it embodies all of Americans' hopes and fears and unresolved issues with the Vietnam War or as the Vietnamese call it the "American war." It feels like I become a repository for other people's sentiments. Many people have assumed that my father must have been in the army and my mother a prostitute. This is often what is behind the question, "how in the world did your parents meet?" The idea that my father was a civilian, and my mother worked at a travel agency in Saigon would never have crossed their minds. So most of the time people can't really tell I'm Vietnamese until it's revealed--this usually happens after the "what are you anyways" and well frankly I can't tell how ignorant people until it's revealed either. I met this sweet older white woman a professor in grad school, and when it was revealed that I am part Vietnamese she came over and grabbed both of my hands and got real real close and leaned up into my face--I know I can rarely say someone leans UP and into my face. She looks into my eyes and she says really slow and drawn out, "I protested that war." Well...okay. Good for you? My people thank you. Sometimes, it's more awkward than others. I offered to give a young woman a ride to the eastside from the westside, I say young because she was my age. She was making small conversation you know, as we are buckling in, "I just got back from Vietnam." She turns to me and looks, "YOU were in the war??!" Apparently, she was missed a few history classes. And fellow Angelenos know how long that ride was. Once, when I was in my early 20's an older man saddled up next to me at the bar. He was clearly intoxicated and for some reason felt compelled after the mixed race reveal to tell me he had served in Vietnam. He proceeded to confide in me that when he was in Vietnam, he had raped a young Vietnamese girl. Not only did he regret his actions, but had spent the past 25 years wondering if that very act had sired a child and whether that child would have grown up to look like me. Look, I'm just trying to drink my bourbon, I wasn't asking to be your confessional. Something about me being mixed race seems to invite people both American and Vietnamese to blurt out their secrets, dump their fears, guilt--and frankly, I was tired of it. I was tired of carrying other people's feelings and sentiments. So I created a multicity durational performance piece to gather those thoughts, feelings, and sentiments and put them to rest.

A Vietnamese suitcase is a generally speaking a cardboard box. The "suitcase" serves a particularly temporary purpose, unlike the somewhat indestructible western version of the suitcase, made for on-going travel. I position myself at locations around various cities; the sites in each city include the federal building, the Vietnamese neighborhood and a Vietnam Memorial. I travel between these sites by public transit over the course of one day.

Photo by Robert Lau

Photo by Robert Lau

People are asked to share their thoughts, feelings, and memories of Vietnam. I chose not to talk, instead using a flyer and gestures to communicate. I ask people to share these thoughts, feelings and memories by writing them on joss paper and placing the joss paper in the "suitcase." I carry these sentiments with me throughout the city.

At each Vietnam Memorial, I perform a mourning ritual where I burn incense to honor the Vietnamese who were killed in the war.

The durational performance was performed in three cities—Los Angeles, Chicago, and Washington, DC. In each city I start my performance at a federal building, and then travel to a Vietnamese neighborhood and end at a Vietnam memorial with a ritual.

Photo by Jules Rosskam

While I was burning incense at the Chicago memorial, police officers came up to me and asked what I was doing. I explained it was a performance, and I was burning incense to honor the Vietnamese who died in the war. The officer asked if I had a permit. "Do I need a permit to honor the dead at a memorial?" The officer said he would check and shuffled off. Later I heard him caucusing with a few other officers, "Well, she's not doing anything illegal, she's just praying," and they let me be. In front of the White House was a bit trickier. The secret service was concerned that I was standing in front of the White House with an empty box. I assured them the box was filled with sentiments. They did not appreciate the humor. And at Maya Lin's Vietnam Memorial, I was soon asked to leave by the National

Park Service. Apparently you do need a permit to honor the dead, at least if you are going to burn anything. They gave me a number to call. Maybe one day I will do another performance documenting the process of getting a permit to honor the dead at a memorial.

Photo by Alex M. Lee

I created an installation with the joss paper and the documentation of the durational performance.

Photo by Robert Lau

After visiting all three cities, I returned the joss paper and suitcases to Vietnam. In Hanoi, Vietnam, I created a final ritual performance. Using the text from the Joss Paper and a translator, I read the sentiments in English and Vietnamese, then I burned the Joss papers.

Photo by *Xoi* magazine (Hanoi)

In addition to burning the joss papers, I burned 3 million U.S. dollars in joss paper, at least $100 for every person killed in the war, US or Vietnamese, military or civilian. I then repatriated the ashes of the joss papers and scattered them during the festival of Vu Lan, the Day of Wandering Souls, a lunar holiday. The performance series follows the migrations and forced immigration of Vietnamese diaspora in the reverse.

The Melting Pot in Housewares Has a Slight Crack

Matthew Olzmann

down the middle. I'm one half something.
One part stained glass window. One part

three-hour infomercial. A crucifix hangs
in my chest like a heart. Chamber music.

One part Mestizo. One part mezzanine.
I know where the checkout lane is.

Your mother spends and spends and spends.
My father says this to me.

He doesn't understand how much I save him,
she replies on her cell phone.

Which floor is Kitchen Utensils? Which floor
is China? Take a credit card and the escalator down.

Do you still go to church on Sundays?
My grandmother asks.

I say the word *assimilation* like a blade
of grass bending. Always bending. A hundred rows

of flickering TVs for newscasters to pronounce
immigration as if they were born thousands

of years ago. Here. In the theater of household
appliances, people see my brother and I and ask:

Which one was adopted? Which floor is Electronics?
Which floor is Hardware?

Where's a nail gun when you need one?
We're standing between departments.

We were born in different strip malls,
both in America.

Yes. I know most of the Lord's Prayer, how to hook
up a DVD player, how to disappear.

In Halves

Matthew Olzmann

> *Half. Meaning everything.*
> ~Jon Pineda

here is the apple sliced through
the center~ its core. one half
brown in the sunlight, so still, almost invisible,
a meditation made of sound. The other is
made of fumes, like snow, it understands
silence. the chill of wind.
I've known the soil the sky
and the glass neither half empty nor
filled with lightning.
and broken. I was born in halves and
I've branded myself with separate sections.
my patron saints of doubt. I've known that
this skin this halo
this earth has been opening
has been accelerating like the chambers of a heart.
toward a boiling point. there is no question.
there's no explanation for the flesh
the slight exterior the body
that insists on remaining demands to continue: divided
somehow mine and somehow whole.

They Say, You Can Be Whatever You Want

Matthew Olzmann

but not the computer terminal, the encryption
or the access code. You can't be
the plasma TV or the signal it receives.
Not the candle or its flame~which is starved
for something more than the wick.
Not the light it casts against the plaster.
Not the plaster. You might be the silhouette.
You might be confused~maybe.
But you can't be the stone castle in the fishbowl.
You can't be the water, the sunlight, the algae
against the glass. Lose your desire to
become the sand, the heat, the scorpion's tail~
an object with a definite name. It ain't happening~
not in this life, friend. Not the undertow
or the Mariana Trench. You can't be the voice
that tells you to define yourself against all you are not.
Instead, you'll be an equation, variables
on both sides of the equal sign. You'll be known
by percentages: one part root winding through soil,
one part map with borders yet to be named.
And no, you can't be the map. But you can take
it with you to church. Yes, *holy* is a word.
You can worship even when they say you can't
be the pulpit, the pew, or the collection
basket passed from hand to hand. Not the hands.
Not the newspaper or the dent in the door.
Not the dog bowl. Not the fuel cell.
You can't be the odd months that extend
beyond the calendar pages, toward the horizon.

But you *will* be a part of that horizon,
of the storm on its ocean, of the island in its storm.

Katawan: A Collection of Body Parts

Giovanni Ortega

Cuello
on the verge you sucked
Vato Vampira's sweetness
Cabarnet evening

Tenga
naririnig ko
ang kanyang mga sigaw
sa aming kama

Calves
there lies laps that flow
a Tiger spun the track marks
Azteca whimpers

Pecho
I rained inside you
and spread the border language
Mecca stares rug burns

Eyebrows
Smoke slowed 'tween his brows
Flint lit our conjoinment high
His smile withstood time

Saliva
Sepia Photos speak
a steam room of cocoa sweat
the griot asleep

Pezon
Taino Lisbon
frolicked among duck feathers
Arriolas dried

Pelvis
Equator chose me
Mariachi sings circus
reared street decadence

Throat
passed out down under
acidity flows well here
the head pounds below

Follicles
Snoring in my arms
Burped tremors each time we kissed
She left before us

Nariz
La Virgen watched us
Velas flamed our bodies high
Bikini Nena

Ojos
Looking back behind
Pause a few paces ahead
children scream outside

A'ama
La Cumparsita
floated when our fingers locked
the rest is hidden

Skin
a rupture insight
darkness wrapped my torso round
straight in to the night

Spine
his back glittered stars
mapping the waves of our swim
irradescent light

Pezuña
His eyes pierced my lips
intoxicating spearheads
locked between wet toes

Hips
glass in the ceiling
salsa knocked on windowsills
rug burns on my shin

La Boca
the bridge crossed my groin
unable to surpass heat

Juarez thrusts drumbeats...

Crickets

Giovanni Ortega

Crickets sing jazz solemnly
in the backyard of my infirmary
picadilly candles hung on their antenaes
honeymoon of silence i bring inside the footseps of my ceiling tears clung
on my bloodshot eyes
afraid to drip into the hardwood floors of my chest
i pound i pound i pound
no ones home

just this jazz that the cricket sings

AHF

Giovanni Ortega

i feel comfort from strangers who draw my blood
whether it be Mormons or Texans
waiting for answers you have yet to ask
the smell of chlorine and disenfectant
calms my every pores
A Kiwi smiles

as he touches my face with his voice

Baraka

Giovanni Ortega

Letters danced on the walls
as Gavinda walked through
his 6 year old body tossed
by the soccer ball on his feet
alternating steps
as hijabs and kufis Assalam one another
the sweltering heat of Medina
is a perspiration present
Dates parade the bazaar
and citrus smoke fills the aire
Habibis are lost with each other's company
and I am intoxicated with a man
whose eyelashes reach towards Mecca
as he utters those mistaken calligraphy
Gavinda reaches out to him
"Would you like to play soccer?"
the earth shook,
it rattled

the way you wake yourself from a nightmare

Sandra Mizumoto Posey

I sat waiting for him at a little independent coffee house on Colfax Avenue. I ordered a large açai smoothie (because I buy into all that bullshit and I don't eat right so I figured the extra Amazonian nutrition boost would do me good) and a spinach feta scone, because they were out of vegetarian quiche. "I'm at a table by the door," I texted him, seconds before he walked in and spied me. He smiled nervously and looked a bit like a ferret, his teeth yellow like pieces of corn. Not at all like his photos, but after all they had been pretty small given I could only look at them on the screen of my phone. The perils of Tinder. Well, I thought, it might be a nice conversation.

He ordered a drink, then sat down beside me at the small aluminum table. He was carrying a bag of books from the local bookstore, so I asked him what he'd gotten. He pulled out a vintage copy of *The Analects of Confucius*. That started him talking about his deep and abiding admiration for Asian culture. He began telling me about the martial art he pursued—I don't recall which martial art it was because at that point I started to check out a little and attempted sip my thick açai smoothie with extra force to expedite its progress through the straw. Damn. Why did I have to order the large?

He pulled out his phone and began to show me photos from his last trip to Japan. "I go twice a year," he told me, boasting, "I go to get the shit beat out of me by my Senseis and to absorb all the culture."

Please don't guess that I am Japanese, please don't guess that I am Asian.

I kept fairly quiet, asked polite questions, and otherwise kept to myself for fear that some stray facial expression or bit of personal revelation might point to my inherent Asianness. Sometimes, I've found, the only people who can spot it immediately are either other mixed race people like me or these Asianophile men. It's like a secret Spidey sense: they zoom in on it, latch onto to you, then begin to exoticize you. I'm not sure which is more disturbing, being told by someone that I don't look Asian at all or being told once they find out, "Oh yes, I can see it in your almond eyes or the color of your skin." My heritage, I want to tell them, my experiences, and the people I call family are not something you can understand or discern by the shape of my eyes or the color of my skin. Nor is it something you can rule out because of them.

I kept sipping my smoothie. Hard.

If he found out I was Japanese, it was likely one of two things would happen: he would either strive to teach me about Japan and its culture or he would try to ascertain what aspects that he so admired I personally embodied and embraced. Neither, I figured, was at all his business.

Ironically, or perhaps not so much given it is such a common phenomenon when I go out on dates, he didn't really ask much about me at all. He only asked what I taught. I told him Women's Studies. He began to explain that he didn't know too much about that, which was actually a more refreshing approach than the one he had been taking as the expert on all things Japanese. I quickly responded, however, that he needn't worry that I was going to spend our time together teaching him about it because that was what I had to do everyday for work, and I didn't have any inclination to do it in my free time. That might seem a bit abrupt, but you have to understand that I've spent more than one date either trapped into being challenged about some aspect of feminism which I then have to parse out and explain or defend, or being stuck outlining the basics of Women's Studies 101 during a time when I just want to meet someone nice who is interested in me.

And yes, I am half Japanese with a mother from Japan, so I do have exposure to that culture and embody some elements of it. I am also a Women's Studies professor and that is part of my identity, given I spend most of my waking hours occupied with some aspect of it. But neither of these things is me. They are the roots of and the manifestation of some of my abiding concerns, issues, and inclinations, but they themselves are not what motivates me from day to day. All of that is much more complex than some perceived genetic relationship to the philosophy of martial arts or even my personal identification with feminism.

I moved to Denver five years ago, simultaneous with my split from my partner of twelve years. I traveled from Los Angeles, where I had friends and support networks built over a lifetime, to a smaller city where I knew no one. I swear the dating pool is more limited here, even in a town touted in the media as "Menver." But dating is, I've found, is difficult in the era of Tinder and OKCupid, especially when you are divorced, older, and have a young child. While an incident at a restaurant--where the waitress checking I.D.s literally yelled out to her fellow servers what my birthdate was and said, loudly, "Can you believe how old she is??"--tells me that I look fairly young for my age, there is no hiding your age on the internet. Your choices are to reveal it or lie. I refuse to do the latter, and so I think that I don't even come up under the search parameters of most men, who, according to all the data, trend toward dating younger women even when they themselves are older. When I do connect with someone (usually by me reaching out to them rather than the other way around), some tell me I am too old, some say they don't want to date someone with children, and some say they still want to have children of their own (which is just another way of saying I am too old). The men that have children of their own often are either parents of college-aged kids (who therefore don't want to deal with the logistical complexities of having young children around all over again) or they have, in a weird twist of divorcee fate, the exact opposite childrearing schedules. Being a parent also means my time is limited, so these arduous smoothie interludes listening to rhapsodic musings on Asian culture or having to defend and explain the content of my day job can be particularly tiresome.

People tell me I don't need a man to be happy. Hey, I'm a Women's Studies professor. I think I know that glib little piece of traditional wisdom. I'm not arguing that I do. But I also know that people are not meant to live their lives in isolation. Remember those psychological experiments where they deprived baby monkeys of physical contact to see how it would mess them up? Yeah, after five years in Denver, that's me. I need good, close friendships in my life and a sense of community. Occasionally, it would be nice to have someone hold me so I don't regress into that deprived baby monkey state. If I'm lucky one day I'll find another partner, someone to wake up with, or perhaps just someone to share the mundanity of my days with or vent with when I'm down. I'm tired of sharing everything with the emptiness of my Facebook wall because I have no one to talk to in person. It's a little sad, frankly. But so far, the alternative has been isolated interludes with the likes of this guy, the one carrying *The Analects* under his arm.

Eventually I forced that entire smoothie down my throat and excused myself by saying I hated to cut our time short, but I was a bit stressed because I had work to do. As I bussed my own dishes, I wondered, in passing, if Amazonians get as annoyed when people order açai smoothies and attribute unspecified healing properties to them. Probably. We all have our moments, I realized, of exoticizing people and things in order to fill the gaps where otherwise our own lives are lacking.

this english language

Amal Rana

this english language
trips me up
confuses me
with everyday banalities
commonplace pleasantries
full of empty meanings
hollow echoes
of sentiments not truly felt

this english language
envelops my taste-buds
dulls my senses
wreaks havoc with my bones
numbing
every sensation
every desire
every nerve ending
with passionless power

this english language
slowly rips apart
those ancient mother(s') tongues
burning deep inside my throat
ebonyred embers
glowing silently with rage

lately words trip over each other
lips
stumble
stutter
stammering
to remember
this english language
colonizing tongue

foreign and unwieldy
freezing all it touches
with a cool white mist
tasteless and greedy
reaching in to grasp
that which still remains from the old world
nestled deeply under strange vowels
a-e-i-o-u
grammar lessons
and tales of white-skinned jinn
that covered the land in blood

Untitled Essay

Mia Riverton

For my mother.

As a child, I followed the same routine every night in preparation for bed. After taking a bath, I put on my pajamas, brushed my teeth, and jumped into my beloved canopy bed. I waited under the covers patiently, with the lights off and the door slightly ajar, allowing a small but comforting sliver of light to stream into the bedroom. In a few minutes, without fail, I heard my mother's light footsteps as she ascended the stairs to my room and tapped softly on the door. Every night, I called out "Come in," and she entered my room and asked the same question.

"Are you ready to be tucked in?"

Without a word, I obediently rolled over onto my stomach as my mother sat down on the edge of my bed. She always began slowly, scratching her fingernails lightly up and down my back, trailing her fingertips along my spine and around my shoulder blades. She hummed or softly sang Chinese lullabies to me, tracing patterns with her fingers in time with the rhythm of the melody. Then she began to scratch my back in earnest, appeasing all of my "itchies." I lay perfectly still with my eyes closed, calmed by my mother's soothing touch. My body relaxed completely, though I never drifted off to sleep. My mind sometimes wandered, as I daydreamed or thought about the events of the day. But if I sensed my mother begin to slow her movement, I immediately opened my eyes and solemnly pointed out all the new itchies that I had developed on my back. She dutifully scratched each one, making absolutely certain that it was gone before she moved on to the next.

Sometimes we played a game~she traced out words or Chinese characters on my back, and I would guess what they were. Sometimes, when neither of us was very tired, she surprised me by tickling my sides, sending both of us into fits of giggling~a sort of conspiratorial hilarity that always ended with me flinging my arms around my mother's neck in a grateful hug. Sometimes, she would tell me stories as she scratched my back, excitedly whispering to me the adventures of the Monkey King, whose naughty antics

I always secretly admired. But after a while, we always grew silent, quietly enjoying each other's company. It was then that I was conscious that I loved her, with that sort of fierce, protective love of which only children and mothers are truly capable. When she finally rose from my side, my mother leaned over and brushed my cheek with a kiss. On her way out, she always paused in the doorway and spoke to me in the musical tones of her Mandarin accent.

"Good night, my daughter."

As I grew older, my bedtime routine changed. I substituted a morning shower for my nightly baths. In addition to brushing my teeth before bed, I engaged in all the ritualistic exfoliation and purification of the complexion that accompany female adolescence. I started sleeping with my door closed, sometimes locked. And at some point during my middle school years, I decided that I was too old to be "tucked in." When my mother knocked on my door, I called a cheerful "Good night." The first few times, she stood outside my room, patiently waiting for me to invite her in. When I did not, she murmured a gentle "Good night" in reply and slipped noiselessly back down the stairs. After a while, she stopped coming up to my room altogether.

When I came home for Thanksgiving vacation during my first year of college, I had been away for three long months and was ready to be pampered by my family. On my first day at home, my grandmother stuffed me with her gourmet Cantonese cuisine. My father handed me some extra money ~ an "allowance supplement," as he phrased it. My little brother even offered to let me borrow his Game Boy, in a moment of uncharacteristic generosity. My mother was surprisingly quiet, although she seemed happy to see me.

I had taken an early flight home that morning, so I was tired and decided to go to sleep rather early. As I climbed into my now canopyless bed, I heard my mother's familiar tread on the stairs. After a brief pause, there was a tentative knock on my door.

"Come in."

My mother entered the room and looked at me bashfully, tucking a stray hair behind her ear with a self-conscious smile.

"Are you ready to be tucked in?"

Silently, I rolled over onto my stomach and closed my eyes. She sat down beside me and awkwardly stroked my hair. The familiarity of her touch stirred something within me; I turned my head on the pillow and looked into the beautiful, serene face of my mother. We gazed at each other for a while, and after a few minutes she began to graze my back with her fingernails. She scratched lightly at first, as always, then more vigorously. Neither of us spoke. It was not until she rose from my bed that I realized there were tears in my eyes. She paused in the doorway, casting a long shadow into my bedroom.

"Good night, my daughter."

Son of a Janitor

Tony Robles

The house of a janitor is supposed to be clean. One would assume this to be true because the janitor performs his duties with the sacred mop, broom, and toilet brush. My father was a janitor for some 20 odd years at the San Francisco Opera House. It would be 10 years before he'd realize his dream and start the "Filipino Building Maintenance Company" and go into business on his own. At the dinner table he'd ask me questions such as, "What did you learn in school today?" I've always been somewhat of a bad listener. "Nothing" I'd reply-I always replied nothing-not that I was indifferent to school-even at a very young age. Yes, I was very aware of the things they were doing to me in school and after the bell rang I'd let it fall from my mind like some brown, withered old leaf falling off a tree-destined to be stepped on my some kid on their way home. I always liked the sounds those leaves made. My father always told me if I didn't do well in school, I'd end up cleaning toilets all my life. My father didn't graduate from high school, and I guess he carried that with him. Somehow he felt that the high school diploma was a key-some kind of rocket fuel which would kickstart you into the realm of possibilities. Somehow that slice of paper with what-ever burned into it would bring you closer to your dream. It was an access pass of sorts. "Do you know how to clean?" Dad would, on occasion, talk shop with me-an 11- or 12-year-old kid with no work experience. "Yeah, I know how to clean," I'd reply. Okay, he'd say, how do you remove chewing gum from a carpet? Dad would slip in the hypothetical in this manner. I was supposed to use logic and deduction in finding the correct answer.

"I would take a pair of scissors and cut the gum off..." At this point my father would belch or fart, or perform both simultaneously. Shaking his head he'd say, "It's very apparent and clearly evident that you don't know anything about cleaning. The way to remove gum from a carpet is to take an ice cube and place it on the gum. Wait 'til it hardens, then remove it with a putty knife." I never asked him what to do if you didn't have an ice cube-perhaps I should have. My father would proudly demonstrate his expertise-explaining how to remove wine stains from a carpet or the correct way to vacuum a rug. "You have to use nice long strokes in the direction of the nap of the carpet. Nice long strokes until it makes you feel good..." By the end of his speech, my food would be cold but my father would urge me to "eat all that food on your plate, or I'm gonna knock you upside your head." He had a great sense of humor.

The one thing I was fairly proficient at was cleaning the toilet. It was one of a couple of chores assigned to me. The other chores were drying the dishes and vacuuming. My father didn't clean at home~he left that duty to my stepmom and me. Why would he want to bring his business home? I remember once during the Christmas season my father worked during the showing of the *Nutcracker*. This meant lots of kids. Dad not only had to mop floors and empty trashcans, but he had to get on his hands and knees and pick hundreds, perhaps thousands of sunflower seed shells. He came home exhausted, complaining that those kids made him "sweat his butt off" that day. At home, my father took to gardening, which proved therapeutic. He would take a spray bottle and sprinkle water on his plants~large and unique cacti, whose spines climbed the walls. He'd sometimes shoot me in the head or the behind with a narrow stream, intended for nobody but me. I'd hide behind a cactus or palm plant, but he had good aim.

Toilet duty, for me, was a peaceful duty. It was a simple thing~take some cleaning solution, pour it in the bowl, take your toilet brush and start scrubbing. I had a certain finesse, or technique, to my bowl cleaning system. Depending on my mood, I'd employ several different methods. There was the "Around the world in a day" method, in which I'd use wide, circular motions with my toilet brush in order to bring out the luster and shine of the pot. It was almost like stirring a bowl of soup. I also called this method, "Stirring a bowl of soup." I also employed the "splish splash" method, in which I'd very rigorously scrub the toilet all over, creating a small puddle at the base of the bowl. Again, it was a good system~although a bit messy. I was a quick learner. My father only had to show me how to clean toilets once~after that, I was on my own. My favorite method was "The Beethoven." I coined this particular method, "The Beethoven" because it could be both graceful and rigorous, depending on my state of mind. I would use the toilet brush like the conductor of an orchestra; slow and graceful with a calm rippling effect~etching an invisible melody, which seemed to outshine the other porcelain in the bathroom. Then I'd get more rigorous, splashing and creating waves~a crescendo and the finale~the flush. Those remain to this day some of the most creative moments of my life.

My father continued after me about things over the years. I can't blame him really. I wasn't particularly talented, but I managed to get out of high school and college. The getting out was the most rewarding part. When we eat dinner these days, he doesn't ask me about what I learned in school, which is good because I remember nothing. But the one thing I do remember was cleaning those toilets. And believe me, it's helped me a lot more.

The Land of Dead Children

Genaro Kỳ Lý Smith

The dust children work the black market selling stale cigarettes,
hard chewing gum whose wrappers are as difficult to peel as wallpaper,
and canned sodas no longer spit and fizz forth suds when tabs are pulled.
The packaging long empty of the promise of what was once good,
what was once desirable and quenching is all that remains.
They tote and hawk their wares on street corners,
hover over customers at soup stalls, hindering their next bite or sip of broth;
they huddle in foyers of hotels, the farthest they are allowed to enter
though vacancies are abundant.
Every day they go out, their hair brown or red, stringy or curly,
Afros their mothers never learned to comb and treat or plait.
They go out with eyes green or black, skin freckled, tanner, noses wider,
and the only thing they have of their mothers' are the eyes.
They go out as *con lais**, and though some are white,
they become the new niggers of Nam.
Their childhood ended having to learn the importance of pitch
to a language that requires stressed syllables.
Their faces have lost the softness essential for innocence,
and they speak with a harshness forced from wanting to be heard
over the din of the city's futile dreaming.

At night when they return home to their mothers, they eat and understand
that the silence between them is their mothers' definition for *sorry*.
The children have learned never to ask about fathers they do not remember,
fathers whose names they cannot pronounce,
fathers who once cradled them to sleep
while whispering what their promised lives would be like in America.
They have learned their mothers' disappointment
harnessed over their shoulders
and in their furrowed brows,
the shame they inherited of how American men really are.
The mothers see the ones they once loved in their children's faces

* half breeds

when they watch them sleep at night, and the mothers wonder,
Are their children's dreams filled with fathers whose faces they recognize?-
do they sit on their fathers' laps while driving tractors?
The mothers wonder if in these dreams they hold their fathers' hands
on the first day of school, maybe cry when the fathers leave for work.
Or maybe they do not cry knowing their fathers will come pick them up,
eager to show them the colored construction paper cut-outs of birds with wings
too small to take flight, of their pet dogs, cats, and rabbits
with too many whiskers drawn,
or turkeys with each tail feather cut out and pasted on their backs;
they come running out of the schools eager to tell their fathers who they sat next to,
which friends they traded or shared their lunches with,
ready to tell them about all the things they learned that day.

Craycism

Sebastian Speier

Craycism is seven boxes of crayons, each aligned with a continent's ethnic majority. Within each box is the regular twenty-four crayons you would find in typical package of Crayola Crayons, except one color has been changed to the name *Skin*.

In the Asia box, the yellow color has been renamed *Skin*. Similarly in the Africa box, the dark brown has been renamed *Skin*. Other boxes in the series include *America: Post 15th Century, Native America, Europe, South Asia,* and *Other*. In Other the user is able to create their own skin color by blending white, black and pale tan.

In response to the civil rights movement of the 60s, Crayola changed the name of the "*Flesh*" crayon to "*Peach*." Renaming this crayon was a way of recognizing that skin tones vary. But the color tones weren't changed to reflect an equality to be able to make a variety of real skin tones. Satire has long been a channel for voices within civil rights activism, and here it is meant to skewer the ignorance imposed by Crayola during the civil rights movement. On the bottom of each box it reads "*Now geographically correct.*"

The second piece in this body of work is the *Skin Carton,* which consists of eight crayons all using the same pigment. The oil-based pigment was created through a Behr color scanner to read the exact color of my skin. Although the crayons are labeled Skin Color 1, Skin Color 2, Skin Color 3, etc., they are all the same pigment. This is a reference to Crayola's *Multicutlural Crayons* carton which only includes eight different tones. In their attempt to make their product more politically correct, they do the opposite by limiting consumers to eight hues that represent all of humanity's ethnicities.

The users are then encouraged to use these crayons to color a coloring-book of sixty-four illustrations of my face, thus interpreting my very skin color.

This sculptural installation is an ongoing work dealing with cultural identity and immigration policy in multicultural societies.

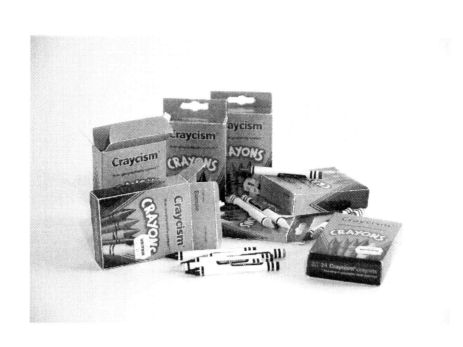

Cabbit

Jeff Chiba Stearns

"What Are You Anyways?"

Jeff Chiba Stearns

I've been asked the quintessential mixed-race question, "So, what are you, anyways?" a lot over the years in regards to my multiethnic appearance. As a teenager growing up in the 80s in the predominantly Caucasian city of Kelowna, BC, it was a question I felt like I answered on a daily basis. Now as a 36-year-old adult living in Vancouver, I realized that I haven't been asked "What are you?" in a really long time. As someone who has spent a lot of time contemplating and reflecting on their racial identity and being highly involved in the mixed-race community across North America, I often wonder how I would answer this question today.

I guess I would say, first and foremost, I am a filmmaker, animator, documentarian and artist. I am also 100% Canadian, 100% Nikkei, 100% Japanese Canadian, 100% German Canadian, 100% Russian Canadian, 100% English Canadian, 100% Scottish Canadian. What I am not is half- nor am I a fraction or stuck in between a hyphen. Personally, I don't like fractions because I've learned that when I break myself down into halves or eighths, others perceive my multiethnic identity as weak or diluted. I'm neither this nor that, but if you squint really hard I probably could be. And even if some people see me as being mixed, or mixed race, or biracial, or multiracial or multiethnic–I consider myself pretty complete. For me, being mixed does not mean I am mixed up...and if I do refer to myself or others as being mixed, I'm usually referring to being beautifully blended both on the inside and out.

When I want to feel a sense of community, I'll refer to myself as a hapa or a hafu, or sometimes I'll feel more of a sense of community referring to myself as a human. At any point I like that I can choose to identify with anything I feel like; my ethnic heritage, my background, my culture, my nationality, my philosophical views, my age, my music, or my hairstyle. I like to make media about my identity because I feel it's important to meditate on existence. For me, existence is identity, and filmmaking is meditation. It's important to question who you are constantly because it is a large part of existing.

I've accepted that as long as there are borders and boundaries, people will always be curious about why we look different. Thus, I don't mind if people ask me "So, what are you?" as long as they're okay with me asking them "So, why are you wearing that hideous jacket?" In 2005, I had a chance to explore my multiethnic identity in my short "hapanimated" film, *What Are You Anyways?* This little animated film would take off internationally and forever label me a mixed-race advocate. Even after all these years, I'm still not sure how I feel about being called a mixed-race advocate.

What Are You Anyways?

However, being a so-called mixed-race advocate helped mature my thoughts on multiethnic identity, and I realized the importance to continue creating media on the subject. Multiethnic people are thirsty for media that reflects their experiences and identities. Thus, in 2010, I released my first feature documentary entitled *One Big Hapa Family* (www.onebighapafamily.com) that questions why everyone in my Japanese Canadian family married interracially after my grandparent's generation, and how their mixed kids perceive their unique multiethnic identities. After 31 years of existence, I talked to my parents for the first time about their marriage. They told me that they do not see themselves as being in an intermarriage—they just see

themselves as a Canadian who married a Canadian. I like that. I wish the world were more like my parents.

Sure, I don't speak Japanese, but neither does my mom. I'm fourth-generation Canadian (Yonsie) and I have no idea who my family is in Japan. Although I do believe it is very important to know your history and heritage, I think it's more important to know yourself first. Sometimes I look in the mirror and ask myself if I am an ethnic minority or a person of color or if I secretly wish there was a Hapa Island. Then I rub my eyes and realize that the Canadian government already classifies me as a visible minority and there are Hapa Islands. They're called Hawaʻi, and I'm not from there but it is a nice place to visit.

After much contemplation, I have decided that my feature documentary will deal with topics of multiethnic identity, and I have come to terms with being a mixed-race advocate. Entitled *Mixed Match* (www.mixedmatchmovie.com), the documentary will explore the need to find mixed ethnicity bone marrow and cord blood donors to donate to multiethnic patients suffering from life threatening blood diseases such as leukemia. Many people do not realize that patients who need a bone marrow or stem cell transplant must find their genetic "twin," someone with a similar mixed-race ancestry, which at times has been compared to winning the lottery.

Imani Cornelius, an MDS (Myelodysplastic Syndromes) patient, and her family, searching for a match.

The film is an important human story told from the perspective of youths who are forced to reflect on their multiracial identities through their deadly illnesses, and how their mixed-race heritage threatens their chances at survival. For the film I've partnered with Mixed Marrow (www.mixedmarrow.org) to help raise awareness for this important cause. After filming for over four years, I already know this will be the most difficult film I will ever make, but it will also be the most important. I now realize that "What are you?" isn't just a question of curiosity but rather a reason to join a bone marrow registry, a reason to donate a baby's umbilical cord blood, and a reason to help save lives.

Noted scientist Dr. Paul Terasaki with Jeff Chiba Stearns and Mixed Marrow Founder and Director, Athena Asklipiadis

Snaikel

Jeff Chiba Stearns

Excerpts from "White and Wrong: Mostly True Stories"

Jason Sublette

Tropical Paradise

So it's not bad enough that we don't go to church, don't eat biscuits and gravy, have no interest in scouting, don't have a family portrait on the wall, will not pronounce our state "Muh-zur-uh," don't like the rodeo, and just plain don't look right, but now we're going to have a real Hawaiian luau in our backyard. Luau = murdered pig + giant fiery hole in the ground + massive Hawaiians & Samoans chugging beer + singing & dancing – good sense. All of this = astounded small town neighbors holding their collective breath.

Wildman Ricky Yomoto, my father's unlikely pot-bellied beer-swilling fish eye-sucking chain-smoking womanizing best friend, aims a .22 pistol between the eyes of a huge pink & black pig that's tied to the elm tree. He fires the gun and vaults onto the back of the pig like a rodeo cowboy, savagely sawing its flabby neck with a gleaming hunting knife. The pig screams. Blood spurts, pumps, then pours out onto the yellowed grass. My father, the distinguished college professor they all call "Doc," watches in horror his son and daughter watching in horror.

Later, while my proud father tries not to cringe as he helps shave the dead pig with yellow Bic razors, my mother practices the Hula in front of the bathroom mirror. My sister and I can only look at each other helplessly and sigh. Why can't we all just sit around watching M.A.S.H. like normal families?

But a day later, after the murdered pig has been shaved, hacked, sliced up, wrapped in banana leaves, and cooked underground overnight, and while our friends are saying grace in their formal dining rooms before they begin eating bland meatloaf and mashed potatoes, my sister and I smile impossible smiles, the grease glistening on our fingers, stringy pork melting in our mouths, wildman Ricky strumming his beat-up ukulele, muscle-bound Vai Uili expertly twirling a flaming baton and stomping the ground so hard the walnuts fall off the trees. Billy, Derwin, Tifa, Lorna, Maureen, Kimo, Meia, Paki, Ligo, Dexter, Leleia, Etawali: thick brown brushstrokes on this bright white canvas that is now our universe.

We dig our dirty toes into the fine sand of this improbable back-yard beach and lean into each other. We are an island. At least tonight.

Game, Set, Match

Yesterday my father shows us his new apartment, explains that we can come over after school any day that we want. *Everyday* if we want, and I think, *yes, it will be everyday.* And although his belongings are stacked head high in the living room, I still can't tell this embarrassing news to my friends with their perfect *Leave it to Beaver* families. I know people will read about it in the newspaper though, and juicy news travels fast through the aisles of Hy-Vee. I know they'll say it's because we aren't Christians. And I know everyone will blame my flashy Korean mother because, let's face it, there's white and then there's wrong.

But today things are looking up. I'm in the 12-and-under finals of the American Cancer Society tennis tournament. I'll be playing Brandon Stick, a lousy player with Fila tennis clothes and three Prince racquets. I know he gets private lessons from a college player. I will delight in beating him.

But right before the match begins Brandon speaks to me for the first time ever. Me, the scrawny, slant-eyed nobody? He tells me that maybe I could spend the night at his house tonight, after the match and all. We'll get pizza, watch cable, play his pinball machine. Pinball machine! I say *sure,* trying to remain cool. I know that I'm blushing. Brandon Stick is beyond popular, has legendary make-out parties in the finished basement of his huge house.

The match begins. I'm distracted at first, worried about what I'll sleep in tonight since I don't even own pajamas. And will I need my own money for the pizza? Will I need quarters for the pinball machine? I lose the first few points. But pretty soon I settle down and it becomes obvious that Brandon can't handle my forehand. I hit deep to his backhand and when he blocks back short sitters, I pound the ball to the forehand corner. I'm careful to not act too happy about it and I tell him *good shot* whenever I can. I let him win one game per set and we're finished in forty minutes. 6-1, 6-1. We shake hands at the net. *It was just a lucky day for me,* I say. As I crouch at my tennis bag (which is so obviously just my mother's burgundy airplane carry-on), I close my eyes, tell myself *relax, don't act squirrelly.* I snap out of it when I see a blur of Brandon's legs as he dashes to his father's white custom Econoline with the shiny mag wheels. He jumps in, and they speed away. I'm puzzled at first, but then I tell myself that they're probably just going to go pick up the pizza. So I wait in the stands. One hour. Two hours.

Then I get it. I've lost by winning. So I walk home alone with my first-place trophy. That's something anyway. But as I turn onto Florence Street, I spy my gangly sister struggling under the weight of a heavy crate of my father's books. As she drops it in the trunk of the car she pitches forward, her skinny brown legs lifting up off the gravel for a split second. My father's wedged between the opening of the front seats laying his suits across cardboard boxes in the back, the setting sun reflecting off his bald spot. My mother takes impossibly tiny steps toward the car like she's in slow motion, struggling to hold the bushy Boston fern shoulder-high so it doesn't drag on the gravel. I wonder if she's wondering whether her mother-in-law was right in opposing their marriage. Maybe the races shouldn't be mixed. And what will become of her mixed-breed children, especially now that they'll be from a broken home? Maybe she thinks a good German wife would have been better for my father. And then I wonder too, is my mother to blame? Does she want too much in life? A career, respect, excitement, equality, love, romance, and family. Or maybe she's right. Maybe this town has ruined our family. Maybe my father moving us here for his selfish reasons made happiness impossible.

I look at the three of them not looking at each other, and I shake my head no. I pitch my trophy in the neighbor's bushes, turn around, and begin walking back to the courts. There is no winning today.

I would have killed to be Muhammad Ali. I wanted his grace, his bravado, his toughness. He was everything I wasn't, everything I would never be. My father and I watched every Ali fight on *Wide World of Sports*, cursing obnoxious Howard Cossell anytime he criticized "The Greatest." Between rounds we boxed wearing my father's foam Tae Kwon Do gloves. I danced around my father, firing left jabs at his big nose, stepping in for my overhand right. On that rare occasion when I penetrated my father's defense and he pretended to be dazed, I stopped, looked out at an imaginary crowd, threw my gloved hands high into the air, and bellowed, "I'm a baaaaad man!"

And I believed it.

All of a sudden I had my chance to use what I knew were prodigious (yet untested) boxing skills. My friend Michael got sucker-punched in the locker room by mouthy Jerry Pruett. Michael crumpled against the tile wall, covering his bewildered face with his hands. Blood dripped between his fingers and dotted the concrete floor. Jerry Pruett pranced around the locker room saying, "Who's Next?" I cracked my knuckles, chuckled to myself, then pounced. I quickly snapped two jabs at his thin lips, and when he covered his face, I delivered a right uppercut to the solar plexus. As he bent over gasping, I smashed his right ear with a looping left that sent him to the floor. The astonished boys looked at what I had done and slowly backed away into the gymnasium. I shuffled my feet, thrust my hands into the air, and yelled, "Get up sucka, and I'll whup you some more!"

The only problem was that all this happened later that night in front of the bathroom mirror. I was glistening with sweat, bobbing and weaving, taunting and sneering, jabbing and hooking—no one. Eight hours earlier in the locker room as my friend bled on the floor and Jerry Pruett challenged us all, I could only clench my fists behind my back and imagine doing what only I knew I could. In the bathroom, though, I danced and punched and battered Jerry Pruett. I made up a rhyme about his mother. I was undisputed champion of the world—the slant-eyed Ali.

A few weeks later I switched on the Boom Boom Mancini-Duk Koo Kim fight by accident. Mancini was supposed to be the real-life Rocky Balboa, but I wasn't impressed. He just looked like one of those short-fused boys who got into scraps on the playground. But when I saw Kim, his flat Korean face and his compact muscled body, I cringed. I yearned for lean sinewy muscles like Marvelous Marvin Hagler and Thomas Hitman Hearns. I wanted to look like the young lean Cassius Clay, not this ovalish miniature Sumo wrestler. Good God! Was this what I would become in a few years? This ugly junebug, this wild javelina?

Mancini was surely no Ali, not even close. He looked sloppy, slow, almost dirty with that mop of sweat-soaked hair. He couldn't dance. He wasn't fast. He threw sloppy, wild combinations. But Kim was even worse. He was a relentless bulldog. He marched deliberately into Mancini's flurry of fists and took it round after round. His fat face swelled up. His narrow eyes puffed up like they had been erased. But he wouldn't go away, wouldn't just go back to where he belonged. He kept coming. Kept punching, kept getting punched.

How many times had I been called Jap, nip, gook, Chink, dink? How many times did I stare into the mirror waiting for my father's prodigious German nose genes to rescue my flat face? And how many times did I answer the same stupid questions? *No, it isn't hard to see. No, I don't shave my arms and legs. No, I don't speak another language. No, I don't eat raw fish. No, my father didn't adopt me.* So fuck Kim and fuck me, I thought. I began cheering for Boom Boom.

In the late rounds when Kim finally tired and Mancini began beating Kim senseless, I jumped up and started punching the air wildly. I threw crazy roundhouse rights and flailing left hooks. I growled. I kicked at the couch. I spat on the floor. And when he pummeled Kim with thirty-nine unanswered blows to the head in Round 13, I shouted, "Kill him! Knock his fucking head off!"

I swear, though, I didn't know he was *really* killing him.

344

I couldn't have known his brain was already bleeding as he crumpled to the mat in the fourteenth round, that he was already dying as he pulled himself up for more punishment. I didn't know anything about the blood clot. I didn't know he had scrawled "Kill or be killed" on his hotel lampshade.

I didn't know referee Richard Greene would take his own life three months later, that Kim's mother would kill herself four months after Greene, that Boom Boom Mancini would sink into a serious depression when the dust settled. I certainly never dreamed that twenty years later I would stand helpless over my own near-dead mother after she swallowed a bottle of pills, feeling exactly the way I felt on November 13, 1982, when they carried Kim out of the ring already in a coma: Waylaid. Complicit. Sentenced.

Understand that when I woke up that morning I didn't know that I would help kill him.

Believe me, nobody told me that I wouldn't always hate my face, that eventually I would be proud to put kimchi in my grocery cart, that two days before my marriage I would have *husband* tattooed on my hairless arm in Hangul, that one day I would try to claim Michelle Wie, Ahn Hyun-Soo, Daniel Dae Kim, and Karen O as my own, that on my 35th birthday some high school boy would abruptly stop his Cadillac Escalade just to point his finger at me and yell out, "Fucking Chink!"~and I'd be glad for the imprecise recognition. How could I have ever known all of this then?

Kim, I didn't mean to hate you. I just wanted to be Ali. I just didn't want to be me.

I am not a bad man.

The Gift Horse of War

Julie Thi Underhill

Freshly graduated from a small liberal arts college an hour away from Seattle, I moved to the city to find a job after college. During the last year of my degree at Evergreen, I'd studied documentary film and video. For my final project, in the spring of 2000, I began a family history documentary focusing on the American war in Việt Nam, interviewing both my refugee mother and my U.S. Army combat helicopter pilot stepfather, reading everything I could get my hands on, realizing the difficulty of making a film about an open wound of ongoing unfinished business. Even my classmates pitied me for needing to do work on the war in Việt Nam. Beside their self-aggrandizing music videos and abstract experimental films, my work was far too raw, too serious. The more sympathetic of these classmates would pat me on the arm and say, their voices leaden with gravity, *sorry you have to do this*. Fifteen years ago, the American war in Việt Nam was in the past, too far behind us to be real anymore. My young college classmates saw my interest in Việt Nam as a relic of something they could barely comprehend, having no direct memory of that era themselves. And the other veterans' kids sometimes quietly thanked me for the work, but no one lingered to engage it.

As I neared graduation I realized that this project would be an unwieldy way to introduce myself to potential employers in Seattle, where I would soon move. I feared if they knew too much about this project, they wouldn't know what to do with my work's emphasis on war or even with my own personal connection to war, as the daughter of a refugee from Việt Nam and an American civilian contractor working in Việt Nam after the withdrawal of U.S. troops, who evacuated together during the Fall of Sài Gòn. Raised also by my stepfather, the six-year U.S. Army combat helicopter pilot in Việt Nam and Cambodia, war was never something "left behind" in another land and in another time. War literally came home to roost, with maps of bombing missions and arrogantly armed intentions to "save" Việt Nam coming to life and argued beneath our patterned plates at the dinner table, at the family altar, in our nightmares. My close friends knew about this upbringing. Yet at age 24, I was new at navigating the tensions between private withholding and public revelation. As I relayed an "inedible" story about the reverberations of war, while screening my film *Spoils* the spring of 2000, I asked my audience about the transmission of such life histories~ "where does it go when it leaves you? Who~what~happens to it?"

Within a couple of months of making my video diary *Spoils*, I sensed that my deep connection to war, and interest in Việt Nam, could be a potential liability as I searched for a job as a new college graduate. So in my cover letter and resume, I didn't go into the content of my recent work but emphasized those skills and techniques I'd learned in the film/video program at Evergreen. I left out that emphasis on Việt Nam, on war, to be more marketable to employers, as entry-level film and video jobs were hard to come by in Seattle. I approached this dilemma not just as a new college graduate, but as someone accustomed to having my body and life history sometimes "read" by others in invasive and condescending ways, so it seemed that the less potential employers knew about my personal background and connection to Việt Nam, the better.

After cutting negative for a while~real negative, on a hot press bench with cement~and after doing some production assistance for a music video company, I finally found a job as a stock footage librarian in a documentary production company in north Seattle. I quickly began editing video, though, without being paid for that part of my job description. They'd call themselves makers of "natural history documentaries," and their many state and national park documentaries attested to that. Yet their documentaries about some of those state and national parks also addressed the Native American inhabitants of that land in the most exoticizing and demeaning way possible. As it turns out, the company made most of their money off these sorts of "Indian" documentaries. All my training in school on reflexive ethnography~on the ethics of documentary~had preemptively critiqued the very work I would be doing the next year. And as a co-creator of these images, I felt complicit in their offensiveness, which stirred a moral conflict within. It was difficult to complain, however, during an economic downturn in the film industry in Seattle, and with so many other college grads searching for work. Since work was so hard to come by, I tried to swallow how it felt to return every morning to those dimly lit and cold editing rooms, doing work I could hardly respect.

Despite the company's stated intentions, cultural sensitivity was in short supply around those parts. While working on a Chaco Canyon project one day, I transferred digital video interviews with Zuni, Hopi, and Pueblo elders. After doing painstaking graphic design reconstructions of Chaco Canyon's most prominent structures, I was excited to finally hear the voices of descendants of the people who had traded in this important prehistoric site in New Mexico. The production company's owner, Gray, complained that I took too long making sure each entire interview had been captured. "You can just cut them off," Gray growled. "It's not like they can answer the question that you ask anyway, without going on and on about nothing." I was stunned that Gray didn't realize that he'd asked them the most problematic questions possible while interviewing them, including, "Do *you* think white people should be allowed in Chaco Canyon?" Sadly, the elders had to talk around the fact that it didn't truly matter what they thought about white folks visiting (or filming) Chaco Canyon–white people had taken over all the sacred sites in Native America, not just this one. They could not reply, *We have no choice, and must pretend to be inclusive of ethnic tourism of our ancestors' architectural wonders and holy places.* Gray retorted and laughed that Native Americans "have pretty much been our problem to begin with." By "our" he meant white America.

In a similar vein, Gray later remarked that "some Indians" had complained because he'd used the same ghost footage of an improperly attired Native American in all of his films. By ghost footage I mean that my boss had asked a Native American man to dress up in the old fashion of his tribe, before filming that man in front of a blue screen. He then had one of his editors remove the blue screen and reduce opacity on the man's footage to turn him into a "ghost." Gray then put that same man digging up something out of the ground in his continuous films, one after the other, no matter which part of the country that man's people were supposed to have lived. The man's translucence–and reduced opacity–made him a ghost image, in film terms, yet I meditated on the double meaning of ghost. He was, in fact, the descendant of people who had been slaughtered during the process of settler colonialism, during the various wars and extermination policies that made "manifest destiny" a cornerstone of European conquest of North America. And yet this man's generic quality and translucent figure as a "ghost" image, in the context of a documentary film, made him part of the cultural imagination which had long failed to distinguish between different Native American peoples, and which failed to see how these "mysterious" peoples' disappearance had *anything* to do with white people.

One day, Gray even tried to convince me to dress up as a Native American woman so he could film me in front of that same blue screen, to make me into a ghost image. My boss intended to have me remove the blue screen and shrink myself down in postproduction, to make myself walk around Chaco Canyon as the impostor ghost of a former inhabitant of the ancient settlement. "Oh, I get it," I replied wryly. "You take someone who is sorta brown and make them small enough, so they look like other sorta brown people." Oblivious to my sarcasm or sense of irony, Gray laughed heartily and said, "I hadn't thought about it that way before, Julie, but I guess you're right!" The next day a cardboard box appeared in the hallway, with the words "INDIAN KIT" writ large in uppercase black block letters. I looked inside to see a burlap sack, a matted and gnarled black wig with a grey stripe–no doubt from a Halloween witch's costume–and a conch shell and various pottery and basketry items, none truly indigenous or even hinting at authenticity. The tattered burlap sack–my "Indian" clothing–was particularly problematic. I held it up, noticing that its prior occupants were potatoes, not Native Americans. Great, I thought. The ethnically indistinct brownish girl gets to reenact the cultural stereotypes of a white man who secretly believes that Native Americans have been "our problem" to begin with, but who actually capitalizes off of the disappearance of these "mysterious" people. And by letting him film me, I would be further complicit in his representational violence. My sarcastic reply must have saved me, however, since he never pushed filming me, even though he brought the costume. I never knew, though, when he would ask again. The "INDIAN KIT" box loomed large in the hallway, threatening me every day.

While I was growing up my refugee mother had always told me that we, the Chăm ethnic minority, are the equivalent in Việt Nam to the Native Americans here. "We were the original inhabitants before the Vietnamese," she had explained. Yet at that job in Seattle, where cultural sensitivity was already in short supply, I'd managed to keep my own identity somewhat vague. Gray and his wife, Dale, the office manager, never asked me much about my life, my studies, or my interests. They knew that my mother was from Việt Nam and my dad was an American man from the United States, but that was about it. Then halfway through my year working at the production company, I'd begun collaborating with a Việt Nam veteran on a documentary project that would bring together Vietnamese and Salvadoran women for postwar reconstruction talks. Finally, I thought, I am returning to the real work. I let my employers know that I would be reducing my hours a bit in order to work on this project. During my last semester in college, that family history documentary had opened up so many unanswered questions for me—about history, about healing—and I was desperate to have these questions addressed by working on relevant films. So I returned to the war work and began conducting interviews with people who might illuminate the conflict in El Salvador, which I knew next to nothing about, at the time. An NPR reporter friend of mine living in Mexico, Gerry Hadden, introduced me by email to someone who'd worked for the Truth Commission for the war in El Salvador, and during one spring weekend I flew stand-by to Mexico City to visit with Gerry and to do further research.

The following Tuesday I was at work again in Seattle, at the production company, where Dale, the office manager, inquired about my trip to Mexico. I told her about the documentary project, bringing together women survivors of the wars in Việt Nam and El Salvador for postwar reconstruction talks. Vaguely bored, she replied, "Exactly how did war affect your family again?" I took a breath, met her gaze, and considered my options. When people ask me a question like this, I have to carefully assess their interest and commitment before responding. Does someone ask such questions to truly understand the situation better? Or to put me on some sort of mental map of scales of victimization and regret? To peg me as a symbol of the failures of U.S. intervention, in a war the U.S. could never proudly claim to have "won"? Yet this woman I worked for was asking how war affected my family. Despite my fears about revealing too much to employers who might not understand, I gave Dale the benefit of the doubt, too generously, it would turn out.

"Well, my mother was the wife and then widow of a commanding officer in the South Vietnamese Army. She was basically in the army herself. She snuck supplies through enemy checkpoints, she identified dead soldiers' bodies, and she eventually brought her husband home as a skeleton after he was killed in action, after thirteen years of marriage. She lived during constant warfare, since she was born during the French Indochina War. She was always under attack, for thirty years. Female family members were also raped during and after war." In the tone perfected from *years* of trying to make my story easier on people, palatable even, to avoid the compassion fatigue of glassy eyes and pat-pat-pat on the arm just before a quick escape, I continued my story as casually as possible. Yet I also told the truth, as had been requested. "Our family was impoverished by constant warfare, and then disrupted by the evacuation. My mother was separated from her eldest children for sixteen years. During that time, one of my sisters was given lethal injection by government doctors, on account of her mixed race identity. And everyone in the family still suffers from PTSD and depression, including secondary trauma to the children born here."

Although I'd tried to keep the story factual and not emotional, Dale stared hard at me, resentment gleaming in her eyes. "Well, Julie. *You're* going to have to remember, if it wasn't for war, *you wouldn't be here.*" Her final four words were heavy with spite and condemnation. In her glare, I was just my mother's daughter, with the U.S. nation-state an unwilling rectifier of the problems associated with spilling not only blood, but also seed, in a quagmire of a nightmare of a memory. In that moment I realized that my boss's wife looked at me and saw bar girls gyrating, U.S. soldiers patronizing prostitutes, the shame of having one's unsolved problems coming home to roost. She didn't even bother finding out how her preconception aligned with my own story, if at all, with that eyebrow-raised smirk, "So, how did your parents *meet?*" She'd already decided against something honorable, even tolerable. In her eyes, I was evidence of unwarranted compassion for my mother and her home country, whose erasure was evident in Dale's words, "if it wasn't for war, you wouldn't be *here.*" Here, here, home of the free and brave, not including us. Apparently, my maternal family and I did not deserve the asylum granted us. Now it was my turn to have glassy eyes. I was too stunned to answer her. I somehow excused myself and escaped back into the cold darkness of the editing suite.

+++

The following day Henry, my half-time coworker, came to the editing suite. Henry was in his 40s, with a cousin who'd been MIA in Việt Nam since during the war. Henry and I had talked before about the war, and we shared a similar political outlook. I sensed he'd have some compassion, so I decided to relay the previous day's discussion with him. "Henry," I whispered, "I have to tell you something, but you can't say anything to anyone." Dale was just down the hall in the front office, and could walk by the postproduction suite at any time. I told the story in hushed tones, in one long breath, hoping to get it all out before she walked past us to hear.

As I told him the previous day's events, I noticed Henry's face getting red. He is naturally quite fair in his complexion, so the crimson hue surprised me. And then he did something which I could have never imagined or predicted. He threw his head back to scream, "Thank god for Henry Kissinger!"

"Shhhhhhhh, Henry!" I whispered fiercely. Yet he put up his finger, interrupting my interruption.

"Thank god for Richard Nixon!" he screamed even more loudly, echoing down the hall, reverberating throughout the production company, past the "INDIAN KIT" box in the hallway. Henry finished with his loudest pronouncement yet. "You wouldn't want to stare the gift horse of WAR in the mouth!"

I felt dizzy, my blood draining, my intestines knotting. But amidst my fear and horror I also realized~with increasing clarity, as the years pass~ that his sarcastic angry protest defended my right to live, as a child of that "contentious" war, in this country. And true to the historical amnesia in the front office, Henry's compassionate insurrectionist outburst was never addressed. The gift horse of war galloped past Dale without even stopping— it was never intended for her, was it? She never confronted me, nor did her husband, over Henry's yelled defense of me. And yet I knew, without a doubt, that this whole episode signaled an end for me at the production company in north Seattle, even more than the "INDIAN KIT" had.

I quit that job within a few months, after saving up enough money to do a postwar study tour throughout Việt Nam, my second trip to my mother's homeland. This journey was my perfect send off–the most fitting way to say farewell to that dimly lit editing suite. On the postwar study tour through Việt Nam, traveling with veterans and protesters and historians, I wasn't a ghost likeness when I knelt in ceremony within a tower in Mỹ Sơn, built by my Chăm ancestors in 200 AD, the longest continuously occupied temple complex in Southeast Asia. That day I promised those ancestors I would never forget that I am still here, despite five hundred years of conquest and assimilation by the Vietnamese who settled the Chăm kingdom, despite a century of warfare in Indochina by colonial French and imperial U.S. powers, despite the postwar displacement of my family, and despite successive houses of amnesia upholding the conqueror's rationale that they had to destroy the entire village in order to "save" it.

Originally published by NAIL magazine

Es Tu Origen/It's Your Origins

Alberto Vajrabukka

Escaping Madrid's sun,
we wander in dim coolness
among the displays of the *museo*
and the smartly-dressed guards

Dark-skinned Santo Niño figurines
watch over silver and turquoise here
from behind alarmed plexiglass sheaths
As indifferent and eerie
as their fairer and dustier twin that is perched
5,000 miles away atop
my Tita's, my compulsive collecting auntie's
walnut veneer console table
standing guard over
The Price Is Right

And the silver goblets and baubles,
they ask if you're a long lost cousin,
also midwifed into the world by raw indio hands
It and the turquoise laugh over this
our chance meeting
so far from Taxco

We rush past the arms and armor
but you point out the high vaulted ceiling
remarking how long it takes
to cross the hall
and how clean the blades look
for a three hundred-year-old sabre

I pose next to some colorful canvas maps
of *California, Nueva España, and Bahia de Manila*
and a guard rushes forward, shaking his head
When you put your camera away

he smiles sincerely
his fricative *gracias*
at once both sexy and funny to us

      Gracias
De Nada ¿De donde sois? Where you guys from?
Asks the PhD student much later at a bar
as he buys us *coronitas*
Broken Spanish from a *mexicano*
and an *asiatico* named Alberto
have piqued this castellano's curiosity
stirred his interest
      We share our trip to *el museo*
We laugh together
and he remarks how he doesn't know
his own history
Smiling, you tell him
      Es tu origen

Alberto Vajrabukka

Ten9Eight

A Breath of Fresh Air   **5April/05**

Tranquil Color

Organic Wood. Origami
Stripe. Hanging Capiz. Ethnic
Flower. A New Warm Finish
For You.

Loose
Hot live
Flesh
Pulsating with
Each sigh rising
From the release
Pulse   Of tendons
Sigh   Ligaments
Ease   Diaphragm
Each   Taking in
The sky and
Let fly
Arrow
Of spine at
My red root
Hunkered
Deep into
The earth
Seated
On a drum
In a fox
Hole at
An opera box
Curtains
Part
Spot
Light
wide
on
the hot   pulse
live   sigh
loose   ease
in   each
side
out

EASY
SPRING
CLEANING

Hot New Products
To Transform
Your House

Do You Mind?

Meditation: A Balancing Act

**You Can Be The
Next Pope**

**Extra: Where Is
Your Durable
Power of Attorney
for Healthcare?**

Joy $US
Peace $CAN
Health Y JPN
Security € EU

Relax! Refresh!

Three Two One. A new bed, love, religion.

My Mother Not My Mother

Kieu Linh Caroline Valverde

My mother did not raise me during my first few years of my life. Though not physically present, she remained central in my thoughts and fantasies of family. One of the earliest memories of my mother was when I was about four or five years old. It took place in the suburbs of Sài Gòn where my grandparents, the people who cared for me from the time I was an infant, decided to retire. It was a stark departure from the downtown Sài Gòn home I grew up in, so much so that I took to calling our new home, "the countryside."

Walking out of my favorite shop in the "countryside" where I could buy Ritz crackers one at a time due to U.S. Army PX spill-out, I thought I saw my mother getting into a black sedan. I ran quickly to the car to catch her, but the car sped off. I didn't stop running though. Maybe the distance was only blocks, but it seemed like miles by the time I realized I could not catch up with the black sedan. In my mind, it was my mother in that car, and she did not stop for me. She intentionally left me.

The odd thing is, I only recognized who I thought to be my mom from photos my grandmother showed me. "This is your mother in the United States... She sent you pretty dresses from there... She loves you very much." So that's how it went—packages from my mother in the United States, pictures of a truly gorgeous woman who rivaled any glamorous movie star. She was a mythical figure, a ghost, a mother I longed to see and know.

When that black sedan rode away, my dreams disappeared. I cannot properly express the hurt and pain associated with the feeling of abandonment that day, but I can say, I truly believed my mother left me—again. By the time the sedan was out of sight, the sting of the loss struck me almost immediately. The grieving lasted seconds, then I quickly told myself, "I no longer have a mother." From that day on, I willed her out of my life. I would still recognize that others would see her as my mother, but I would know in my heart, she already relinquished that right when she drove away. That set the tone for our relationship thereafter—which is not entirely fair to my mother. In the mind of a child though, I needed to build a defense mechanism to safeguard myself.

It would have been like this for a very long time, I think, if it were not for the fact that Sài Gòn was sure to fall, and my mother decided to return from the U.S. to take me out of Việt Nam. It happened quickly. She showed up at my grandparents one day when I was 5 years old. Her visit was brief. Then the next time I remember seeing her was when we left the country together with my new stepfather. We flew to Hong Kong, then visited my stepfather's family in the Philippines before settling in Oakland, California.

I felt excited to travel to so many new places and meet nice new people. It was not until we settled in Oakland that I really became homesick. I missed the tropical weather. I desired the array of fruits that was nowhere to be found in my new home. I longed to be back in Sài Gòn, where the toughest part or the day was having to choose from dozens of noodle dishes or different colored sticky rice for breakfast. Most of all, I missed my grandparents, the only caretakers I really knew. I missed my grandfather's loving embraces after walks to school. I even missed my grandmother's rough handedness when she routinely scrubbed the dirt from my skin.

In place of the familiar stood my mother. We could have not been more different. She was the Southerner that spoke like what my grandmother may have called the fish market lady. Her use of the Vietnamese language was casual, informal, with sprinkles of words I was not allowed to use. Then there was me, the "Northern Princess," which my mom took to calling me to jest, but I never quite got the joke. I insisted on my mom addressing me a certain way, the Northern way, the proper way, the right way. She was not use to a little girl bossing her around. This also set the tone for our relationship until this day.

My mother, still in her mid-twenties when she retrieved me, was not use to having a child tell her how to parent. In general my mother was not use to having a child around. She left me with my paternal grandmother when I was an infant and went on live her life. This thought use to bother me a lot, but then I did not have the full story. I would not have the full story for another thirty years. Those decades in between were filled with much daughter-mother angst. I could not understand her inability to mother, nor her desire to be free, to be free of me. I could not justify the erratic behavior that ended up in thunderous slaps across my face and then blood pouring from my nose. I particularly could not understand how she made up family dynamics and history and insisted and then beat me to play along.

When I learned of the possible reasons why she behaved that way, only more questions arose. My mother was 18 when she met my father. By all accounts, he was the dashing helicopter pilot from a good family and spoke in that alluring Northern accent that made the women swoon. My mother was the gorgeous, free-spirited Eurasian from a working class family. Her beauty was so exceptional that her images adorned all the popular photography shops in town.

It could have been a charming union, except unbeknownst to my mother, my father was a married man with two young kids. So after a period of courtship shrouded in lies and mystery, once revealed, he broke my mother's heart. She quickly found a way to leave town, fearing she could not refuse him if nearby. Smitten, love-struck or in lust, he found her and flew his helicopter there to retrieve her. According to my mother, she lost her virginity to him that night, and I was conceived.

My father was not looking to impregnate his lover and so made an attempt to push my mother to get rid of me. Nothing worked, and I was born nonetheless. That should have been indication that their union was not one of love but something more unromantic. Still, on her end, she was in love. So she continued the affair and became pregnant again. This time, efforts to terminate the pregnancy worked. I often wondered what if I had a brother or sister from my mother and father. Possibly, we could have comforted each other through the trying times. We will never know.

I had a rather odd beginning, even for Vietnamese patriarchal standards. Normally the man would announce to his wife that he has a paramour, and she would be absorbed into his family along with the child. The wife would have no choice but to agree. This would not be the case with me, however. My father's wife refused to be put into that situation. It caused her a mental breakdown but once recovered, she was firm; she would never accept the other woman and the bastard child.

It would have to be my mother to make the tough decision to leave the tragic situation. She broke off the affair. Unable to take me in completely as his child, but also unwilling to let me go entirely, my father convinced my mother to leave me with his mother to care for. He rationalized that my mother was still young, barely out of her teens, and could have a legitimate relationship elsewhere. My mother believed maybe it would be best I was raised in a wealthy and educated household, allotting me a position of social acceptability and opportunities to advance in life. She sadly relinquished me to my father's parents.

This was a great source of sadness for her. She said he told my grandmother this would only be a temporary situation and that some day she would come for me. Weeks thereafter, she would stand across the street looking into my grandparents' home to catch a glimpse of me. Though enjoying her new position as the It Girl in Sài Gòn and flying around her world due to her job with the airlines, she really did believe we would be reunited. When it was certain the country would fall, she came as promised and whisked me off to other country, another home.

I feel for my mother when I hear this story and many more stories expressing her love for me. They are often murky when compared side-by-side with my own experiences with my mother. Though I do not doubt my mother loves me, I also know I was not suppose to be here, in her universe, in her space, in her heart. She often told me that she was entirely too young to have a child, and that why could we not be sisters instead? Naturally, as that little girl perpetually running after my perceived mother in the black sedan, my only thought is, "But I just want a mother."

As it would be between us, we were a mother who loved her child but did not have the capacity for her, and a daughter wanting a mother-a mother her way. Our tragedies are not entirely unique, though admittedly it does have it atypical components. It is difficult to comprehend entirely. But always the sociologist, I have on occasion tried to relate to my mother. No,

I try to really put myself in situations where I am forced to endure or make sacrifices I believe my mother may have had.

Once such incident took place when during on long-term stay in Australia, I was able to meet one of my mother's childhood friends. She relayed to me much of my parents' affair, but what was most intriguing was her relationship with a young boy before my father. Apparently, my mother and Nha Trang's most eligible young bachelor were in puppy love. He came from a distinguished family so when he asked his parents to marry my mother, there was concern. They said she was too beautiful to make a suitable wife, so that proposition ended. They could have easily said she was not from a good family and was a bastard child of a Frenchman as well—which was not entirely correct but probably was more of the perceived truth behind their dismissal than my mother's exceptional beauty.

In thinking about this, I wondered how much family social-economic background makes a difference. Coincidentally at the time, a Vietnamese American professor was pursuing me based solely on my reputation as a scholar and that I was easy on the eyes. I was actually quite put off by him initially. I did not and do not date scholars as a rule, and his stalker-like mode of courting was distasteful. But what caught my interest was the way he stressed his family standing in all our brief conversations. He was puffing his class status to appeal to me. Normally this would repulse me, but with my mother's story fresh in my mind, I allowed this person to pursue me. It ended quite disastrously, not so much because of my mixed class and racial background, but rather because of my perceived politics, of all things.

Possibly because I feel for my mother deeply and want to make sense of her that I go to such extremes and allow myself these social experiments. They are not logical or healthy, but at the time they were opportunities to learn. Possibly I wanted to develop a narrative of my mother's upbringing that could somehow justify how she relates to me so oddly. We really did not have an ideal mother-daughter relationship, whatever that is to mean or look like. Sometimes, it is simply impossible to dig and pry to understand another soul. Maybe it is in the nonsense that all things make some sense.

It is like a dream I once had. I was dying, and my mother was by my side. I asked her with a deep sadness, "Why did you not love me or never were a real mother to me?" She answered, "It is because I am not your real mother. My sister is your real mother." She was referring to the aunt I remembered who always treated me lovingly. With that explanation I felt the skies open up, and I could make sense of the world. A weight was lifted, and I then understood, "But of course, you were never my mother, that is why..." Then I died.

Ethnic Cred

Jane Voodikan

i knew from a young age the simultaneous power and limitation of disadvantage. at the end of a long summer day spent roller-skating with my friend, right before we got back into her house, i fell to the ground, slamming my kneecap against the concrete. i couldn't walk at all–any impact to the joint was excruciatingly painful. that was a friday evening.

when saturday rolled around, i still hadn't recovered enough to walk. i started fantasizing about broken bones and doctors and crutches. battle signs. status signs. it was painful, yes, and it sucked to not be able to get around, but, boy, would it be cool if everyone else knew it too.

it didn't happen. by the time monday rolled around i was able to walk again, and so my injury was all for naught–no cool points gained whatsoever.

majority-minority dynamics mean that, in these days of alleged "multiculturalism" and hating the man, it's not "cool" to be white, which has made me wonder recently, every time my ethnicity is brought up or i clarify that i'm not, in fact, "white," does it mean i'm just grabbing for those cool points again?

depending on where i am the question comes up with more or less frequency, though it happens to be that since i've been in china for the past three years, the fact that "half my blood"[1] is chinese seems to be a point of interest.

now more than ever, i get stuff like this a lot:

you don't look eurasian. you're half-chinese? really? you don't look like it! i thought, maybe, in the eyes. you look eighty percent white and twenty percent chinese. i never would have guessed it!

in fact, during my lifetime, though i've frequently been asked the quintessential "mixed" question–*what are you?*–there have only been a handful of people who have been spot-on about my ethnicity. one was in a crowded nightclub in hong kong.[2] another was a fellow hapa and activist herself, who after 30 minutes of talking to me, suddenly gasped and asked, "are you biracial?" and one was an apparently vagrant woman in a BART station in san francisco who had been talking to herself and then approached me and asked, "are you half-chinese or japanese or something?"

the mixed-race business, for me, extends beyond the appearance-related issues--the questions and the stares when you're in public with the parent whose genes receded in your DNA, the funky hair stuff, the "all mixed-race people are good-looking" myths, but still, the surface seems to be the starting point for all mixed-race discourse.

i am the quintessential "racial spy."[3] i apparently don't "look chinese" (whatever that means), and i wasn't raised speaking chinese, and most people just don't seem to believe i'm really chinese at all, which makes me wonder of myself, am i just a poser out to get some ethnic cred?

at this point, i'm not even sure that i "feel chinese."

here, there is a big distinction between "chinese" and "foreign." that's problematic for those of us who are ethnically or racially chinese but were not born or raised here. sometimes i play my "chinese card" when protesting against the generalizations foreigners make about "chinese." their response is always an attempt to distinguish "chinese" the nationality from "chinese" the ethnicity.

on the other hand, my mother is chinese, as in, was born and raised in china, and though my (white) father, by his own admittance, views her and the rest of us as white, i don't think any amount of fetishizing and as-similating, can completely wash over the impacts of early-age socialization.

the hatred and intolerance goes both ways. when my mother chose to marry my father, her father refused to attend their wedding, so disgusted was he that she would marry out of her race. and so from before i was even born, it was set up that this intermingling was unacceptable. my grandfather did give my siblings and me chinese names at birth, but i never used mine until i came to china. on the other side of my family, it was always my blond-haired, blue-eyed cousins who were the prized grandchildren.

so it's also hard when, from chinese people here, i hear stuff like: nobody would ever consider you chinese.[4]

because that automatically files me into the same category of all the other foreigners here, many of whom are imbibed in what i'd call subtly racist politics or simply haven't been exposed to dealing with cultures other than their own, and i believe a large part of that is rooted in their whiteness and their seeing themselves as completely separate from anything remotely chinese. so when foreigners go on about "the chinese this or chinese that" or when foreign women automatically assume i'm part of their sisterhood and share their rage against chinese women and say things like "us white girls," i take exception. because while i can't say i'm chinese and expect to be taken seriously, i don't feel like i'm "one of us white girls," either.

even on the global stage, where white isn't actually the majority race in terms of numbers, white culture and ideology has managed to posit itself as dominant, a thing to aspire and subscribe to as a norm.

this rage against the whiteness resonates down to my core, down to my very self and family. i have language envy when i meet bilingual hapas or asian americans. okay, admittedly, i could have done more to progress my knowledge of chinese in college, but really, it's still no comparison to speaking a language from childhood. and yeah, my mother doesn't even speak mandarin; she speaks a sub-dialect of cantonese, but this knowledge doesn't comfort me, either, especially when i'm in hong kong or guangdong, surrounded by cantonese speakers, and all i can think about is the only explanation i was given as to why my siblings and i were raised in an english-only household (in the words of my father): "i didn't want to be a foreigner in my own home."

i often wonder how people's perceptions of me here would be different were i a native cantonese speaker instead of merely being able to count to ten and wish somebody good tidings for new year and clamor for a red envelope.

it wasn't always this way. i used to be a staunch defender of the "my race [implying, then, everybody else's, as well] is not a big deal" theory, and had enough attitude to retort "human" when somebody asked "what are you?" but then i had to go and move to china, and that just seemingly opened up a whole can of worms.

we forget often that there aren't these hard lines, that race isn't something that can be fit into those checkboxes. one of the most thought-provoking questions i've been asked about my being in china was whether i felt that having chinese heritage gave me more of a right to be here, a place where many westerners enjoy the economic benefits of the exchange rate and numerous privileges[5] that their foreign passports afford them.

i originally came here as an english teacher, believing that my relevant education, experience, and training earned me a position in the field. but i quickly found most anybody who looks white and holds a passport from an english-speaking country can get a job teaching english here. so do i belong here any more than the rest of them? well, i can't deny that my "whiteness" isn't getting me paid.[6]

but maybe i could say that for me, being here runs deeper than just, at worst, drinking, sleeping around and traveling, and at best seeing and experiencing "another" culture. it is, after all, a culture in which i hold a share of belonging.

i didn't get the crutches. but maybe the ethnic cred is my own to decide upon.

---

1. i don't even know how to describe my "chineseness" accurately and fairly. i feel that no matter how i do it i'll be stepping on somebody's toes who might be more "authentic" than me. is it culture? ethnicity? race? i'm not sure what any of these mean or how they are supposed to manifest themselves in a person. therefore i'm just going to stick with blood, which actually sounds ridiculous to me, but i think is something nobody can really dispute.

on that note, the label "half" is pretty annoying, too. "you're half," one of my (full) chinese-american friends says. as if my incompleteness as chinese extends to my very incompleteness as a person.

2. hong kong, with its chinese roots and past as a british colony, is a world capital of "east-meets-west."

3. "racial spy" is a term i originally heard on new demographic's podcast "addicted to race." it refers to the experience of one's appearances not corresponding to others' expectations of a member of a particular racial group's appearances.

4. translated from my non-native (and probably shitty) mandarin: "are you a chinese person or a foreigner?" "foreigner!" "why don't you have blond hair?" "you really look chinese!"

5. these range from "hard" privileges, like ease of finding a job in certain industries, the most notorious being teaching english, to the "soft," like receiving special treatment from everyone from restaurant owners to governmental authorities because of the perception that foreigners don't understand china.

6. this was the "shocking" revelation that was the title of an article in a feminist publication called *LOUDmouth* in which the author confesses her realization that as a white english teacher in japan, she was inextricably part of the neocolonialist system that heralds english (and, by extension, whiteness) above all else.

The Hapa Hydra

Chloe Worrall Yu and Mylo Worrall Yu

The Hapa Hydra is a hybrid of mythical creatures that come from different cultures that represent all the backgrounds in our lives. We have two blended families. One is our mom who is Vietnamese and Pennsylvania Dutch (German)/Quaker (British)/Scots-Irish and our step-dad who is adopted and is Filipino, Spanish, and Australian (and our little half-sister). The other is our dad who is second-generation Chinese Canadian and our step-mom who is Japanese (and our two little half-sisters). Our lives are like this creature, with all these cultures and stories put together to make us who we are, which is pretty cool.

One head is the Loch Ness Monster, which comes from Scotland. The second head is the Dragon, which appears in Vietnamese, Chinese, Japanese, Filipino, Germanic, English, and Welsh myths. "Dragon" is the translation of Mylo's Chinese-Vietnamese name. The last head is a Sarangay, which is like a Filipino Minotaur.

The body of our hapa creature is the Phoenix, which is in a lot of mythologies. Chloe's Chinese-Vietnamese name translates as "Phoenix."

Finally, the tails are from Kitsune, a mythical fox in Japan.

We like our mythical creature because it has so many abilities and comes from lots of places, like we do.

We think you should make your own hapa mythical creature too!

Ingredients of Contents

Ethelyn Abellanosa is a sometime artist, writer and crafter whose work explores her identity as a mixed Asian American woman dealing with size/weight obsession. In her professional life, she's worked for several museums in arts administration and operations and has served as a Seattle Arts Commissioner. Her volunteer work includes curating and promoting artists of color.

Neil Aitken is the author of *The Lost Country of Sight*, winner of the 2007 Philip Levine Prize for Poetry, and founding editor of Boxcar Poetry Review. Of Chinese and Scottish-English descent, he was born in Vancouver, BC and has lived in Saudi Arabia, Taiwan, and various parts of western Canada and the United States. His poems have appeared in *American Literary Review*, *The Collagist*, *Crab Orchard Review*, *Ninth Letter*, *The Normal School*, and elsewhere. A former computer programmer and a Kundiman fellow, he is presently completing his PhD in Literature and Creative Writing at the University of Southern California. His current manuscript, *Babbage's Dream*, recently placed as a semi-finalist for the Anthony Hecht Prize and his chapbook, *Leviathan*, will be published by Hyacinth Girl Press. www.neil-aitken.com

Kevin Minh Allen was born Nguyễn Đức Minh on December 5, 1973 near Sài Gòn, Việt Nam to a Vietnamese mother and American father who remain unknown to him. He was adopted by a couple from Rochester, NY and grew up in Webster, NY with his two younger sisters. In 2000, he moved to Seattle, WA to pursue a life less ordinary. Kevin is a poet and essayist who has had his essays and poetry published in numerous print and online publications, such as *Eye To The Telescope*, *The International Examiner*, and *Northwest Asian Weekly*. He had his first poetry chapbook published in July 2014, *My Proud Sacrifice*. http://myproudsacrifice.tumblr.com/

James Lawrence Ardeña has been in arts organizing with isangmahal arts kollective, LA Enkanto Kollective & Mixt Up Productions. Originally a spoken word artist and poet, he still dabbles in the visual realm of cultural critique via mixed media resin assemblages. His current creative pursuits include gardening, foraging, fungi, and being an uncle. He manages the Multicultural Center at Shoreline Community College and is on the Board of the Puget Sound Mycological Society (PSMS). He is one of the original editors of the Mixed Up Trilogy of chapbooks in which he & Brandy hand-sewn over 700 chapbooks while bleeding for art just a wee bit.

Sandy Sue Benitez is the founder & editor of *Poppy Road Review*, *Black Poppy Review*, and *Flutter Press*. Her latest chapbook, *The Lilac City*, was published by Origami Poems Project. Sandy's most recent work has been published in *The Artistic Muse: Pohemians*, *Houseboat*, *The Missing of the Birds*, *The Kentucky Review*, and *The Blue Hour*. She's been nominated for the Pushcart, Best of the Web, and Best of the Net. Sandy resides in Southern California with her husband and two children.

Tamiko Beyer is the author of *We Come Elemental* (Alice James Books, 2013) and *bough breaks* (Meritage Press, 2011). Her poems have been published or are forthcoming in *The Volta*, *Tupelo Quarterly*, *Quarterly West*, and elsewhere. She is the Deputy Communication Director at Corporate Accountability International where she harnesses the written word to challenge some of the most powerful and abusive corporations in the world. She lives in Dorchester, next to the Neponset River, in a former chocolate factory. Find her online at tamikobeyer.com.

Sumiko Braun is a Los Angeles-based poet, writer, filmmaker, performing artist, scholar, and community advocate. She is a UCLA graduate student pursuing a Master's degree in Asian American Studies. Her "in between" perspective and experience as a class-shifting queer mixed race womyn of color and single mother drives much of her work. Inspired by the power and radical ability to transform culture and society through storytelling and art, Sumiko is oddly best known for her acting role in the sci-fi cult classic *Sharknado*.

Leilani Chan is an award-winning performance artist, actor, playwright, director, cultural worker, and Founding Artistic Director of TeAda Productions. TeAda Productions exists to enrich the repertoire of contemporary works created and performed by people of color. Leilani and her partner, Ova Saopeng, are currently traveling the country developing *Refugee Nation*, a multi-disciplinary performance based on the stories of Laotian refugees and their descendants from around the country. This project received a Rockefeller Foundation MAP Fund and a NPN Creation Fund in partnership with OUTNORTH, Highways Performance Space and *Legacies of War*, an education and advocacy group around the removal of UXOs from Laos. Leilani is a Department of Cultural Affairs Artist-in-Residence and has toured nationally with her solo work "E Nana I ke Kumu." Her performance installation "Life as a Dashboard Hula Dancer" has been presented as part of Guillermo Gomez-Peña's La Pocha Nostra at LACMA in 2005 and FITLA 2004. Ms. Chan has worked with Hawaiian and multi-racial communities to develop community-based performances and has she been presented at Borderlands Theater, Highways Performance Space, JACCC, Grand Performances, the Getty Center Museum, and at many other college campuses and performance venues across the country. Leilani has directed new works by Robert Karimi at Out North in Anchorage, Alaska and Kristina Wong at REDCAT, [INSIDE] the Ford, and at La Peña Cultural Center. Ms. Chan has also worked with numerous arts organizations throughout the country including Center Theatre Group, New WORLD Theater, Great Leap, Highways Performance Space and many others. Leilani obtained her MFA from U.C. Irvine in 2004. Ms. Chan is on the national steering committee for the National Asian American Theater Conference and Festival and for *Legacies of War*.

Tricia Collins is a director, actress and screenwriter. She was selected to participate in the Bell Media and WGC Diverse Screenwriter's program and holds a Master of Arts from Ryerson University's RTA School of Media. *Reach*, a short film inspired by her late father's receding memories, has screened at the WIFT International Showcase, Vancouver International Women's Film Festival, the Vancouver Asian Film Festival, LabCab Festival, the Female Eye Film Festival and the NSI online Film Festival. Her one-woman play *Gravity* has toured internationally to Trinidad and opened Carifesta the Caribbean Festival of the Arts in Guyana, garnering high acclaim. In 2006 her magic realist play *Dreaming Elevators* was produced by La Luna Productions and was directed by the late and great Lorena Gale. As an actress Tricia has had numerous lead acting roles on stage and screen. Ms. Collins has been a theatre and multi-disciplinary artist in Vancouver since graduating with a BFA in theatre from Simon Fraser University. She is also the project director for #HerDigitalVisions, a social/digital media production program for girls facing cyberbullying.

A San Franciscan born in Australia, Wei Ming Dariotis is an Associate Professor of Asian American Studies, with an emphasis on Asian Americans and Chinese Americans of Mixed Heritage and Asian American and Chinese American Literature, Arts, and Culture, at San Francisco State University. With Laura Kina and Camilla Fojas, she co-coordinated the Inaugural Critical Mixed Race Studies Conference, at De Paul University, 2010. Wei Ming Dariotis co-edited, with Laura Kina, *War Baby/Love Child: Mixed Race Asian American Art*, an art exhibit (De Paul University Art Museum, Chicago, & Wing Luke Museum of the Asian Experience, Seattle) and a related book (University of Washington Press, 2013). She is the Special Guest Editor of the 2012 issue of *Asian American Literatures: Discourses and Pedagogies*, on Mixed Heritage Asian American Literature, and contributed poetry, written with

Isabelle Thuy Pelaud, to the *Asian American Literary Review Special Issue on Mixed Race* (Fall 2013). Her poetry has been published in *Mixed Up*, *580 Split*, and *Yellow as Turmeric, Fragrant as Cloves: A Contemporary Anthology of Asian American Women's Poetry*, and exhibited at the Asian American Women Artist show, "Hungry Ghost" (2012).

Melinda Luisa de Jesús is Chair and Associate Professor of Diversity Studies at California College of the Arts. She writes and teaches about Asian American cultural production, Filipina/o American culture, youth and pop cultures, monsters, and race/ethnicity in the United States. In 2011-12 she was the Fulbright Visiting Scholar at the Centre for Women's Studies, University of York, UK, where she convened the international conference, After Girl Power: What's Next? in February 2012. She edited *Pinay Power: Peminist Critical Theory, the first anthology of Filipina/American feminisms* (Routledge 2005). Her writing has appeared in *Approaches to Teaching Multicultural Comics*; *Ethnic Literary Traditions in Children's Literature*; *Challenging Homophobia*; *The Lion and the Unicorn*; *Meridians*; *MELUS*; *Radical Teacher*; *The Journal of Asian American Studies*; and *Delinquents and Debutantes: Twentieth Century American Girls' Culture*. She is a mezzo-soprano, a mom, an Aquarian, and admits an obsession with Hello Kitty.

Alison M. De La Cruz is a theater maker, cultural producer, facilitator, writer and community-centered dramaturge living in Los Angeles, CA. SUNGKA was Alison's first solo theatrical work, produced by the Japanese American Cultural and Community Center in April 2000 as part of the JACCC's FRESH TRACK Series and produced at East West Players' David Henry Hwang Theater. SUNGKA sold out and a second late night show was added. In the 15 years since SUNGKA first premiered, De La Cruz has been busy. Read more about her at www.alisonmdelacruz.blogspot.com or tweet her at TweetsbyDeLa.

Cheryl Deptowicz-Diaz was transplanted at age eight from Manila, Philippines into FilipinoTown, Los Angeles, California. She was active in the political social movement from 1994 to 2004. She became a California-licensed attorney in 2007, representing those marginalized by the legal system. Her poems are mere rearrangements of diary entries, fears, and dreams, written to make sense of her place in society, heal pains, and honor memories. She lives in Southern California with her husband and Mexi-Pino son.

Lance Dougherty is a graduate of California State University Northridge with a degree in Sociology and a minor in Asian American Studies. His father was an Irish Navy man from Rhode Island, and his mother from the small island province of Capul, Philippines. He grew up in Stockton, California and still calls it his home even though he now lives and works in Las Vegas.

Andrea Duke was born and raised in Vancouver, B.C. She holds a Bachelor's of Science in Biology and Psychology at the University of Victoria. Her mother's grandparents immigrated to Canada from China, while her father's parents immigrated to Canada from England and Scotland. Most recently Andrea has lived and worked in Rio de Janeiro and Toronto. She is always on the move and still considers Vancouver home.

Dr. Angela "El Dia" Martinez Dy is a mestiza Pilipina American poet + writer, student, educator, and hip-hop femmecee. An original member of isangmahal arts kollective, seminal voice of the millennial Asian American spoken word and performance movement, she later co-founded Youth Speaks Seattle, serving as director from 2005-2009. Angela is the co-creator of Sisters of Resistance, an anti-imperialist pro-vegan radical feminist grime and hip-hop blog serving intersectional feminist insight to more than 20,000 visitors worldwide per month (www.sistersofresistance.org). Born and raised in Seattle with her heart in Manila, she lives in England and has a PhD from Nottingham University on intersectionality and digital entrepreneurship. She is continually developing individual and collaborative projects with an international network. Connect with her on Twitter: @eldiadia.

Hillary LP Eason lives and writes in Washington, DC.

Sesshu Foster has taught composition and literature in East L.A. for 30 years. He's also taught writing at the University of Iowa, the California Institute for the Arts, the Jack Kerouac School of Disembodied Poetics and the University of California, Santa Cruz. His work has been published in *The Oxford Anthology of Modern American Poetry*, *Language for a New Century: Poetry from the Middle East, Asia and Beyond*, and *State of the Union: 50 Political Poems*. Local readings are archived at www.sicklyseason.com. He collaborates with artist Arturo Romo-Santillano and other writers on the website, www.ELAguide.org. His most recent books are the novel *Atomik Aztex*, winner of the Believer Magazine Award, and the hybrid text *World Ball Notebook*, winner of the American Book Award.

Margaret Gallagher lives in Vancouver where she spends most of her time making radio at CBC, raising her delightful daughter, and (when time allows) obsessing about cooking. She considers herself half Indonesian-Chinese, half Irish-American, and completely Canadian. She hopes to one day master the art of Indonesian cooking, and to keep her house tidy.

Shamala Gallagher is the author of a chapbook, *I Learned the Language of Barbs and Sparks No One Spoke* (dancing girl press, forthcoming 2015). Her poems and essays have appeared or are forthcoming in *Black Warrior Review*, *VOLT*, *Verse Daily*, *Copper Nickel*, *Multi-Ethnic Literature of the United States*, and elsewhere. Shamala was born in San Jose, California to a South Indian mother and an Irish-American father. She received her MFA from the Michener Center for Writers at the University of Texas-Austin and now lives in Athens, Georgia, where she is pursuing a PhD in English and Creative Writing at the University of Georgia.

John Endo Greenaway is a self-described hapa-sansei who lives and works in the Metro Vancouver area. Born in London, England to a Japanese Canadian mother and an English/Irish Canadian father, he has spent the last 55 years trying to figure out where he fits in. He will let you know when he does. In the meantime, he toils in the cultural mines as a graphic designer and as managing editor of *The Bulletin*, a job for which he holds no qualifications whatsoever. Nevertheless he has held the position for over twenty years. And there's more... As a founding member of Katari Taiko, Canada's first taiko group, John has spent the past 35 years exploring this Japanese-inspired but uniquely Asian Canadian art form. He currently is a member of Sansho Daiko, which allows him to wield very large sticks in the name of art.

Hazel H. Hill is chillin', looking for good coffee, and trying to grow her 'fro. Peace.

Jason Kanjiro Howard is Japanese Irish American financial advisor, filmmaker, and a die-hard SF sports fan. He has over 22 years experience in the financial services industry by helping families and individuals with free, comprehensive financial plans. His office is in West Los Angeles. As a filmmaker, he finds financing for films as an executive producer. His dramedy entitled *I'll See You in My Dreams* premiered at the Sundance Film Festival on January 27th 2015 and will be in 15 cities across the country on May 2015. He is also the EP for the horror film called *The Rake*, which will begin shooting in Chicago in 2015. He is also producing a documentary about the band Sublime and Slightly Stoopid.

Born and raised in Los Angeles, Catherine Irwin is a Filipino-Irish-Chinese American poet and literature geek. She is so excited to be part of a hapa line-up of writers. Currently, she is an Associate Professor of English at the University of La Verne and lives with her husband and daughter in Claremont, CA. She can be reached at tirwin@laverne.edu.

Michelle Tang Jackson is a hapa writer and performance artist. She currently resides in Washington, DC, where she is a theater-maker and teaching artist. She believes in the disarming power of comedy, em dashes, and making the art you want to see in the world. She shares her work at www.maketheartyouwant.com.

Sherlyn Jimenez remains in awe of trees and plants. You'll find her with her hands in the soil growing things. Her memories are invariably connected to food.

Dr. Peter Nien-chu Kiang (江念祖) is Professor of Education and Director of the Asian American Studies Program at the University of Massachusetts Boston where he has taught since 1987. Peter's research, teaching, and advocacy in both K-12 and higher education with Asian American immigrant/refugee students and communities have been supported by the National Academy of Education, the National Endowment for the Humanities, the Massachusetts Teachers Association, the Massachusetts Association for Bilingual Education, and others. At UMass Boston, he has received both the Chancellor's Distinguished Teaching Award and Distinguished Service Award. Nationally, he received the Distinguished Scholar Award from the American Educational Research Association's Special Interest Group: Research on the Education of Asian and Pacific Americans in 2013 and the Lifetime Achievement Award from the National Association for Asian American Studies in 2014. Peter served for six years as chair of the Massachusetts Advisory Committee for the U.S. Commission on Civil Rights and eight years as co-president of the Chinese Historical Society of New England. He holds a BA, EdM, and EdD from Harvard University and is a former Community Fellow in the Department of Urban Studies and Planning at MIT. He is mixed-race Chinese and Scottish American, born in Boston.

Daniel Takeshi Krause's work has appeared in two languages, three countries, and four dimensions. His work has been performed or printed most recently in *Versal*; at The Banff Center in Alberta, Canada; in *A Bad Penny Review*; and *Sugar House*

Review. He completed his PhD in Literature and Creative Writing at the University of Utah. He currently lives and teaches in Southern California.

Noemi LaMotte-Serrano does not write nearly as often as she should. She grew up in the city and is trying to figure out how to raise two boys and three pitbulls in suburbia. She subsidizes this existence with a very boring corporate job, which requires she cover her tattoos and attend meetings where people say things like "root cause analysis" and "strategic metrics" while she Googles "bukowski quotes." She is embarrassed to know too many people who use "your" instead of "you're." She likes lifting heavy shit and having bigger muscles than people who bore her. Her favorite compliment was once being called disarming. When she does make time to write, she does it here: https://whatbeautifuldisaster.wordpress.com

Claire Light is a Bay Area writer and cultural worker. She has worked for 18 years in nonprofit administration, particularly arts in the Asian American community. Her MFA in fiction came from San Francisco State University, and some of her fiction is published in *McSweeney's*, *Hyphen*, *Farthing*, and *The Encyclopedia Project*. A short collection of her short stories, called *SLIGHTLY BEHIND AND TO THE LEFT*, was published by Aqueduct Press in 2009. She has taught writing to teens, college students, and adults, and occasionally blogs for no one's edification but her own.

Marjorie Light, aka Gingee, is a Los Angeles native whose artistic journey has taken her from spoken word poetry and publishing her own zine, to DJing, producing and solo musical performance. DJing and producing since 2003, she is known for her unique take on electronic music, which blends elements of global bass, world music, and hip hop, combining ancient influences and modern sounds into her own style.

Cassandra Love's first book of poetry, *Swagger is a Woman*, is available through Mouthfeel Press. She was a 2008 PEN USA Emerging Voices Fellow and her poems have been featured in journals and anthologies, some of which include: *Forth Magazine*, *Haight Ashbury Literary Journal*, and *Mezcla*. She also hosted the radio show "For the Love of Poetry" on BlogTalkRadio. Cassandra studied literature and played basketball at Yale. With a mother who emigrated to LA from Manila, and a father from North Dakota, Cassandra finds truth in fluidity, ambiguity, and the space between spaces. She lives with her two children and fiancee in Los Angeles.

Pia Massie is a multi-media artist whose work has been exhibited in festivals, museums and galleries throughout North America and Europe, including the Museum of Modern Art, NYC; Musée Cantonal des Beaux Arts, Lausanne; and the grunt gallery in Vancouver, BC. Her work has received multiple awards, including the American Film Institute's Independent Filmmakers award (LA), Prix St. Gervais (Geneva) and Prix de l'Institut de Design de Montréal. Massie's projects have been funded by grants from the Canada Council, BC Arts Council, the National Film Board, the Mass Council on Arts & Humanities and the Rockefeller Foundation among others. Her writing has appeared in *Ricepaper* magazine, *Adbusters*, and *DAMP*, an Anvil Press book.

Kelty is a landscape architect and Partner at PFS Studio where she specializes in projects dealing with the public realm and public art both locally and internationally. Her project work includes the West Don Lands Public Realm Strategy, Lower Don Lands, Gardiner Expressway and Harbourfront Competitions in Toronto; Lansdowne Park in Ottawa; and Blue Mountain Central Park and Sun Palace Venus and Mercury in China. Kelty was the editor of PFS's recent monograph, *Grounded*, and has written on diverse topics all related to the production of emergent landscapes that engage cultural and environmental ecologies. Her writing has dealt with issues ranging from hefted sheep and animal urbanism to invasive plants in public policy. Her landscape architectural and artistic work has been exhibited in Vienna, Berlin, New York, London, Montreal, Toronto, Vancouver, Seattle, and Minneapolis.

Trina Mendiola Estanislao has been a Special Education teacher for the last eleven years. She specializes in helping eighth graders figure out Young Adult Fiction is cool beans, but mostly she is the mom to a Minecraft-crazed five-year-old and a ten-month-old who is all slobber and sweetness. She dreams of finding the time to write again, even if it's somewhere in between soccer practice, Science Fair projects, and blowing raspberries on aforementioned slobbery sweet child.

Rashaan Alexis Meneses has received fellowships at The MacDowell Colony, The International Retreat for Writers at Hawthornden Castle, Scotland, and is a past recipient of the Jacob K. Javits Award. With work forthcoming in *Kartika Review* and *BorderSenses*, her writing has been featured in *New Letters*, *Kurungabaa*, *The Coachella Review*, *Pembroke Magazine*, *Doveglion Press*, and the anthology *Growing Up Filipino II: More Stories for Young Adults*. Named a finalist for A Room of Her Own Foundation's The Gift of Freedom Award and the Sundress Best of the Net Prize, she teaches as Adjunct Assistant Professor for Justice, Community and Leadership at Saint Mary's College of California. Bay Area-based, you can find her hiking the trails and paddling the waters any chance she can get. http://rashaanalexismeneses.com/

Dorian Sanae Merina is a poet, journalist and educator. He's the author of two books of poetry, *The Changegiver* and *Stone of the Fish* (Rosela Press), and a spoken word album, *Heaven is a Second Language*, a collaboration with DJ Highend. He composed and performed the poetry for the short film, *Migrations*, which won the 2008 Poetry Foundation Award. As a journalist, he's reported from the Philippines, Indonesia, Thailand, New York, and Los Angeles on many issues, including immigration, climate change, religious conflict, farm labor, and World Cup soccer. Currently, he's working to document and preserve the indigenous oral poetry, called Laji, on his family's ancestral islands in the Philippines, through film, audio and translations.

Shyamala Moorty is a founding member of the Post Natyam Collective and a CORE artist with TeAda productions, where she combines her backgrounds in Indian and western dance, theater, and yoga to create transformative performance works. Acclaimed as a "tour de force" by the *Los Angeles Times*, Shyamala has toured her solo and collaborative work across the U.S. as well as to Canada, Europe, and India. Her performance work is featured in the seminal books *Desi Divas: Political Activism in South Asian American Cultural Performances* (2013) and *Contemporary Indian Dance* (2011). An MFA graduate from UCLA's World Arts and Cultures program, Shyamala trained in the classical Indian dance form Bharata Natyam, under Medha Yodh and Malathi Iyengar. She performed Indian folk and classical dances for ten years as a member of Iyengar's Rangoli Dance Company and for seven years as a soloist and principal dancer with the Aman International Music and Dance Ensemble. Shyamala currently is an Adjunct Faculty at West LA College and a teaching and performing artist with the AMAN Dance Educators. She is touring "Super Ruwaxi: Origins," a live comic book story about queerness and the immigrant experience, and "Stories...On the MOVE!" a fun for families exploration of Indian mythology and its connections to the world today. She is a resident of Long Beach and is a two-time recipient of the Long Beach Professional Artist's Fellowship. For more information visit www.postnatyam.net and www.dancingstorytellers.com.

Stephen Murphy-Shigematsu is a psychologist at Stanford University and author of *When Half is Whole: Multiethnic Asian American Identities*.

Mark Nakada is an americanadian, Okinawan, Danish, sansei teacher and writer based in Vancouver. He is now working on his 75th anniversary Spam collection.

Lynda Nakashima is a visual artist whose work includes drawing, block printing, video, and animation.

Victoria Namkung has written for the *Los Angeles Times*, *USA Today*, *The Huffington Post* and *Los Angeles*, among others. She earned her Master's degree in Asian American Studies from UCLA and appears in Mike Epps's AOL Originals series, *That's Racist*. As a commentator, she has been featured in the *Wall Street Journal*, *TIME*, and the *Chicago Tribune*. She lives in Los Angeles and is the author of the forthcoming novel, *The Things We Tell Ourselves*.

Debora O is a mixed race writer and educator who lives in Vancouver, Canada with her lovely hapa partner and their "hapa squared" daughter. Her family hails from two peninsular countries—Portugal and Macau. The draw of the briny estuaries and the lull of the ocean currents will always keep her close to the shores of any country. Debora is also a lover of scuba diving, snorkeling, and frolicking in the surf. Meditation and yoga come a close second.

Genevieve Erin O'Brien is a Queer Vietnamese/Irish/American artist, culinary adventurer, community organizer, and educator. O'Brien lives and works in Los Angeles and Ho Chi Minh City, Vietnam. She holds an MFA in Performance from the School of the Art Institute of Chicago. In 2009 O'Brien was a Fulbright Fellow in Vietnam. O'Brien uses performance, video and installation to explore notions of "home" and "homeland." Her conceptual and durational performances, one-woman shows, as well as installations and videos, have been presented at galleries and public venues both nationally and internationally. O'Brien is a 2014 Armed With A Camera fellow awarded by Visual Communications in Los Angeles. Her most recent short film, *For The Love of Unicorns*, is currently making the rounds to a film festival near you. O'Brien was an artist in residence at "Thank You For Coming," a Los Angeles experimental food and art gallery, and a commissioned artist for the Los Angeles Music Center "2014 Encounters." She is lecturer in Asian American Studies at Claremont Colleges, UC Irvine, and UC Santa Barbara. She believes in unicorns and also loves noodles and dumplings. www.erin-obrien.com

Haruko Okano is a Japanese-Canadian interdisciplinary artist who was raised from a young age through the Caucasian foster care system in Ontario. She lost her mother tongue and contact with other Japanese Canadians until late into her teenage years. She considers herself a cultural hybrid. While one foot is firmly planted in the dominant society, her other is lightly placed within the Japanese Canadian community. Born in Toronto, Ontario she moved back to Vancouver in the early 1970s in search of Japantown, her cultural community which had become physically invisible, her people scattered and assimilated into the social fabric of Canada. A political activist, advocate for the arts and human rights, she spends much of her time shaping her lifestyle in harmony with the sustainable principles of a healthier earth.

Matthew Olzmann is the author of *Mezzanines* (Alice James Books 2013), which was selected for the Kundiman Prize. His writing has appeared in *Kenyon Review*, *Brevity*, *New England Review*, *Poetry Northwest*, *Gulf Coast*, *The Southern Review*, and elsewhere. He's received fellowships and scholarships from the Kresge Arts Foundation, The Bread Loaf Writers' Conference, and Kundiman.

Giovanni Ortega wrote *ALLOS: The Story of Carlos Bulosan* and *Crier for Hire: Iyakan Blues*, which was commissioned by East West Players Theatre Co. He has performed and spoken at over 300 organizations, universities, and prisons in North America with various one-person shows, including *Playfair*. In 2013 he took the literary artist category for FPAC Pahayag Project with *Leaves from the Silverlake Barrio*. Giovanni is also a Visiting Assistant Professor in Pomona College. His new play, *Tug of War*, will premiere in Chicago for CIRCA Pintig this May 2015. For more info go to www.giovanniortega.com

Taro O'Sullivan is currently the Executive Director of the Labor Community Services, where he leads the non-profit services for the Los Angeles County Federation of Labor, AFL-CIO. Prior to his work in Los Angeles, he brings nearly 20 years of work in the non-profit and labor sector as a political advocate, diversity trainer, columnist and author. After working on the Gore/Lieberman campaign, Taro took his three children and left the United States for Canada where he remained for nearly ten years. There, he was the executive director of the Service Employees International Union, Canada. He was also the Executive Director of ASIA, the Asian Society for the Intervention of AIDS in Vancouver, British Columbia. He served on the Board of Directors of the Asian Heritage Month Society, the Japanese Canadian Citizens Association; the Asian Writer's Workshop and served on the city of Vancouver Mayor's Special Advisory Committee on Diversity Issues. Some of his public appearances include keynote speech at the 60th Anniversary of Executive Order 9066, which imprisoned over 120,000 persons of Japanese ancestry during WWII at Manzanar Relocation Center in the California Mojave desert, keynote speaker for the 58th Hiroshima-Nagasaki Commemoration for the Physicians for Social Responsibility, Dialogue for Peace, Oct 2001 with panels from the Muslim leadership and Japanese American internment survivors regarding 9-11 and Islamaphobia. Taro wrote a weekly column for nine years for the *Asian Reporter* and other ethnic papers including the *Rafu Shimpo*, the oldest ethnic daily in the country published in Los Angeles. Taro was born and raised in Tokyo, Japan. He is fluent in Japanese. He now lives in Los Angeles.

Tony Osumi is a Hapa Yonsei who lives in Culver City, CA with his family. He teaches 3rd grade and in the summer is active with Camp Musubi, a Japanese American heritage camp based in Little Tokyo. More of his writing and artwork can be seen at www.kuidaosumi.com.

Stevii Paden earned her undergraduate degree in history with concentrations on the Vietnam War and religious studies. She currently works in Data Management Services at Penguin Random House. Somewhat of a crazy plant lady, she spends a lot of time fussing over each of her named succulents. In addition to her plants, Stevii enjoys caring for her animals, Scrambles and Sybil, and her boyfriend and their house. When she isn't busy fussing, you can find Stevii trying to enjoy the great outdoors, running on her favorite trails, climbing, or on rare occasions, crocheting a never-ending blanket.

Sandra Mizumoto Posey has been writing and performing since the early 1990s. She is currently single, living in Denver, and working as an Associate Professor of Women's Studies at Metropolitan State University of Denver. At any given moment, you can find her pining for any number of things, for example: a date that doesn't suck (gender TBD), a publication they will let her use in her promotion dossier, a better mood, and a good middle school for her daughter. If you know how she can attain any of these things, let her know.

Amal Rana is a queer, mixed race, Pakistani Interdisciplinary Poet and Arts Educator born in Jeddah. She currently lives in Vancouver, Unceded Coast Salish

Territories. She is an alum of the VONA Writers of Colour Residency and Banff Centre Spoken Word Program. Her work has been published or is forthcoming in numerous anthologies and journals including *Adrienne: A Poetry Journal Of Queer Women*, *Writing the Walls Down: A Convergence of LGBTQ Voices*, *Your Voice Tastes Like Home: Immigrant Women Write*, *Plentitude Magazine* and online platforms such as *The Feminist Wire* and *Love Inshallah*. She has presented and performed in various cities in Canada and the United States. In a time when even exhaling while being Muslim seems to have become a crime, she sees poetry as an act of sedition and collective resistance. She is the producer/host of Bolo Azadi, a radio project featuring Queer and Trans Indigenous Artists and Artists of Colour (QTIPOC). She recently co-founded Just Write, a monthly writing space for QTIPOC writers, and facilitated the first free queer and trans youth writing workshop series in the Vancouver. She continues to work with others in the community to curate arts events centering voices of marginalized artists. rosewaterpoet.com.

Actress-writer-producer Mia Riverton made her feature debut with the critically acclaimed and award-winning film *Red Doors*. A singer-songwriter since childhood, Mia wrote and performed songs for the film's soundtrack. She also co-created a TV pilot for CBS based on *Red Doors*. More recently, she produced and co-starred in independent film *Capture for Circle of Confusion* with director Georgia Lee. Other feature film roles as an actress include *Spare Parts* with George Lopez and Jamie Lee Curtis, *4 Wedding Planners* with Illeana Douglas, *Open House* with Anna Paquin, and *CEO*, by acclaimed Chinese director Wu Tian-Ming. TV roles include *The Mentalist*, *Leverage*, *Curb Your Enthusiasm*, *Big Time Rush*, *Miami Medical*, *One on One* and *Strong Medicine*. A musical theater buff, Mia has also performed in numerous plays and musicals around the country. Originally from Indianapolis, Mia is the product of a Chinese tiger mom and a Kansas half-cowboy-half-American-Indian dad. Class valedictorian as well as captain of her varsity cheerleading and dance team, she was honored as a Presidential Scholar in her senior year. She graduated *cum laude* and Phi Beta Kappa from Harvard University, and she is Founder and President of the Harvardwood alumni arts organization. https://twitter.com/#!/motherhoodisms

Tony Robles is an housing activist and co-editor of *POOR Magazine*, a poor-people led, indigenous people led media organization. Tony is the nephew of legendary poet Al Robles and the current board president of Manilatown Heritage Foundation. He is the author of the book, *Cool Don't Live Here No More-A Letter to San*

Francisco, published by Ithuriel's Spear Press. His poems and stories have appeared in *Growing up Filipino Volume 2*, *Seven Card Stud With Seven Manangs Wild*, *Amistad Journal*, and various other publications. He was nominated in 2010 for the Pushcart Prize for his short story, "In My Country."

Freedom Allah Siyam is the Dean of Students at the Health Sciences & Human Services High School in White Center, Seattle. He's an organizer for human rights and genuine sovereignty in the Philippines by working closely with BAYAN USA.

Genaro Kỳ Lý Smith was born in Nha Trang, Vietnam in 1968. He earned a BA in English from California State University, Northridge in 1993. He later earned an MA and MFA in creative writing from McNeese State University in Lake Charles, LA in 1999. He is the author of *The Land Baron's Sun: The Story of Ly Loc and His Seven Wives* (UL Press). His other works have been published in *Crab Orchard Review*, *Xavier Review*, *Pembroke*, *Northridge Review*, *Amerasia Journal* (UCLA), *turnrow* (U of Louisiana at Monroe), *Scene Magazine*, *dis-Orient*, *Christmas Stories from Louisiana* (UP of Mississippi), *Gumbo: An Anthology of African American Writing* (Doubleday/Broadway Books), *Kartika Review*, *Asian American Literary Review*, and *Blue Lyra Review*. Recently, he received the ATLAS grant by the Louisiana Board of Regents for 2013-14. He has earned first place in the Zora Neale Hurston/Richard Wright Fellowship competition, received both the Louisiana Division of the Arts Artist Fellowship and mini-grant, second place in the Poets & Writers Exchange Program, and second place for his short story "Dailies" in 2008 from the Santa Fe Writers Program. He currently resides in Ruston with his wife Robyn and their two daughters, Layla and Naomi. He has been teaching literature, composition, and creative writing at Louisiana Tech University since 1999.

Michael Tora Speier completed a creative program at Griffin Nursery School in the mixed race mecca of Berkeley, California before emigrating with family to Vancouver B.C. in the late 60s. He is a visual artist and caterer for the arts, and enjoys writing satirical poetry. Email him for a copy of "Good Things: An illustrated guide to Martha Stewart's early Oregonian bong collection and other highbrow paraphernalia."

Sebastian Speier is an artist and graphic designer living and working in New York. Originally from Vancouver, he moved to Montreal where he studied New Media & Visual Arts at Concordia University. After living in Toronto for six years, he has